"My story is not only of darkness and destruction. It is also a story of great hopes that did not die; of lives shattered, of love that was born out of the ashes of war and hatred . . ."

—MAURICE SHAINBERG

BREAKING FROM THE KGB

"FIRSTHAND KNOWLEDGE . . . IMPORTANT REVELATIONS!"
—*Washington Times*

"SHAINBERG HAS AN AMAZING STORY TO TELL . . . An easy reading eye opener that uplifts and enlightens the reader."
—*The Jewish Standard*

"THIS EXPLOSIVE AND REVEALING BOOK IS MORE THAN A SOLID BIOGRAPHY, it is an important historical document written by a man who endured the destruction of his country, his family, and his faith during the brutal Nazi occupation of Poland."
—*Chattanooga Times*

"SENSATIONAL . . . INTRIGUING . . . Clearly, Shainberg is a courageous, resourceful man."
—*The Jewish Week, Inc.*

"A MAN WHO HAS TRAVELLED FAR TO ACHIEVE HIS OWN FREEDOM."
—*New American*

"HEARTWARMING . . . an astonishing, almost unbelievable story . . . *Breaking From The KGB* rings true from start to finish."
—*Canadian Jewish News*

"MUST READING FOR ALL WHO CHERISH A FREE WORLD . . . A most important document."
—JULIUS SCHATZ
Member, United States Memorial Holocaust Commission;
President, National Council on Art in Jewish Life

BREAKING FROM THE KGB

Warsaw Ghetto Fighter...
Intelligence Officer...
Defector to the West

MAURICE SHAINBERG

BERKLEY BOOKS, NEW YORK

To the Memory of My Father

MIKHAIL OSHER SHAINBERG

This Berkley book contains the complete
text of the original hardcover edition.
It has been completely reset in a typeface
designed for easy reading and was printed
from new film.

BREAKING FROM THE KGB

A Berkley Book/published by arrangement with
Shapolsky/Steinmatzky Publishing, Inc.

PRINTING HISTORY
Shapolsky Books edition published 1986
Berkley edition/May 1988

ISBN: 0-425-10697-7

A BERKLEY BOOK® TM 757,375
Berkley Books are published by The Berkley Publishing Group,
200 Madison Avenue, New York, NY 10016.
The name ''BERKLEY'' and the ''B'' logo
are trademarks belonging to Berkley Publishing Corporation.

PRINTED IN THE UNITED STATES OF AMERICA

10 9 8 7 6 5 4 3 2 1

PUBLISHER'S NOTE

The security or secret police apparatus of both the tsarist Russian and Soviet states has had a tangled, confusing history. From its origins under the tsars, when the Okhrana ("the Guard") was formed to uncover assassination plots, to its status today as a worldwide espionage network, the secret police has gone under a variety of names. After the Revolution, the idea of the Okhrana gave rise almost immediately to the Cheka ("Extraordinary Commission") under the direction of the notorious Felix Dzherzinsky, founded on December 20, 1917. On February 6, 1922, following Lenin's death, the Cheka was reorganized as the GPU ("State Political Administration"). A little over a year later, on July 6, 1923, this was changed to the OGPU ("United State Political Administration"). On July 10, 1934, Stalin purged the OGPU and formed the NKVD ("People's Commisariat of Internal Affairs"). From February 3, 1941, this became the NKGB ("People's Commisariat of State Security"). On March 19, 1946 the MGB ("Ministry of State Security") came into being; this was changed on March 15, 1953 to MVD ("Ministry for Internal Affairs"). Finally, on March 13, 1954, the KGB ("Committee of State Security") was formed, and it has persisted until today.

However, for the convenience of the reader, the Soviet police apparatus is referred to as the KGB throughout.

CONTENTS

Preface   1
1. A Traditional Childhood   3
2. Becoming a Man   12
3. First Love   26
4. Case White   35
5. Occupation   42
6. Mularek   51
7. The Ghetto   60
8. A Time to Kill   77
9. Stefan   89
10. Uprising   98
11. Mieczyslaw Pruzanski   106
12. The Road to Liberation   113
13. Berlin is Burning   123
14. Reichstod   132
15. Return to Poznan   141
16. Colonel Zaitzev's Diary   149
17. What the Diary Revealed   159
18. Fascists and Comrades   176
19. Haganah   189
20. Moscow   197
21. The Russians   212
22. Policy Shift   216
23. Imprisonment   220
24. Academy   236
25. Escape to Freedom   244
26. America   256
Appendix   266

PREFACE

This is my record of a turbulent life—of how I, a child of the Warsaw Ghetto, survived the Holocaust; how I became a high-ranking officer in the Polish-Soviet forces; and above all, how I discovered the diary of Colonel Gregory Zaitzev, the Soviet intelligence officer who commanded the infamous Katyn prison camp for Polish officers, where thousands were massacred by the Russians.

The weight of my secret knowledge about Katyn has been heavy, and I decided that it must be lifted from my conscience, that I must bear witness to the shocking truth about that cold-blooded mass murder by the KGB, the Soviet Secret Police. It is time to let the true story be told.

I did not know that I would be rubbing shoulders with history when the first bombs fell on Poland, my native land. My concern was for my family and my own survival. I did not know then that I would assume a new identity, as Mieczyslaw Pruzanski, Pole, Catholic, and underground fighter; nor that I would serve on the staff of an important Soviet KGB officer; nor that I would attend the Moscow Military Academy and eventually rise to the upper levels of the Soviet-controlled KGB.

Not in my wildest dreams could I have imagined myself in a military uniform of captain, entering the Auschwitz concentration camp as one of its liberators or standing next to the highest Soviet and Polish Army officers as they accepted the surrender of the defeated German army.

This then is my story—of the strange, unthinkable odyssey of an Orthodox Jewish boy from the Warsaw ghetto, through the fire and storm of war into the moral wilderness of a double existence. An odyssey that took me all the way from central Poland to the Eastern districts of Russia, then back across the ravaged towns and villages, bombed-out cities and battlefields into the heartland of Nazi Germany; then back to Poland and out of it to Israel; then to my final destination and free haven, the United States of America.

I traveled thousands of miles, on foot, in horse-drawn carriages, in motor vehicles, and in trains. I saw thousands of dead and mutilated bodies, and I am plagued by thousands of memories that continue to assail my mind—of places that are no more, of a Jewish heritage wiped out by the cruel decree of history, and of thoughts about my kin and friends who perished.

But my story is not only of darkness and destruction. It is also a story of great hopes that did not die; of lives shattered but by the grace of God restored, of love that was born out of the ashes of war and hatred, and of men and women who remained loyal to their beliefs and who struggled bravely in the face of death and torture.

Perhaps I have been spared so that I might share this account of turbulent times with the survivors of my generation and with many others too young to have experienced what I went through.

I am no longer a young man, and when people ask me why I have waited so long to tell this story, especially the story of the Katyn Forest massacre, all I can say is that there is no simple answer. For many years I lived in fear of retribution for having learned the dark secret of that Soviet atrocity; I was afraid to disclose the information I gathered lest I endanger myself and the lives of my family and friends.

Today, I feel safe. Others who might have suffered from my revelations are either dead or have emerged from behind the Iron Curtain. With the passing of my brother, Rabbi Dr. Nathan Meyer Shainberg, there remains no one who might be embarrassed by the more intimate parts of this memoir. Today I am no longer held back by friendly counsel and by less friendly warnings about the dire consequences of my revelations. That is why the time has come, at last, to tell the truth.

CHAPTER 1

A Traditional Childhood

I was born October 21, 1919, with "a hat on"—a fetal membrane that covered my head. And anyone born with "a hat on" was supposed to have good luck. That was tradition.

Tradition ruled the community of my childhood. In the Jewish quarter of Warsaw I grew up in an Orthodox family in an Orthodox neighborhood, within the Orthodox tradition—which might have been useful ten centuries earlier but which was now tenaciously observed and perpetuated in utter disregard of new realities.

My father, Mikhail, exercised absolute authority over a prosperous factory that manufactured cardboard packaging, a hotel in Krynica that could accommodate three hundred guests, and a few smaller businesses in Warsaw. He was the same autocratic ruler at home.

My mother, Toba, was the daughter of Rabbi Nute Yudke of Ruzhan, a well-known and respected sage of the nineteenth century and author of several Talmudic commentaries. She assumed the role of Orthodox matron without question. She married by parental arrangement and lived in strict observance of dietary laws and the precepts of Torah and Talmud. She accepted all limitations of her freedom with stoic devotion. She bowed her head to the barber's shears, exchanging her flowing tresses for the plain, dark-brown wig that instantly made her look like a middle-aged woman. Her graceful figure and attractive face were unappreciated in Warsaw's Jewish quarter. Her beauty was seldom remarked on; in time it simply withered away.

My brother, Nathan, was a studious youth. Seven years my senior, he towered over me physically and mentally with his

passionate commitment to learning. I could never understand hi
joy in spending long, weary hours slouched over Talmudic tomes
Little wonder that he became a rabbi in his seventeenth year
while I qualified as a mischievous rebel in my tenth.

I had two older sisters, Dina and Fela, and two younger ones
Guta and Hena. All four meekly accepted the roles assigned to
them by tradition. They were reared to become good, Orthodox
wives who would bear many children and raise them with strict
fidelity to Jewish custom.

I suppose I was the black sheep of the family. My rebellious
nature often put me at odds with my parents and siblings, and I
can't recall any truly intimate relationship with any of them. Not
that our family permitted, let alone encouraged, any of the over
expressions of affection common to other households. Papa's
home was rigid and solemn, requiring formal observance of
assigned roles. Thus I never got to know my family members
beyond the parts each of them played. By the time I had matured
into adolescence, the thunderous weight of history was to crush
any prospects of our getting to know each other.

We lived in a four-story brick house, facing a courtyard along
the busy cobblestoned Gesia Street. Our apartment was comfortably large, a symbol of my father's prosperity. Yet I found little
joy there. Rather, I was drawn to the streets, teeming with life
and excitement, streets that led into the unknown world of a
great and shining city. Warsaw was one of the most beautiful
and shimmering cities of Europe; its Marshalkowska Street, its
broad avenues, parks, theaters, and palaces were unrivaled. I had
always been aware of that larger, strange, forbidden world only a
stone's throw away. Yet for most Jews, even before the infamous ghetto walls went up, Warsaw might as well have been
Peking, Calcutta, or New York.

My life was very regimented. Yeshiva, my religious school,
began at 7:00 a.m. I had no choice but to be prompt, for any
tardiness would be reported to my father. His punishments always exceeded my real or alleged crimes. He would unhesi-
tatingly curtail the few freedoms I had, sparing neither the rod
nor his huge fists.

The students sat for hours on uncomfortable wooden benches.
We were dressed in somber black gabardine suits, tailored centuries ago to make the Jews as inconspicuous as possible in a
hostile society. Now, however, our clothes made us both uncomfortable and noticeable. We walked the streets of our district as

though we had just crossed a time bridge from the sixteenth century.

While my brother before me had been an attentive, even inspired student, I was all too easily distracted by what was happening in the street. I was envious of youngsters who could run and play outside. Their shouts and laughter filled my ears, drowning out the rabbi's voice. As a result, I was on most familiar terms with the rabbi's leather strap. Often, he would administer the punishment with the appropriate Talmudic justification: "Rabbi Judah says: Study with care, for error in the course of study is accounted deliberate sin."

Once I was foolish enough to complain to my father about the severity of the rabbi's punishment. I soon found out, however, that such complaints only placed me in double jeopardy. I collected new punishments with compounded interest—more blows and bruises on my face, arms, and shoulders. From then on, I submitted to the Yeshiva's justice without murmur.

With the exception of a two-hour lunch, which was also closely supervised, the Yeshiva classes lasted until 7:00 p.m., when I could go home, do my chores, and go to bed. The one day off from Yeshiva, the Sabbath, did little to heal my wounded pride or satisfy my yearnings. From the opening prayer and candle-lighting on Friday evening, through the next twenty-four hours, I was a prisoner. Except for the services at the synagogue, I was confined to our apartment, where my activities were restricted to meals, sleeping, prayer, and contemplative silence. There was nothing in me that could share the great spiritual joy many others found in the celebration of the Sabbath; for me it was sheer misery.

Sometime around my tenth birthday, my father finally discovered that the word of the Lord simply wasn't getting through to me. He decided that I must be a slow learner and, to remedy the situation, he hired a tutor from the Yeshiva to give me additional instruction at home, from eight to ten o'clock in the evening, six days a week.

My tutor was a dark, hairy man who soon revealed his unusual fondness for little boys. He insisted on sitting close to me during our tutorial sessions, which were conducted in the privacy of my room, and, at times, he would reach out his hands to touch me. I found this repulsive, and learned more about diplomatic evasion than I did about the Talmud.

The cat-and-mouse game with my tutor exploded beyond the walls of my room on the evening before Hanukkah. My tutor made a particularly brazen approach to me, moving to touch my private parts. I screamed, "You dirty old man!" and ran out of the room.

He pursued me, calling me all sorts of names, like "monstrous little atheist" and "scoundrel." My father appeared out of nowhere, halting the chase. I knew that if I as much as suggested my tutor's impropriety, I'd be compounding my punishment once more. So I remained silent while my tutor glibly lied about the incident, telling my father that I was a hopeless case who refused to accept his instruction.

My father dismissed the tutor for the evening, asking him to return for the next session. I was then summoned to my father's room. His justice was swift. There was no questioning. As I looked into his cold, harsh eyes, his powerful right palm smashed into my face. I crumbled to the floor, tasting the salty warmth of blood in my mouth as my father left the room, slamming the door behind him.

The following morning I could not eat breakfast. As I sat at the table, my mother saw that I could not open my swollen mouth. I trembled and cried. For the first time since I was an infant, she held me closely, trying to console me. "Oh, please, Mama," I said, "please find me another tutor."

She promised to talk to my father about it, and I left for the Yeshiva, nourishing that small hope in my heart. I sat in sullen obedience through the day's classes, worrying about what the tutor might say to my father, hoping my mother's promise would bring me relief. Nursing my wound, detached from my fellow-students and the rabbi, I daydreamed about the city. In my mind, I escaped from the darkness of that building into the broad expanse of the park—I didn't even know its name. Even the rabbi must have had some compassion for his injured student, for he left me alone that day, not calling on me for a single response.

Classes were dismissed early so the students could go home and light the candles for the Hanukkah Festival of Lights. As the other boys spilled into the streets, rushing home, a couple of them asked me what had happened. I was not in a talking mood. My pain went much deeper than a swollen cheek.

I started for home, but suddenly changed my mind and wandered off aimlessly into the heart of the city, beyond the edge of the Jewish district. I stopped in front of a small café, brightly lit up and full of gay noises and music. A few couples strode arm-in-arm down the street, and one of the young women blew me a kiss. I trembled with pleasure. I wished I were older and like them, free to come and go as I pleased.

There was a certain holiday mood in the city—perhaps because it was Christmas, or perhaps that was the way Warsaw lived.

I pulled up my socks and loosened my jacket in a feeble attempt to appear older and more casual. After all, an attractive young lady noticed me—I was somebody! Besides, since I would eventually be punished for my wanderings, I might as well make them as worthwhile as I possibly could. So I roamed the city, crossing a nameless bridge and marveling at the size of the Vistula River. I walked past resplendent palaces in the park and gaped at the great churches and the tall buildings. The lights, the traffic, the throngs on crowded avenues—it all added up to such excitement that I felt as if I had been transformed into a real man, a man-about-town, strolling the busy streets, greeting strangers who nodded back in approval. Yet, at the same time I dexterously slipped into dark alleys whenever I saw a policeman who might inquire what a boy of my age, particularly a Jewish boy, was doing out alone on the streets at that hour. I bought some chocolates and paraded along the sidewalks, relishing my new-found freedom, intoxicated with the throbbing hum of the great city. I never knew this kind of world could exist.

I soon grew tired. I was weary from walking and almost dazed by the marvels that bombarded my ears and eyes. But I was afraid to return home or visit our relatives in the city. I wanted to put off the punishment for my escapade.

Ironically, my haven that night was to be a religious institution—a synagogue I had spotted. I peeked inside its unlocked door. It was dark and empty. Quietly, I slipped into my refuge and found a bench. It was not as soft as my bed, but it was not as hard as my father's hand. Almost instantly, I fell into a deep sleep.

I awoke with the first light of morning, straightened my clothes, and slipped out to the street. I had a full hour of wandering before I was due at school. I watched the horsedrawn milk wagons making their rounds through the cobblestone streets, delivery boys distributing newspapers to vendors, and street cleaners pushing their brooms along the gutters, preparing the city for a new day. I watched the city stretch and rise as it came alive that cold December morning.

I reluctantly found my Yeshiva, sat on my bench, and maintained the silent aloofness that had seen me through the previous day. The classwork had not really begun in earnest when my father barged into the room and demanded that I accompany him outside. I was too worried about the impending punishment to pay much attention to the surprised stares of my classmates as I made my way around the desks to the door.

In the corridor, my father began shouting at me, demanding to know where I had been all night, and why I hadn't come home, and whether I had slept in the streets.

"I slept in a synagogue, all night . . ."

"Liar! Liar!" he screamed, as his muscles tensed, aching to lash out at me.

Remembering the power of his angry hand, I pleaded with him to hear me out before passing judgment. I described the synagogue in great detail, identifying the precise bench on which I had slept. He withdrew his poised arm as he considered the truthfulness of my report. Perhaps he decided that I might be telling him the truth after all, for he nodded his head, apparently recalling some of the details of this synagogue at the edge of our district. A faint smile crept up his face. The crisis was cracking. He seemed ready to listen to my side of the story. I hastened to press my case:

"I hate my tutor, Father. Please find me a new one and I promise I'll study as hard as I can. Please, Father."

"All right," he said. "I dismissed him last night."

In a rare gesture, he affectionately patted my head.

"Come home after school today. You hear?"

"Yes, Father," I said. "Yes, yes."

The rabbi, sensing my troubles, did not call on me again, enabling me to pass the day in city dreams. I was rather pleased with myself. I had ventured alone into the great unknown, the world of Warsaw. I had defeated my lewd tutor, and earned tokens of affection from my father and mother.

It was a banner day—that is, until I started to leave school. My old tutor came up to me, enraged by his dismissal. He loudly prophesied before all my classmates that I would grow up to be a useless bum and a criminal. But I no longer feared him. He was not my teacher at school, nor was he my tutor at home. He had no power over me. So, as he continued to taunt me in front of my class, I shrugged off his tirade, and my cool response impressed everybody.

My homecoming that evening was the happiest event of my childhood. I was the prodigal son who came back, the sheep who returned to the flock. Both parents spoke to me with something like affection. Even brother Nathan's scholarly austerity softened as he welcomed me with a warm smile. As soon as our parents left the room, my sisters set upon me with a hundred questions. I was the center of their attention. I confided to them about the mysterious woman with rouged cheeks and silk stockings who had thrown me a kiss. This made them squeal so hysterically that my father reentered the room demanding to know what all the commotion was about. We lowered our voices as I went on with my tale of nocturnal wanderings through the city, holding them spellbound. I slept well that night, feeling secure and content in my home and with my family. It was—for me—a novel experience.

Two days later my new tutor arrived, and to my considerable relief, I found him to be an intelligent and quiet man, concerned only with my education. I liked him.

A few days after my triumphant return home, our rabbi at the Yeshiva announced to my class that he was organizing a new anti-Zionist youth movement and was looking for recruits. The rabbi was a very pious man, dedicated to the prevailing opinion within Orthodox Judaism that there would be neither salvation nor a homeland for the Jews until after the arrival of the Messiah. The rabbi believed it was his divinely ordained duty to work against the spread of secular Zionism.

My father, of course, was in complete agreement with the rabbi. The Messiah would come in glory one day and rescue His chosen people. Until that day, however, the Jews had to endure their fate and put their faith to the test in heathen lands.

But I was becoming a man of the world. I had walked the streets of Warsaw and had even caught a blown kiss from a painted woman. I felt shackled by the restraining traditions of Orthodoxy and was suspicious of the rabbi's vehemence against Zionist Jews. In class, I questioned the motives for the anti-Zionist movement and declared that the Zionists were fighting the injustices we had suffered for the past two thousand years. Surely the rabbi knew of the pogroms and persecutions of Jews in Christian countries. Why shouldn't the Jews try to return to the security of their own homeland? I was sure that it was not merely the hand of God that dispersed the Jews from Jerusalem. It was the sword of Rome. And as the Jews had returned from Egyptian and Babylonian captivity before the coming of the Messiah, why should we not have the right to deliver ourselves from the present Diaspora?

The rabbi was shocked by my audacity. After a moment of silence, he said, "We must wait. We must wait for the Messiah."

The news of my debate with the rabbi reached home before I did, and my father was waiting for me. We sat and talked. Apparently he had finally realized that I was not a troublemaker, but only an outspoken boy. He was naturally on the rabbi's side, and he kept reminding me that I was the grandson of the great Rabbi Yudke and should not dishonor his memory with my radical ideas. The Jews, he reminded me, had survived forty centuries by clinging to the Holy Word, and the impertinence of a mere youth was no match for the collective wisdom and tradition that went back several millenia. But my father understood that my questions and doubts came from the heart and were not inspired by the devil, as the good rabbi believed. There was tension, to be sure, but we were beginning to communicate with each other.

As time went on, the family settled back into its routines. I dutifully attended the Yeshiva every day, hating every minute of it, impatient for the day when I would be old enough to make my own decisions. Rebellion was bubbling quietly within my mind. The warmth and attention I received after my disappearance had long since evaporated. I was hoping that my mother would treat me the way she treated my sisters, and hug or kiss me once in a while. But her religious convictions demanded that she regard me as a man. From the time I turned five years old, she was not supposed to touch me or appear half-dressed in my presence. No, I was not caressed by either of my parents. But at least my father was now reluctant to beat me.

Then it happened. It was a Wednesday evening, a year later, three nights past the last lights of Hanukkah, on a cold mid-December night. There were quite a few people in our apartment—some kind of social gathering of my parents' friends. Suddenly, my mother collapsed.

She was carried to her bed amid great commotion. People gathered about her and I tried to get through the crowd. I saw my mother reach out her arms toward me in response to my cries of "Mama, Mama!" But I was stopped by strong hands. The women milling about in the room could not permit me near my mother, who was not completely dressed. I did manage to see her smile and her waving hand which then fell limp upon the blanket. Unfortunately, I couldn't be with her when she died.

Much later, I learned that my mother had been six months pregnant when a doctor told her that she must abort the child or die. An abortion had been performed, but instead of saving my mother, it killed her.

I did not realize how much I loved my mother until she died. Indeed, the only moment of tenderness I can recall was her comforting me the morning after my father had struck me down. I grew up realizing that Nathan was her chief joy: Nathan, the rabbi and scholar; Nathan, the torchbearer of family honor; Nathan, the model son. My mother had been a real Yiddishe mama, dispensing religious advice, marital advice, medical advice—you name it—to all who sought it, and sometimes to those who didn't. I was sure she had a mysterious messenger service to God. In short order she could deliver an appropriate and practical religious comment for any situation.

At her death, when she reached out to me, I thought she had some final word for me, something that I would carry with me for the rest of my life. And I still feel a certain bitterness toward those who held me back from her.

After her death, I became the big brother of the household. Nathan was too involved with his religious scholarship to attend to the mundane needs of his sisters, and my father's businesses took much of his time.

I was approaching my thirteenth birthday. It was nearly time for me to accept the responsibilities of manhood.

My being born with ''a hat on'' was supposed to bring me luck. But luck, good luck, seemed to evade me. The only luck I seemed to have was the luck of a Jew, the luck of an outcast.

CHAPTER 2

Becoming A Man

The age of thirteen is an important milestone for a Jewish boy. It is the year he makes his Bar Mitzvah, the year he is admitted into the adult community, the year he becomes a man.

But before my time came to take the official vows of manhood, I performed one more act of youthful rebellion. It happened in the summer, during those idyllic days when the vigor of youth could not be contained within a classroom. My Yeshiva did not accept the radical theory of progressive education which provided a summer vacation for young students. If the hard wooden benches of the Yeshiva were uncomfortable in the winter, they were outright torture in the summer. The heat forced us to open the windows, filling our stuffy classroom with fresh summer breezes. The cries of other children at play in the streets were too much for us to bear.

One night, I organized a meeting with five of my classmates, and we drew up a plan of action. All the other schoolboys in Warsaw had vacations; why shouldn't we?

The next day, with myself as spokesman, we stormed the principal's office. I astounded the man by announcing that we were a committee of six formed to plead for an eight week summer vacation. We were entitled to this holiday, I pointed out, because other schools granted it, and weren't we the equals—if not the superiors—of other students?

The principal's face turned so red that I was afraid he might pass away like Mama.

"Troublemakers! Bolsheviks! Bums!" he exploded, flailing his arms wildly and throwing us out of his office. He pursued us down the corridor with a vengeance. We were sent home for the

12

rest of the day, a punishment that was envied by all our classmates who didn't have the chutzpah to join our cause.

Our revolt didn't end there. One week later, we constructed a
huge sign illuminated by electric bulbs. We installed it outside
the school and managed to hook it up to an electric streetcar
wire. The blazing lights spelled out this revolutionary message:

WE ARE KIDS. WE'RE ENTITLED TO HAVE A VACATION LIKE
ALL THE OTHER KIDS IN THE WORLD.

The sign caused a sensation. Passersby stopped to read it.
Some laughed; others shook their heads in disapproval. The
school officials were not amused by our prank.

Our principal called the police and demanded that they come
and remove the sign. The police, who were very anti-Semitic,
were delighted to hear of dissension among the Jews. They
refused to take the sign away unless they were paid. The school
was forced to pay them an outrageous amount to remove the
abomination.

It was fun while it lasted, which was only a few hours. When
I went home that evening, the atmosphere reeked of tension. My
father and brother greeted me icily. I knew that my punishment
was going to be severe.

At 11:00 p.m., I got undressed and started to go to bed.
Suddenly my brother rushed at me and held me down while Papa
gave me about forty lashes on my bare behind with his thick
leather belt. I screamed loudly, but nothing helped. Soon I was
hoarse from screaming. It was the worst beating of my life and it
kept me awake all night with pain. At that moment, I can
truthfully say that I hated Papa and my brother, and wished I
could run away and never see them again.

The next morning, I was too sick to go to school. I had a
temperature of almost 104. My prolonged sobbing brought my
oldest sister Dina to my room. She didn't ask what had happened;
she just cradled my head in her arms and begged me to stop
crying. But I couldn't stop, so she joined in. We made quite a
ruckus with our wailings, which attracted my brother's attention.
He stuck his head in the door and laughed. "Punishment is good
for the body," he pontificated, "and it helps to purify the soul."

By sunset, my temperature was over 104. My back was
swollen and I couldn't sleep from the pain. Finally, when I could
stand it no longer, I started screaming, and a doctor was called.
His diagnosis was that I was so badly bruised I would have to

remain in bed for several weeks. He scolded my father and brother for having brutally beaten me and admonished them not to repeat this punishment, or he would have to report it to the authorities.

I was bedridden for three weeks. Every morning at 9:00, the doctor arrived to massage my back and change the dressing on my lacerations. My father came into the room only when the doctor was there; otherwise he ignored me. My sisters, however, made up for his callous behavior by spending as much time with me as they could. Their attention was comforting.

My confinement gave me time to think and to formulate a strategy. When my sores healed and I could walk again, I went directly to my father. "I'm not going to Yeshiva anymore," I said firmly. "If you force me to go, I'll run away from home and you'll never see me again."

My father rose from his armchair and scowled at me. "What have you become—a revolutionary who doesn't need his family anymore?"

"I'm thirteen years old and I can make my own decisions."

"All right, enough, enough. But at least finish this year for your Bar Mitzvah. Then you can go where you want."

"No. I won't go back to that slave school."

"And where *do* you want to go to school?"

"I want to go to the Tachgemoina Gymnasium." (This was the equivalent of a high school.)

He bristled with indignation. "Atheist!" he cried.

"I'm not an atheist. I'm a human being and I want to be treated like one."

My firm attitude ruffled Papa. "And what will our people say when they see you wearing the uniform of a Christian?"

"It's not a Christian uniform. It's a school uniform without the ball and chain that goes with the Yeshiva uniform. It's a Jewish religious school! It just isn't Orthodox."

He pleaded, "What will the community think if you go to school with a gang of Reform Jews? They have denied their faith. They don't keep the Sabbath properly. They have lost their spiritual values. The Reform Jews are outcasts! Hillel says, 'Do not withdraw from the community.' "

I snapped back at him, "Hillel also says, 'Do not judge your comrade until you have stood in his place.' Please try to see it my way."

I had never dared to speak so openly to my father before.

He realized that there was nothing more he could do about me.

"All right," he said wearily. "We shall visit the Holy Rabbi Abraham Mordeccai Alter of Ger to seek his wisdom before the matter is settled."

Four days before Yom Kippur, we drove thirty miles out of Warsaw to see the Holy Rabbi. My father, brother, and I stood on a long line of thousands of Hasidim waiting to greet the rabbi. We stood for hours with all those people, each of whom had traveled a long distance just to be touched for a moment by the Holy Man's mystical wisdom. Slowly, we inched forward. When we got close, I could see him considering the myriad problems thrust before him, weighing arguments and offering solutions that were said to be both just and benevolent.

Finally, we stood before the Sage. The Holy Man asked my Papa if anything was bothering him, and he replied that he was having trouble with me. "He doesn't wish to attend Yeshiva any longer." He pointed an accusing finger at me.

I was asked to step forward and the rabbi gave me a penetrating look. His tired, wise eyes focused on my face. As our eyes met, I felt him probing my mind, almost as if it were a physical contact. I realized that he could discover any secret I harbored simply by gazing into my eyes. I felt moved and ready to surrender to his power. Then I noticed something like a smile on his face. His lips twitched and there was a twinkle in his look. He touched my shoulder gently with his pale, soft hand and turned to my father.

"Let him go to Reform Yeshiva," he said. "He will be all right. I can tell from his eyes that he's a good boy. Don't worry about him."

I was so overjoyed to have the rabbi on my side that I practically shouted at him. "Thank you very much, Rabbi. I promise you that I'll be a good Jew."

My brother was crushed by the rabbi's words. He didn't speak to me or even look at me all the way home. I had the sweet taste of victory in my mouth, and I didn't care what my brother or Papa thought.

This was a whole new life for me, and it spelled freedom. I cut my long earlocks, went to the gymnasium school, made new friends, and, for the first time ever, felt like a free human being.

After my first term in the new school, I brought home an excellent report card which made my father very happy. At the dinner table one night, Papa was so pleased with my progress that he said to the family, "Maurice has become a very good boy. He's good for God and good for life."

My relationship with my brother also improved at this time. One day, he went so far as to ask me for a favor.

"I've received my orders for a military physical. Would you go with me to the Military Health Committee?"

"Of course," I said, secretly delighted to be taken into his confidence at last.

All twenty-year-olds went before this board for a physical to see if they were eligible for service in the Polish Army. My brother was already an ordained rabbi and did not wish to be drafted into the Polish Army, which was notoriously anti-Semitic. He had been on a starvation diet for three months and could no longer walk alone. I had to help support him, taking along a bottle of kosher milk to sustain him.

I waited three hours outside the Health Committee building while he submitted to the rigorous physical. Finally, he came out with a smile on his usually dour face. "I'm free," he said. "I only weigh 110 pounds, and they won't draft me." I never saw my brother happier.

"Let's not go home yet," he suggested. "I want to go to the Mikvah and bathe in the hot waters." I was not permitted inside, so I waited under the trees for him. After immersing himself in the holy waters, he came out and started to walk toward me. Suddenly, he fainted. I couldn't revive him, so I ran inside the building and found a doctor.

"This poor boy is half-starved," the doctor pronounced. "I'll give him an injection; then he must get something solid in his stomach."

As soon as my brother regained consciousness, the doctor gave him some soup and urged him to stop starving himself. With my help, Nathan was able to get home safely.

At this point in my life, Nathan's approval meant the world to me. Yet I did not consider him a good person. He was everything I abhorred: he was a religious fanatic who lacked a warm heart and thought only of his calling. But he was my brother and I loved him.

After so much unhappiness in my life, playing soccer in school was a great joy. For years, while I was stuck in classes at the Yeshiva, I had enviously watched boys in the street playing soccer and other sports, and it pained me not to be able to join them. At the Warsaw Maccabi, a sports center, I finally had my chance to play, and soon became one of the best players on the junior team. My athletic ability gave me great self-confidence and made me very popular with my classmates.

Of course, playing soccer once again got me in trouble with Papa. The team played on the Sabbath, the day that I usually attended synagogue with him. But I had to be at the stadium by 11:00 a.m. and therefore had to stop going to synagogue. This upset Papa very much.

I tried to placate him by saying that I wasn't missing synagogue—I was attending the Reform synagogue with my classmates before we left for the game. This was a lie, and I think he saw through it, but he pretended to believe me. It was the first lie I had ever told him and I was plagued by guilt for some time. Whenever we lost a game, I was certain that God was punishing me for my falsehood.

One day, while on the way home from a game with some of my friends, we saw a huge crowd waiting to enter one of the Warsaw theaters. We asked one of the men on line what the big attraction was and he replied, "Ze'ev Jabotinsky is speaking."

"Who is this Jabotinsky?" I asked jokingly, as my friends snickered. "A Jewish comic?"

The man paid no attention to our disrespect. "He's the leader of the World Jewish Zionists," he said quietly.

"Oh, I'm sorry," I said. "I would like to hear him speak."

"The lecture is sold out," the man said.

We made an attempt to buy tickets anyway. When we failed, I convinced my friends that I knew of a way to sneak into this theater. Once, when I had played hookey from the hated Yeshiva, I had sneaked into this movie house to see *The Invisible Man*, a film that had fired my imagination. To be able to make oneself invisible like Claude Raines seemed to me the most wonderful thing that could befall a human being. I took my friends to a back door which was unattended, and we managed to sneak in. We milled around with the crowd and stood in the back of the orchestra, where no one questioned us.

Jabotinsky turned out to be a skinny zealot with glasses and dark blond hair. He was a forceful, dramatic speaker who shrieked when he wanted to stress a point. He won over most of the audience, and he overwhelmed me.

The essence of his talk was that Israel belonged to us and that we had to fight to regain it. All Jews must live together in peace in their homeland. We should not attempt to buy back the land that is rightly ours, but must fight for it. And the world had to help us.

Jabotinsky was critical of Great Britain for closing the gate on the Jews. If anything happened to the European Jews because of the burgeoning of Nazism, the speaker said, Britain would be to blame. The British had promised to readmit Jews to Israel, but they had not kept their word.

One prediction that Jabotinsky made that afternoon terrified me and the rest of the audience. He said: "If the Jews do not leave Europe in the next few years, they will all be liquidated by Hitler."

On the way out, I told my friends that this man had so impressed me that I planned to join his organization. When I was 16, I became an active member of his group—Betar Ket Moranov—and began to spend every night at its headquarters. Soon I was wearing the organization's brown uniform on special occasions.

One of my friends at this time was a man named Max, who was one of the chairmen of Brit Achail, an Army organization for older men. He was a close friend of Jabotinsky's and took me to see him one night at the Hotel Bielanska. I was so in awe of the man that I was tongue-tied when we met.

Jabotinsky shook my hand warmly and thanked me for all the help I was giving his group. "Max told me that you wanted to ask me some questions," he said, trying to put me at ease with a smile.

"I'm nervous because I admire your ideas so much," I stammered.

He smiled affectionately. "Would you like to go to Israel?"

"Of course—that's my dream."

"Your father should send you—he has money. Why doesn't he invest money in Israel instead of in Poland? His capital would be safer there."

"My father won't invest in Israel because, like most Jews, he's waiting for the Messiah to liberate us."

"That's been the main Jewish problem for two thousand years. We've been waiting for someone else to do the job for us."

Jabotinsky sat down and told me a story. "One day, I met an American capitalist, and for three hours I tried to convince him to invest part of his fortune in some *yeshuvim* [new settlements in Israel]. He was Jewish and listened to me with interest. Finally, he said to me, 'You've convinced me.' He took a dollar bill out of his pocket and handed it to me."

"I would have thrown it back at him," I said heatedly.

Jabotinsky shook his head. "No, that's not the correct attitude. I took his dollar because I have no right to refuse *any* amount for this cause—no matter how small. Some give a little; some give a lot. I accept everything, because I know that I can't depend on funds from most religious Jews. They refuse to contribute anything for the building of Israel. Soon they're going to discover that it's not only too late to help Israel—but it's also too late to help themselves."

I asked him what his economic plans were for Israel.

"The big problem at the moment is how to help European Jews survive. Our economic plan for Israel is capitalistic control by the government. We are not against organized, productive cooperatives in communities. Government support helps the economy in every way to keep the highest standards for the country's citizens. We have a culture and civilization that are more remarkable than those of some nations. But why aren't Jews more united? Why are we spread all over the world? Why do we allow Great Britain to dictate to us? Do you know who our king is? He's the King of England. He sets down the quotas for us: how many Jews can live in Israel, how many can die for Hitler. We must fight for the admittance of all Jews to Israel, before they can be slaughtered by Hitler. In 1917, the British foreign secretary, Balfour, issued the Balfour Declaration vowing British support for a Jewish national home in Palestine—but this promise was never kept. Now it's up to us to act."

When it was time for me to leave, Jabotinsky thanked me for coming. "I am honored and delighted to meet the grandson of a highly respected rabbi."

I responded with "Tel Hai," a Zionist greeting. I had enjoyed our conversation and felt prouder than ever to be associated with him.

Meanwhile, at home, my path was continuing to diverge from my family's. My father remarried, and this time he chose a woman completely different from his first wife. Leah was a far cry from my pious mother. Although she came from a religious Jewish family, she was vain and worldly. She spent hours admiring herself before a mirror. She came from a poor family and now suddenly found herself transported from a small, narrow bed to a luxurious, king-sized model. She also found herself with an eight-room apartment and two maids—one for cooking, the other for cleaning.

My father gave her everything she wanted: fashionable new clothes, a mink coat, new furniture, and costly perfumes. She gave him a boy and a girl.

Leah was only 29, considerably younger than Papa. She was a

sexy, large-breasted woman, and we children were thoroughly
repulsed by her. I especially disliked her. I didn't want another
mother; one comparatively perfect mother had been quite enough.

After she bore my father two children, we pretended to ignore
them. But they were so handsome and lovable that whenever my
stepmother went out, I couldn't resist playing with them. When
she returned, I resumed my silence. I never initiated a conversation with her until after Hitler had invaded Poland, and that
was the only good thing that ever came as a result of the Nazis.

Love seemed to be in the air before the Nazi tornado. My
brother married a brilliant doctor of chemistry who was the
daughter of Shulem Kaminer, publisher of the religious newspaper *Der Yid*. My sister Dina married the son of the rabbi of
Shedlec, an apprentice lawyer named Joseph Goldman.

Meanwhile, my sister Fela changed radically and spoke only
Polish and French, abandoning Yiddish completely. She started
dating a Polish boy, and I served as their go-between. Whenever
he wanted to see her, he would give me the message and I would
pass it on to her.

One day, her boyfriend asked me to go upstairs to our apartment and tell Fela that he wanted to see her immediately. She
went downstairs, and that was the last we ever saw of those two.
They obviously eloped that afternoon and most likely ended their
days in a concentration camp. I have never been able to find a
trace of either of them.

I continued to be actively involved in Jabotinsky's organization. One incident that I have never forgotten happened just
before the Hanukkah, the holiday that commemorates the historic
fight waged by the Maccabees for their freedom in Israel. This
observance was a traditional holiday for Jewish youngsters all
over the world. We wore our Betar uniforms, marched in parades, and attended festive dances at night. It was a jubilant day.

A few weeks before the holiday, I was leaving our apartment
in my brown uniform. I ran into my brother on the stairs. He
took one look at my outfit, and—without a word—punched me
brutally in the face. I managed to run down the stairs and out the
door. My brother opened a window on the landing and flung my
military cap after me.

My face was covered with blood, and several people passing
by stopped to offer their help. I told them I was all right and
cleaned my face as best I could with my handkerchief. When I
entered our group headquarters with a bleeding face, all activity
stopped. My comrades were horrified.

"My brother attacked me," I said, "because he's a rabbi and despises this uniform."

When my friends heard that, they were more eager than ever to fight for our cause to free Israel. Our military leader, a lawyer named Biderman, called me into his office and asked, "Do you want us to get back at your brother?"

"No," I replied. "He's my brother—and I love him."

He gave me an approving look. "You're right. We have more important things to do now than fight religious fanatics. But if you ever change your mind, let me know, and we'll take care of him." We came to the conclusion that Zionism was a difficult concept for many religious Jews to accept, for it was an affront to their main hope in life, the coming of the Messiah. We agreed that we must tolerate the disapproval of our Jewish brothers, for part of our mission was to protect them. Someday, perhaps, they would see the virtue of our activities. Someday, perhaps, they too would want to live in a Jewish State.

I belonged to Kvutza Gimel (Group Three) whose leader was Yitzak Isolucki, better known today as Yitzak Shamir of Israel. On a number of occasions, it was he who called up my father demanding to know why my brother, Rabbi Nathan Shainberg, beat me when he saw me in the Betar uniform. He also directed some of the exercises for Betar youth groups, which were held in my father's villa in Michalin, some 15 miles from Warsaw. Of course, all such activities were kept secret from my brother and father.

A few weeks later, during Hanukkah, we made a public display of our strength and dedication. We worked hard preparing for the day. It rained heavily, but this didn't dampen our enthusiasm. We marched in a parade, took part in all the festivities, and attended a dance in the evening. Our national leader even joined in the festivities, despite the deluge. We all got drenched, but that didn't stop the dance. It was one of my happiest evenings.

Several days after our holiday, we had a violent incident at school. Members of two Polish Fascist groups—Falanga and Ozon—threw stones through our windows. Some of my classmates, who also belonged to Betar joined together in fighting our enemies with steel poles. When they saw how we were armed, they tried to run away. Meanwhile, the police came and started attacking the "Jew boys," as they called us, instead of arresting the ruffians who had broken our school windows.

A full-scale riot broke out. Almost the entire student body, as well as the faculty, started battling the police. About sixteen officers were hurt and hospitalized. I guess we won, because only four students required hospitalization.

Finally, the Chief of Police, a charlatan, arrived and quelled the riot. He assumed his usual, transparent role of pacifier, professing to be on our side and against violence. We had to comply with his wishes. He wanted peace, and he had the ammunition to gain it. All we had was the sense to fight for our lives and freedom. I have never forgotten that day, April 26, 1937. It marked one of my first involvements in a physical struggle for my rights.

After the police left, the various organizations involved in the riot formed their own groups and discussed the uprising until late that evening. All agreed on one aspect of the event: the Polish police were not to be trusted.

The riot had a positive effect on all of us. We became more and more zealous for our cause and started to secure weapons and ammunition to make us stronger in the event of another attack. But although we grew stronger, I could not understand why Warsaw Jews could not be more united. Instead of belonging to one strong organization, they splintered off and dissipated their strength. The diverse groups argued with each other and engaged in endless talks about the type of government Israel would have in the future. It was like choosing furniture for a house that wasn't yet built.

Our leader, Ze'ev Jabotinsky, pounded one message into us: we must fight for our territorial rights in Israel and grow strong enough to overpower our enemies. Polish anti-Semitism grew daily. The Polish Senate passed intolerable edicts against our culture, religion, and traditions. For two thousand years our people had eaten kosher meat, which entailed the swift slaughter of animals with a knife. The Poles now purposely forbade that practice and demanded we slay animals by electrocution.

Next, an edict was passed that fifty percent of the employees in any Jewish factory had to be Polish Catholics. Polish factories did not employ any Jews. Even in an apartment house occupied solely by Jews, there had to be a Polish super. Policemen, mailmen, and all government employees had to be Polish Catholics; no Jew could apply for these positions. Priests in their pulpits denounced us and called for our liquidation.

In May 1938, a delegate from the Chemical Labor Union came to Papa's factory and forced him to fire 125 Jews and replace them with Poles. The dismissed Jews represented almost fifty percent of our manpower.

Papa closed his plant for ten days in protest. City officials fined him 10,000 zlotys and warned that if he did not open his plant in three days, the city would take it over and hire only Poles. Papa turned the factory over to me and spent the rest of his days in the synagogue reading the Talmud. Each day, after I was dismissed from school at 1:00 p.m., I went to the plant and stayed there until 7:00 p.m. Of course, we had to comply with the law and fire 125 Jewish employees. This generated bitter feelings in the factory.

The year 1938 was momentous for me in many ways. I graduated from the Reform Yeshiva and entered the Warsaw Polytechnical Institute. Here, in a non-Jewish atmosphere, I began fully to realize the horrible fate that awaited the Jews in Poland.

By order of the anti-Semitic authorities, Jewish students had to sit on the left side of the classroom, apart from the pure, Aryan Poles. I became one of the staunchest foes of these racists. My experience with Jabotinsky's group gave me the expertise to organize groups to fight anti-Semitism, and to my surprise and delight, some liberal-minded Polish students also joined us. I also founded and edited an illegal journal, *Prawo Ludo*, which sounded a militant cry for an end to racism and to reactionary and fascist Polish policies.

It was during my days at the Polytechnical Institute that I started writing to further the Jewish cause. This skill would become extremely useful to me in the black days to come.

Around that time, Lazer Rippel, the leader of our youth organization, enlisted 25,000 youngsters to join a bold pilgrimage on foot to Israel. I was one of the first to sign up for the march. I could no longer bear to live in this country full of prejudice and hatred. In my mind, the Poles were even more anti-Semitic and despicable than Hitler himself.

Of the 25,000 youths who enrolled for the march, ninety percent were from such Zionist organizations as Betar, Tel-Chai, Hagana, Ahiba, Gordonia, and Hashmonea. We were filled with the kind of zeal that must have inspired the Crusades.

On the eve of my departure, my sisters stayed up all night, preparing sandwiches for me. My father watched these preparations in silence. He didn't approve of the march, but he didn't try to stop me.

As thousands of youths assembled for the pilgrimage the next morning, for the first time in my life I felt part of a truly united body. The march would be very long—about six thousand miles—but we would be carried forth by our mutual ardor.

The spectacle of thousands of youths assembled in the street drew a great crowd. Some said we were crazy; others hailed us as heroes for leaving this ugly and bigoted country. We raised our voices in triumphant Zionist songs that were heard all over the Polish capital. The police were powerless to quell us. Our legions numbered many thousands, and 500,000 Warsaw residents were Jewish.

I said goodbye to each member of my family as the march got under way. We walked in a military formation, and our marching songs kept us in step.

But our exultation was short-lived. When we had walked only twenty-five miles, our glorious pilgrimage was halted at Piasecna. There, we were confronted by 2,000 heavily armed Polish soldiers on horseback. Their order was terse and nonnegotiable: Britain had voiced its disapproval of this march to the Polish government, and we were to return to our homes immediately or be arrested.

Our defeat was crushing. All our hopes were shattered with these few words. There was no singing on the return trip; we trudged back to Warsaw like a defeated army.

"I knew the march would be stopped," Papa said when I returned. "It was a foolish project, and it was doomed to fail. Do you think that the Poles would allow the world to think that its youth wasn't happy here? Even though they hate us, they want to save face before other nations."

There was much truth in his words.

Back to the old routine. I returned to school and after classes reported to my father's factory. One of his employees was an avid communist, and I would spend hours with him arguing about racial prejudice. He contended that people should not fight solely for nationalism. They should fight for equal rights in every direction—especially in the economy, the educational system, and society's social structure.

I rebuked him by saying that Poland would never grant Jews equal rights. It was a hopeless cause in this militantly Catholic country. From the earliest grades, Catholic students were taught that the Jews killed Christ and had no place in a Christian society.

My friend told me I was wrong and invited me to attend some open meetings sponsored by the communists. He assured me that his comrades were of all nationalities and religions, and that they would fight for each other's rights. "You don't have to go to

Israel to enjoy equal rights,'' he insisted. ''You and I were born in Warsaw, and we must fight to gain equal rights here in our homeland.''

''How can you fight thirty-eight million fanatics?'' I asked.

''We communists have placed our faith in Stalin,'' he replied, ''who is the leader of the communists the world over. He's not Russian—he's Georgian. And even if I don't live to enjoy these rights, at least I'll die knowing that my children will.''

''Good for you—if you believe that. But I feel that we Jews can only achieve our liberty in Israel. Ninety-nine percent of the Poles hate Jews. And the Socialist Party will fight for equal rights for all—except for the Jews. They hate us so much that when my soccer team plays a Polish Socialist team, we have to lose or get beaten up after the game. They throw stones and bricks at us and cut us with broken bottles. So much for equal rights from the Socialists.''

The only benefit I saw in the communists during those days was that they stood as a vocal opposing force against the Nazis. We had heard many terrible stories about what was happening to German Jews, and we all generally agreed that Fascism was our greatest danger in Europe. Hitler also despised communism, which made Jews and communists share a common danger. A communist's ideal was a long way from my ideal, but as Hitler pressed east, absorbing Austria and Czechoslovakia, it was easy to contemplate an alliance of necessity between Jews and communists.

From the 20-20 hindsight of history, it's easy to see that the communists never had any intention of assisting the beleaguered Jews. But the mood of the hour clouded this vision. We needed allies desperately. If two thousand Polish cavalry could intimidate 25,000 Jews, how could we face Hitler's Panzer divisions? We needed allies, and the only potential ally of any strength in the area was the Soviet Union.

The events of the summit of 1939 crushed these thoughts. Hitler and Stalin had signed a non-aggression pact. Poland was doomed. The fate of Poland's Jews was sealed.

CHAPTER 3

First Love

My first love was a beautiful, blonde Polish girl named Halina, who lived practically under my nose. Our apartment was at 21 Gesia Street, and she lived at No. 25, just a hundred feet away.

Although Gesia Street was ninety-nine percent Jewish, the remaining percent was composed of Polish apartment-house supers, and certain Polish civil workers, like Halina's father. He was a postman, who had to live near his place of work—our Jewish ghetto.

Halina was tall, slim, and attractive with blonde braids and bright blue eyes. We passed each other countless times on the street as children, without speaking. When we were both about thirteen she began to watch me play soccer in the street with some of my friends. We played with a primitive ball made of rags, and we indulged in lots of horseplay.

My friends noticed this lovely girl watching me and started to tease the two of us. But I found her very attractive and it seemed to me that whenever she was there, I played better.

One rainy day, I saw Halina standing under a canopy down the block at 31 Gesia Street, trying to stay dry. "How are you going to get home without an umbrella?" I asked her. There was no reply.

"Sorry," I said. "I suppose you don't speak to Jew boys."

She glared at me. "That's not true. I live among Jews, and I like them. I'm not anti-Semitic."

"Good. Then why can't we be friends? I would like that."

She smiled. "My name is Halina."

"And mine is Maurice. I live at No. 21."

"I know."

26

"How do you know?"

"Because I've seen you since you were small. And I enjoy watching you play soccer."

"You like the way I play?"

"No."

"No? Why not? I'm supposed to be the best player on the team."

"Yes—and you know it. You only play for yourself. You act as if you're the only player out there and the ball's all yours. You should learn some team spirit. You want all the glory for yourself."

"Well, at least you're honest. What you say is true. From now on, I'll try to cooperate more with the rest of the team."

We stood there talking until the rain stopped, and then I walked her home. When we got to her apartment house, she said goodbye but wouldn't shake my hand. I saw her again the next day, but all she said was "Hello." Our relationship continued in this formal manner, and we didn't have another conversation of this nature for another year.

One day, when I was fourteen, I accompanied my sister Hena to a doctor in our neighborhood. She had a bad cold.

When we arrived at his office, I saw Halina seated in the waiting room.

"Hello," I said casually. "Are you sick?"

"No. I'm just picking up some medicine for my mother."

I introduced her to my sister, who immediately started gabbing with her as if they were lifelong friends.

"I didn't know you were one of our neighbors!" Hena gushed. "We could have had such fun." From there they discussed schools they had attended, boys they had flirted with, and mutual friends. I felt left out and wished Hena would get lost. The next thing I knew, Halina was inviting Hena to visit her apartment.

On our way home, Hena asked, "Maurice—how come you're seeing a Polish girl?"

"We're not dating—I'm not planning to marry her. I've only had one conversation with her. She's just a neighbor to me."

"You better not let Papa see you talking to her. He'll *kill* you."

"Don't worry—there's nothing to it."

That remained so for quite a long time. Whenever I ran into Halina, which wasn't often, our conversations followed a similar routine: Hello. How are you? Fine—and you? Fine—thank you. Nice to see you. Thank you. Give my best to your sister.

Finally, when I was sixteen, I got the nerve to invite her to watch me play in a soccer game at the stadium. I told her the game would start at 11:00 a.m. on Saturday.

"I'd love to go," she said. "Will you call for me at my apartment?"

My heart dropped. I had always gone to the stadium with a friend named Leo, who drove me there on his motorbike. Unfortunately, it only seated two.

I explained this to her. "Would it be all right if I gave you two tickets, so that you can take one of your girlfriends along?"

"Are you afraid to be seen alone with a Polish girl?" she snapped.

"No—I wanted you to have company during the game. I intend to meet you when it's over. It really would be more convenient that way."

She seemed satisfied with that explanation and said she would ask one of her classmates to come along.

I couldn't wait until Saturday, and when it finally came, I played one of my best games. We won, thank God, but then I worried how I could possibly find Halina in that crowd of fifteen thousand. I also worried how my friends would react if they saw me with a Polish girl.

I separated from Leo and my teammates and went in search of my blonde. She was waiting outside the locker room with her girlfriend who seemed to be one of those shy, quiet types. That suited me, since I wanted an opportunity to talk with Halina.

I tried to ignore their compliments about my playing, but I was secretly overjoyed that they had noticed my every move. Our team was the junior soccer squad. Next, the seniors would play, and I suggested that we find good seats in the grandstand before it got too crowded. I was hoping her friend would excuse herself, but she had no intention of doing so. We found three good seats, and I bought the girls some ice cream.

We no sooner got settled and Halina started in about my selfish mode of playing on the field. "When will you learn that you're not a soloist? Soccer is a team sport—not an exercise for one. You're a very selfish player."

I knew she was right. Many people had accused me of that, especially some of my teammates.

"I knew you were in the grandstand and I got carried away," I said, not exactly lying.

"I wish I could believe that," she said, smiling.

As much as I liked soccer, I couldn't wait to get away from

the stadium to take Halina to a good restaurant. I knew it meant taking her friend along, but since she never intruded in our conversation, I didn't mind. I wanted to impress Halina with my know-how in a glamorous setting.

"Let's leave and beat the crowds to the trolley car," I suggested five minutes before the game was over. Leo had already left with his motorbike. Halina gave me a knowing smile. She knew that I was still avoiding running into my friends while dating a Polish girl.

The three of us left the stadium. "I'm starved," I said. "Why don't we all go to a nice restaurant?"

"Fine," Halina agreed, "but if we go to the Jewish quarter, we're sure to run into your friends. Wouldn't it be advisable to go to the Polish section?"

I nodded.

"But that poses another problem," said the all-knowing Halina. "You can only eat kosher food, and we can't get that in the Polish section."

"Halina—don't worry," I pleaded. "It's about time I tried Polish food. I think I'll start with some Prague ham."

The girls laughed at this. We were in good spirits when we entered one of the better Polish restaurants. I didn't have to worry about being heckled for dating a Polish girl. No one paid any attention to us. My soccer friends had always told me that I didn't look Jewish and now I was beginning to believe them.

We had a wonderful meal, and I discovered that I really liked the taste of ham. After dessert I asked the girls if they would like to go to a movie. American films were the big thing in Warsaw, and admission prices were very steep. Most of my friends couldn't afford to attend, so I used to treat them. The girls were impressed with my offer, but tendered their regrets.

"I can't tonight," Halina said, "but I'd like to go some other time."

We walked her silent friend home. Then I escorted Halina to her apartment house. She thanked me for the entire day, saying that it was one of the most enjoyable times she had ever had. She also said she would like to go to the movies with me soon, if the invitation was still open.

"Certainly," I said, happy with my progress.

She leaned toward me and kissed me on the cheek. I walked home on bubbles.

When I got to my apartment, I lay down on the sofa and thought about the entire day. It had been perfect from beginning to end—all because of Halina. I realized that I was falling for her. I tried to recall the exact features of her face, but somehow they were blurred in my mind. I knew that she was beautiful, with fair skin, golden hair, and a body I found very attractive. I was lost in rapture over her, and it must have showed.

"Are you sick?" one of my sisters inquired.

"No, no—I'm just thinking about the game today. We won."

"Naturally," Dina said, "you always do."

That night, I dreamt about Halina. Actually, it was almost a nightmare. In my dream, I was playing soccer and spotted Halina in the grandstand. Her presence got me so agitated that I lost the game. "At last," she said to me in my dream, "you let someone else win."

By next morning, I was absolutely smitten with her. My heart was bursting with love, and I detested being apart from her blonde beauty. I had to tell someone about my great love. The only one I could trust was Leo, so I suggested that we go for a ride on his motorbike. We were roaring through downtown when I told him I was in love with a Polish girl. He almost crashed his bike into a pastry shop. He was from a strict Orthodox family, like mine, and my boldness in defying tradition shocked him.

"How can you walk down the street with her?" he asked. "You'll be ostracized, beaten, ridiculed. Your own people are going to hate you, not to mention her family. What's going to happen when your father finds out? You may give him a heart attack."

That thought had crossed my mind, and it made me unhappy. But young love is not easily killed. The more I tried to put Halina out of my mind, the more I thought about her.

"Listen, Leo," I said. "Don't worry. I've been out with her—in the Polish section—and nobody detected that I was Jewish. I think I can pass for Polish."

"Maybe," Leo said, "if you stay in the Polish quarter. But I wouldn't walk in the Jewish section with her. It's too dangerous. Many people know you—and they will certainly report to your Papa that you're dating a Pole."

Giving up Halina was beyond my strength. The next time I saw her I could no longer hide my feelings. "I like you very much," I said.

"I know. It's obvious. Does it show on me, also?"

"Do you mean that you like me, too?"

She nodded. "I've watched you and admired you for years and went out of my way to make you notice me. I can't control my feelings for you any longer. I'm not afraid of loving you anymore.''

She suddenly kissed me on the lips and then ran down the street. It was the first time a girl had ever kissed me like that and I found it blissful. All my life I had been starved for a parental kiss, and now, I had finally been kissed by someone I loved. It was a marvelous feeling. I was giddy for the rest of the day.

The next day, I waited near her apartment house until she came out. I had been there quite a while, but pretended I was practicing my soccer game. I was overwhelmed with emotion when I saw her. ''Why did you run away yesterday?''

''Please don't ask me questions. Let's just walk.''

We walked in silence for ten minutes. ''Could we go to a movie?'' she finally proposed.

''Sure. Why not? What's playing?''

''*Suez* with Tyrone Power and Loretta Young. I'm *crazy* about him.''

I felt my first true pang of jealousy. ''And I'm crazy about her,'' I said defensively. We both laughed.

We sat in the balcony and she reached for my hand. Her boldness took me by surprise, but I found it pleasant. After a while, I observed that she was sneaking glances at me in the dark, so I started sneaking glances at her. By the second reel, we were looking at each other more than at the Suez excavations. Right in the middle of the movie, she kissed me on the lips, then started crying.

''Why are you crying?'' I asked in a loud voice. Some people in front of us thought she was crying because Annabella, who loved Tyrone Power in the film, was killed during a typhoon.

''It's only a movie,'' a fat Polish woman said to Halina. ''Don't cry.''

''Halina, she's not really dead,'' I whispered. ''She's only an actress.''

She squeezed my hand. ''I'm crying because I'm so happy to be here with you.''

''But you know that we can never marry?'' I said sadly.

''I'll never give you up!'' she answered in a loud voice.

''Sssh!'' the audience rasped.

''Why do you love me so much?''

''Because you're the handsomest boy I've ever met. I like you better than *kielbasa*.''

''Kielbasa!'' I exploded. ''You're comparing me to a sausage?''

''Quiet!'' the people around us whispered. But Halina got a

case of the giggles and couldn't stop. We both started laughing uncontrollably and were asked to leave the theater by one of the ushers. We left Tyrone Power on a cliff, gazing morosely at his Suez Canal. What good was it to him? He had lost not only Annabella, but Loretta Young, too. We couldn't have cared less.

"Served her right for being so pretty," I said as we ran out of the movie house. We laughed all the way to her apartment.

"Come on up," she said. "My family's away for the day."

I couldn't believe what I was hearing. Once we got inside the apartment, she locked the door and started kissing me passionately. I was afraid that she might cause me to go too far.

"I'd better go before your family comes home. Your father would kill me."

"Please don't go," she begged. "My parents won't be home for hours. And anyway—I'm not afraid of them anymore."

I decided that if Halina wanted to go "all the way," as my friends on the soccer team put it, her apartment was not the place for it. Before we went too far, I proposed a plan.

"Next week, we're playing a club in Krakow. My father owns a hotel near there, in Krynica, where we could stay. He won't be there, so it's all right. Could you tell your parents that you're spending the weekend with one of your girlfriends?"

"Oh, yes—I'd love to spend a weekend with you. I'll tell my parents that my friend Alma has invited me to her family's home in Krakow. Alma is very reliable. I'll tell her the truth and she'll cover for me."

"Will your parents believe you?"

"Of course. I never lie to them." She smiled slyly, and for the first time I wondered if Halina was quite as wonderful and sincere as I thought she was. Then I remembered how I had lied to my father about attending synagogue, and I forgave her.

"Will I go to Krakow with you and the team?"

"No. You and I will travel to Krynica by train and check into my father's hotel. Then, I'll join my team in Krakow. It's all very simple."

"But if we stay in your father's hotel—won't he find out?"

"Not a chance. The manager there is a friend of mine, and he's very close-mouthed. We have nothing to worry about."

As we continued hugging and kissing, I realized that we did have something to worry about. I felt depressed that stupid racial prejudice would keep us from marrying. I wondered why one world, supposedly governed by one God, had to be composed of so many different races who fiercely despised each other. I was too young to find the answer to that enigma, and none of my elders would give me a satisfactory reply.

When we got to the hotel that weekend, the staff started needling me about my Polish girlfriend. But I gave it right back to them. I reprimanded them for their racism and told them we were all brothers and should all love one another. If I chose to love a Polish girl, she was just as good as a Jewish girl in God's eyes. The staff temporarily minded their manners after my rebuke.

That Saturday, with Halina in the grandstand, I played my finest game. We scored a decisive victory.

After the game, the team went to the Moly Roz Restaurant, a popular eating spot in Krakow. I asked our captain if I could bring along Halina. He said that it was okay with him, as long as I could withstand the heckling and not get into any fights. I offered to sit apart from the team and pay a separate check, but he wouldn't hear of this.

"Sit with us and have a good time," he said. "We'll pick up the check. After all, you were instrumental in our victory."

We had a jubilant time at the restaurant, eating, drinking, and dancing. I thought I could detect some jealousy on the part of some of my teammates, but at least they didn't get nasty about my non-Jewish girlfriend.

When Halina and I returned to the hotel, even the manager, Stefan Zudnicki, whom I considered a friend, expressed disapproval that I had brought a Polish girl to the hotel.

"Why do you want to sleep with this girl?" he asked disdainfully, as Halina stood by.

I was surprised at his behavior. I had always liked this man, but now I felt like punching him.

"Stefan," I said coolly, "I am with her because I love her. We plan to marry someday. There is enough prejudice in this nation without having to suffer more from you."

He apologized, realizing that Halina wasn't just a pickup from downtown Warsaw.

Up in our room, Halina was so in awe of my defense of her that she covered every inch of my face with kisses. We hadn't yet had full sexual relations, and I was glad that we had waited. Still, I was so naive about this experience that I had only the flimsiest notion of how to proceed. This may seem strange for a boy of eighteen, but with my Orthodox upbringing, I had not experimented with sex as early as most boys did. My teammates talked about their encounters as if they were hardened veterans, but I had dismissed their outbursts as empty boasting.

I told her the truth. "You're the first, so I may be nervous."

She answered with a warm, reassuring laugh. This was her first affair too, but I must say that she was much more confident in her performance than I was. We undressed and took a long time exploring each other's bodies. It was a very tender experience. I felt somewhat guilty when it was all over. But I blamed that on my religious upbringing.

Fortunately, Halina appeared to have no regrets, and that cheered me up.

After our exalted weekend, we saw each other as often as possible. I started calling for her at her apartment, and her parents didn't seem to mind. I always brought Halina and her mother presents—candy, perfume, cosmetics, books, and magazines—and that softened the shock of my being a Jew. Halina's mother could overlook anything in exchange for a gift; her father, the mailman, seemed more interested in his newspaper than in anything his daughter was up to.

My relationship with Halina matured me, but it also saddened me. Her feelings for me made me realize how little love I had received from my parents.

Halina and I continued dating steadily. We went to the movies, sports events, restaurants, but mostly, we went dancing. We not only danced well together, but we won prizes for our waltzing. These were the happiest days of my young life, which was soon to turn into a nightmare.

CHAPTER 4

Case White

We had our first devastating shock of war that September of 1939, on the afternoon before Rosh Hashanah. Halina and I were huddled in a doorway on Gesia Street, clinging to each other. A faint roar in the sky grew louder, and Halina started shaking.

"What's that noise?" she asked in a frightened tone.

I stepped out of the doorway and looked at the sky. It was a very bright day, and I had to shield my eyes from the sun. I saw the formations of black specks making their way toward us like great flocks of migrating geese. Halina joined me, and we realized that planes were approaching the city.

"They're German," I said, holding her to me. Before she could say anything, we heard the first bombs fall on the city and we ducked inside the doorway. Suddenly, the city was an inferno. Bombs burst all around us and buildings went up in flames. We crouched down in the doorway and covered our heads—as though that would help if a bomb dropped on us. People were screaming and running about, followed by maddened dogs who didn't know what was going on.

I don't remember how long we stayed huddled there. It seemed like hours. Halina was terrified, her face buried in my chest. A number of buildings on Gesia Street were bombed out and burning. Halina began screaming that her mother was home all alone. She wanted to run down the street to her apartment.

"No!" I insisted, "it's too dangerous. There are dead people all around us." She saw the bodies of pedestrians who had been caught in the bombing and began to cry hysterically. One man had been decapitated, and I turned her face away from the horrible scene.

During those moments, I felt my strongest attachment to Halina. We spoke of love while the bombs fell, eternal love. There was death in the streets, and we knew the wrath of the Nazis was blindly spilling blood. Jewish blood, Christian blood—there was no difference.

I do not know how long the bombs kept falling. Time was suspended. While they continued to explode a blonde Gentile girl shivered in my arms. The air was thick with dust and smoke, and my ears were ringing from all the noise. Hitler had launched "Case White," his code name for the conquest of Poland.

I cannot recall the moment the bombs stopped. I can only remember that the ringing in my ears started to fade and the world around me grew silent. After this brief interlude came a new chorus, filling the air with the shrill sounds of ambulances, police cars, and fire engines. Halina appeared calmer, and I said that we might now make it to her apartment. She took my hand and we hurried down the street. People were still running about in a frenzy. I had read about the last days of Pompeii. It must have been a lot like this. Scenes of suffering and death were everywhere. Tenants were scurrying out of burning apartments, clutching their valuables. Children were sobbing and holding frightened pets in their arms. Water pipes had burst and the streets were flooded.

As we neared Halina's apartment house, we bumped into my friend Leo's sister, Malka. She was standing alone in the street, petrified, as if she had been turned to stone.

"What's wrong, Malka?" I asked.

Still staring straight ahead, she said, "Look! Our house is burning!"

We took her by the hand and walked closer. Her apartment house was a flaming inferno. Firemen and civilians valiantly fought to put out the blaze at 12 Kupiecka Street, but the fire was totally out of control. A number of firefighters were overcome by the smoke and were carried off on stretchers.

"Mama! Mama!" Malka screamed. I tried to calm her by saying that perhaps her mother had gotten out of the building, but she didn't believe that. Every fifth house on the block was blazing.

I joined some men on the roof of the house next door to Malka's and helped to pour water on the flames, but it was like tossing thimbles of water on a volcanic eruption.

When I realized that we were making no headway, I rejoined

my two friends. Malka threw herself into my arms and tried to comfort herself.

"I can't leave here until I find out what happened to my mother," she sobbed.

"Maybe your mother was out," I repeated.

She shook her head. She would not be fooled.

"My whole life is buried in that debris," she said in a dead tone. "How can I walk away and leave it all behind? A few minutes ago, I still had a family. Now, I'm all alone." Her brother Leo had left Poland some days before to join the Russian army.

"Please come home with me," I begged. "There's plenty of room. I know that my father and stepmother will take you in."

Malka looked at me gratefully. I took one of her hands, and Halina took the other. We walked toward my house. Fortunately, neither Halina's nor my house had been bombed.

Helina kissed Malka and tried to offer her some encouragement. "Maybe your mother was out shopping when it happened."

Malka didn't believe a word of it, but said, "Let's go to the shoemaker. His shop faces our apartment house. He might have noticed if Mama went out."

"That's a good idea," I said.

When Malka and I arrived at the shoemaker's shop, he was busy covering his broken window with cardboard. Seeing us he said, "Oh, Malka. What a terrible thing. I saw the bomb hit your house. Thank God you're all right. Come in and I'll fix you some tea."

"Oh, no. Thank you," she replied. "I just wanted to ask you if you saw Mama go out this afternoon? I keep hoping that maybe she was not in the house when the bomb hit."

The shoemaker shook his head sadly. He was silent for a few moments. He motioned for us to sit down on a couple of wooden stools. His wife joined us, with one child in her arms and two others tugging at her skirt.

"Chaya," the shoemaker asked her, "did you see Mrs. Frydman anywhere this afternoon?"

"No, I didn't see her. But when the house started burning, people ran out of it. Perhaps she was one of them. It was difficult for me to tell."

Malka looked a bit more cheerful. "Maybe she was one of the lucky ones."

"I can't honestly say that I saw her," Chaya said carefully.

"There was such panic, and I was so fearful for my children, that I didn't pay close attention to the scene across the street."

Malka got up. "Thank you so much. At least you've given me a little hope. If you should see my mother, kindly tell her that I'm staying with the Shainbergs."

The shoemaker and his wife nodded vigorously. "Of course, of course," they said in unison. "We will certainly give her your message."

Malka gave them my address and thanked them for their kindness.

I suspected that the shoemaker and his wife were being charitably optimistic for Malka's sake, and I admired their humanity.

I took Malka home with me, and my father and stepmother welcomed her as a member of the family. They assured her that she could stay as long as she wished. My stepmother escorted her to one of my sisters' rooms and told her that there were clothes in the closet which would surely fit.

Malka started to cry, overcome by her tragedy and our hospitality. My stepmother put her arms around Malka. After all these years of resentment, I suddenly felt affection for this woman who so easily stepped forward to mother the poor girl.

The following day, Malka was still very low in spirits. She had no news of her mother. She now realized that if her mother had escaped the blast, she would have heard from her by now. Some bodies had been recovered from the fire, but they were charred beyond recognition.

"Tonight is Rosh Hashanah," she said to me tearfully, "and Mama's gone. There's no place left to look for her. What a horrible way to die. Why does God permit such things?"

I tried to soothe her. "Don't give up completely. Let me talk to the shoemaker again. Maybe he's heard some news."

When I went to the shop by myself, I didn't have the nerve to again ask him about Malka's mother. I stood there, waiting for him to give me some news, but he merely shook his head. "These are tragic times. Let's hope that no one else will have to die."

There was nothing more to be gained from this visit. The shoemaker and his family sadly watched me leave their shop. I had planned to visit Halina, but an air raid alert sounded, and I ran back to our apartment house. By the time I got there, my parents and Malka were already huddled in the basement with the other tenants. Malka searched my face for some hopeful sign, but she knew immediately that there was none.

Bombs rained on Warsaw again, destroying more houses and killing more citizens. In looking back, those who were instantly killed during these bombings were lucky. It was a far better and speedier death than the one that awaited most of the survivors.

Once again, our house was spared. But the homes of many of our friends were destroyed.

When the all-clear sounded, we went up to our apartment. We sat at the table, and Papa poured wine in our glasses. He stood and spoke in a sad voice, "And it was evening and it was morning—the sixth day. And the heaven and earth were finished and all their host. And on the seventh day. . . ."

Right in the middle of the Kiddush, the prayer said over wine, another bombing started. My father paused only for a moment, then closed his eyes and finished the prayer.

We were terrified. Malka took my hand and held it tightly. My three-year-old half-brother, Shloyma, started to shriek, "Mama! Mama! I'm scared."

My stepmother took him on her lap and held him close. "Don't be afraid," she kept saying while she rocked him. How could you explain to a child that the Germans were bombing us and that at any moment we might be blown to bits?

In the beginning of September 1939, Hitler's army entered Poland. In seven days the Germans traveled 350 miles on the road to Warsaw. The Polish government immediately mobilized every man from twenty-one to fifty years of age. By this time, my brother Nathan was the leading figure among all the Yeshivas in Poland and was fortunate enough to have a diplomatic passport. He managed to escape to Kaunas, the capital of Lithuania, but he had to leave his wife and year-old son behind in Otwock, 30 miles from Warsaw. My sister Hena went to live with them in Otwock, and while my sister-in-law taught school, Hena took care of the baby.

Later I discovered that the members of a large Yeshiva in Kaunas helped my brother get to Japan, where he lived safely for two years. From there, he went to Shanghai and remained in that city throughout the war. He was made president of all the rabbis who had been lucky enough to relocate to Shanghai.

Back in Warsaw, our days and nights of despair began. A day didn't go by that didn't bring air raid sirens and new devastation. One truly lived for the moment, knowing that any second one might be blown to eternity.

Every time we emerged from our flimsy shelter, another part of our neighborhood had been destroyed. Listening to the radio, we could hear the reports of the tragedy that was approaching us. The Russians had joined the battle on September 17, and were attacking Nazi positions in Poland from the east. On this date, also, the Germans effectively knocked out the Polish army in the field. All that remained were a few isolated units and the Warsaw garrison.

News bulletins grew graver by the day. On September 23, the Germans were approaching Warsaw in battle array, marching in three rows. First came the infantry, leading the parade; then came the motorized troops. All were moving in the direction of Zoliborz, east of Warsaw. The next day, an advance squad of Germans arrived at Muranowski Square with trucks full of bread. While the Nazis distributed the loaves to Poles, playing the role of a Messiah, German photographers filmed the benevolent scene to be used for Nazi propaganda.

That afternoon, I had my first encounter with the violent anti-Semitism that was to come. I was lucky to have been one of the first on line for bread. After I had received my loaf, Stefan Muraz, the Polish son of a super at Muranowski Square, ran into our midst and started shouting to the Germans: "Don't feed them—they're Jews."

The German lieutenant in charge of the maneuver couldn't understand what the young man was yelling. One of Stefan's friends, a Pole named Antek, indicated to the lieutenant in broken German and Yiddish that some of the people on line were Jews and didn't deserve to receive charity. He actually pointed out the Jews to the officer.

"Juden!" the officer snarled when he understood the message. He took out his pistol and started firing at the Jews. They were so hungry that it didn't dawn on them that their lives were endangered. Suddenly, when some of their friends started falling to the ground, dead or wounded, the remaining Jews scattered.

Stefan, Antek, and another of their Polish friends, Franek, were assigned to keep a watch on the line for any Jews who might accidently be given rations. I hid myself in a doorway to watch this miserable scene. No other Jews attempted to stand on that line. I hid my loaf under my jacket and felt grateful that I had gotten on line early. On that day, and all through the war, I often felt that if I had a choice of enemies, I would prefer the Nazi to the Pole. What could be lower than what these despicable people had done?

When I felt that it was safe to leave my hiding place, I walked quickly down the street, trying to look as inconspicuous as possible. I had never understood the allure of hunting—of stalking a poor, defenseless creature and slaying it for sport. Now, it was being done to people. To my people.

I ran up the stairs to our apartment and frightened my stepmother when I burst through the door. "Look Mama—I managed to get a loaf of bread!"

She was stunned beyond belief, not because I had a loaf of bread in my hand, but because this was the first complete sentence I had ever spoken to her. There were tears in her eyes, and I realized how my obdurate silence had hurt her all those years.

Malka was standing nearby and, although she was hungry, she said, "Perhaps we should save it for the Sabbath."

My stepmother nodded and put the loaf in our bread container. I had the feeling that as far as she was concerned, it wasn't the loaf of bread that was important, but my recognition of her. I did not mention the shootings at Muranowski Square.

Within a couple of days, the last Polish army garrisons were dislodged from Warsaw. The Germans moved in and made their presence known with parades and constant patrols throughout the city. They announced a military government and established severe penalties for all offenses. They were methodical and precise. They gave the impression of being thoroughly in control of everything. They claimed to be supermen and acted the role well. There wasn't much talk of resisting them.

On September 27, 1939, Warsaw was the captive of Nazi Germany. "Case White," the Nazi code for the annexation and subjugation of Poland, was complete. Poland began its five years, three months, and twenty-one days of Nazi domination and holocaust.

CHAPTER 5

Occupation

As soon as the Germans occupied Warsaw, they began putting all Jews to work. Early in the morning, I was required to report to the Jewish Congregation Building at 26 Grzybowska Street. When I got there the first morning, the yard was jammed with Jews, all waiting for work assignments. Most were sent to clean up the German barracks on Zamenhof Street. I was assigned to a detail with nine other Jews to work on the second floor of a clothing store near the German barracks.

One day, I observed a fellow worker stealing military caps that had been set aside by a German soldier for distribution to the troops.

I mentioned this to one of my friends. He was shocked. We walked over to the thief. "Are you out of your mind?" I whispered. "Do you want us all to be shot?"

The frightened man gave us an angry glance. "These caps may come in handy for all of us," he said.

I realized that he was looking out for us rather than stealing caps to sell. "Well, that's a different story," I said, putting my hand on his shoulder. "But you'd better get back to work before the guards catch you."

He nodded in agreement and went back to folding garments and stacking them neatly on the shelves.

Later in the day, a German soldier who had placed the caps in a stack returned and counted them. When he found some missing, he flew into a rage and ran out into the square where we were assembled for dismissal. The Gestapo officer in charge of our district, First Lieutenant Rinke, was delivering one of his typical Nazi public relations speeches.

"We are your liberators," he barked at us. "You will follow our orders. We will teach you how to work the German way. Those of you who will not work our way will be shot."

The soldier carrying the caps approached the officer, halted a few steps before him and rendered a snappy salute. "Sir!" he said, "I have some important information to relay to you."

The Lieutenant seemed somewhat annoyed at the young upstart who had interrupted his oration, but as the soldier whispered to him, the officer's face turned radish red.

"What! The Jews stole caps?"

"Yes, Sir," the soldier said.

"I want the detail from the clothing store to step forward," he commanded.

Just before he gave this order, I had realized what was happening and backed away from the crowd. Only nine men stepped forward. I managed to slip away and ran into the building where we had been working. But I was seen by one of the German soldiers, who began chasing me.

The Commandant lined up my nine frightened co-workers and, without even searching them, ordered his guards to shoot. I heard the gunfire from the store. It was dark in that building, but I managed to find an empty carton to hide in.

The soldier who pursued me was afraid to come inside, because the building was bombed out and without electricity. Other soldiers soon joined him and entered the building. Although they couldn't see, they started shooting wildly at the cartons. The soldier who first chased me shouted, "Don't fire—you'll ruin the merchandise. We'll get him in the morning when it's light. He can't get out of here alive."

I was trapped. The soldiers locked the door and left a sentry outside to guard it. I stayed still for what seemed like hours. Finally, I lit a match and looked at my watch. It was 8:00 p.m. I tried opening a window, but it creaked so much that I quickly closed it. I decided to wait a few hours more before attempting an escape.

At 10:00 p.m., it seemed quiet enough to try again. I opened the window very slowly this time. There was grass below, and I figured I could jump down without hurting myself. But there was one major problem. Once I got below, I would have to climb a barbed-wire fence before I was free.

I lit another match and found a long wooden box and some cord. I attached the cord securely to the box and lowered it to the ground. Then I climbed out the window and jumped down. I almost cried out in pain, but muffled my scream. My ankle was twisted, but I lay still, afraid that the Germans would hear me.

I waited a few moments. Then slowly I got to my feet. My ankle was throbbing, but my will to live was stronger than my discomfort. I hobbled to the fence, set up the box, and managed to climb on top of it. I then slung my wide leather belt over the barbed wire so I could lift myself over it. The perspiration trickled down over my eyes, and I had to wipe it away with my sleeve. Then, using all my strength, I vaulted over the top of the fence and was halfway down the other side, still holding onto the belt, when I saw a Nazi patrol car coming down the street, raking the area with gunfire.

I froze, suspended in midair like a circus performer. Fortunately it was dark by the fence, and I again escaped detection. My arms were ready to break and my ankle seemed to be getting worse. As soon as the patrol car passed by, I let go of the belt and hit concrete instead of grass. I landed on my good ankle, or I would surely never have made it.

The Germans had instituted a 6:00 p.m. curfew, and anyone caught in the street after that hour would immediately be shot. I knew the neighborhood so well that I was able to limp along and hide myself whenever I heard a sound. It wasn't too far to my apartment, but just as I was approaching Halina's house, I heard a patrol car on the next block and darted in the doorway. I knocked on the gate and the buildings old watchman woke up.

"Who's there? What do you want?" he demanded suspiciously.

"Please let me in before the patrol car comes," I begged.

The old man peered through the gate, recognized me, and let me in. He put his finger to his lips and motioned me toward the doorway. I looked gratefully at him, surprised that a Pole would help a Jew in trouble.

"Don't I know you, boy?" he asked. "You live at 21 Gesia, don't you?"

I nodded, too frightened to answer.

"Be careful that nobody sees or hears you. And you must leave at six in the morning."

"Yes, yes—thank you. I know the mailman in apartment 5. Can I go up there?"

"Yes—it would be safer—if they let you in."

I thanked him and slowly climbed the stairs to Halina's apartment. I knocked and waited a few moments, but there was no answer. I knocked again, and finally her mother slowly opened the door. She looked terrified when she saw me.

"Go away. How dare you bother us in the middle of the night!" she said shrilly.

"Please, I want to see Halina."

"She doesn't want to see you anymore. You can only bring us trouble."

Through the door, I could see Halina in the other room. But even though she heard my voice, she made no attempt to speak to me. I realized that my being a Jew had finally come between us, despite all her former protestations of not being anti-Semitic. If the Germans hadn't come to Warsaw, our affair might have continued, and we might even have married. That was now out of the question. Her parents obviously were afraid that the Germans would retaliate if they harbored a Jew. I looked through the door at Halina, but she turned her face away. I knew then that she would never acknowledge me again. Her mother slammed the door in my face.

Clutching the bannister, I painfully made my way down the stairs. When I approached the watchman, he said, "Come, you can stay with me until morning." He led me to his sparsely furnished apartment and offered me a piece of brown bread. "Here—you must be hungry."

I greedily reached for the bread. "Why are you so good to me? You know I'm a Jew."

"Son, I'm seventy-four years old. I've seen many things in my life. I've always lived among Jews. They're no better nor worse than any other people."

"There are very few like you left in the world," I said with appreciation.

He smiled and led me to a couch. "Try to get some sleep. I'll wake you in the morning." I lay down and he put a blanket over me. Even though my ankle was hurting, I fell into a deep sleep that lasted until dawn.

The watchman shook me lightly and said, "There's an empty apartment on the top floor—number 60. The door's open. Stay there until the tenants have left for work, then you can go safely."

He handed me another piece of bread, and I thanked him again. This man was truly a saint.

I hobbled up to the empty apartment and looked out the window at the awakening city. I was relieved to be here instead of in that store, waiting for the Germans to capture me. I even managed a soft laugh thinking of their frustration when they searched that place from top to bottom and failed to find me. I could hear those Krauts cursing and fuming at my miraculous escape.

After the workers had all left the building, I went down the stairs. When the watchman let me out of the gate, I gratefully shook his hand. "I'll never forget your kindness," I told him. He made a gesture indicating it was nothing.

There were already many people outside, and I quickly got lost in the crowd. When I approached our apartment house, I was happy to see Malka standing at the gate. Her face brightened when she saw me.

"Where have you been? What happened to you? I've been up all night worrying about you."

"Don't speak. Let's go upstairs fast."

She saw that I was limping and helped me get up the stairs. When we entered the apartment, I was touched to see my stepmother crying and my Papa praying. They were truly concerned about me.

"Thank God!" my stepmother cried, throwing her arms around me. "We were afraid the Germans had arrested you—or worse."

I handed her the piece of bread the night watchman had given me, but she ignored it. "I'm so glad that you're safe."

My father came over and put his hand on my shoulder, a tender gesture that was rare for him. He didn't say anything, but I could tell that he was thankful to see me alive.

We sat down at the table, and I told them what I had been through the night before, all because one man had stolen some caps. I knew that I had to get away from the apartment, and away from Warsaw. The Germans had the names of every Jew working on each detail, and before long they would discover who had escaped their wrath. Then they would come looking for me. If they caught me at home, the whole family would be killed.

"Wouldn't it be better if you hid out in the country?" Malka asked. "You might be safer there."

I looked appreciatively at her. She had paved the way for what I was going to propose.

"I have a plan, Papa. Please hear me out, and don't misunderstand."

"I know. You want to leave." He lowered his head.

"How did you know that?"

"Because that's what I would do if I were you. A young person with your courage should not stay here to have himself killed. My generation is too old to fight the enemy. Your generation must do this. You must submit to God's will. He will help you win. I would not be proud of you if you stayed here only to be destroyed by the Nazis. Take Malka with you, my son, and go with my blessings.''

I could not believe I was hearing these words from my father. This was the first time in my life that I felt accepted by Papa. I embraced him and thanked him for his support.

"This is not goodbye," I said. "I'll be back whenever I can to bring you food and see how you are."

We discussed various alternatives and finally decided that we would be safest if we went to the village of Brezezinka, where a peasant named Mularek might shelter us in his cottage. He was an old friend of Papa's and owed him many favors. We would be a good distance from Warsaw, so the Germans might not have so many troops concentrated there. There weren't many Jews in that area, and perhaps we could even pass as Gentiles. We would go to the Warsaw-Gdansk rail station and try to find an open freight car to sneak into. If we failed in that or if too many Germans were there, we could walk the two hundred kilometers, being careful to keep off the main roads, thereby avoiding German patrols.

I thought we stood a good chance of making the journey because the Germans were preoccupied with moving some troops back to the west, where they still had battle lines facing the French and British. Moreover, those Germans who remained in Poland were a bit heady with their easy conquest, and possibly not as careful as they might have been if they had encountered tougher resistance.

If anyone questioned us, we could pose as Polish peasants who had lost their family in a bombing and were on their way to live with relatives in the north.

"Mularek is a good friend," Papa said. "He won't turn you in to the Germans. But be careful. They may be watching the trains."

"Don't worry. Malka and I are lucky. We don't look Jewish."

"You must save yourselves," Papa said. "You can do much for our people. I will pray for you and Malka, and I know that you will survive. We old people must reconcile ourselves to our lot."

I kissed him tenderly on both cheeks, then kissed my step-mother. She began weeping, and my little half brother, Shloyma, joined in. "Why does Maurice want to leave us?" the boy cried. "Doesn't he love us anymore?"

"Hush, son," she said, then turned to me crying. "We have just begun to understand each other, and now you must leave. It breaks my heart."

How ironic it was after all those years of a loveless family life to be showered with affection when it was time to leave.

"I have to pack a few things," I said, and went to my room. I filled a small bag with underclothes, socks, and shirts. Malka asked if she could take a few things my stepmother had loaned her.

"Of course, of course," Leah said, "They are for you, to keep."

When we had finished our meager packing, we all embraced. My father kissed Malka's forehead. "May God take good care of you," he said, then he gave me his blessing.

We walked down the stairs slowly, and I could still hear Shloyma whimpering. I wondered if I would ever see any of them again.

When we started down Gesia Street, we noticed groups of people huddled around the newest proclamation that the Germans had posted on the sides of houses.

"Let's read the latest from the Nazi butchers," I said to Malka.

"You read it; I don't have the stomach for it."

I managed to force my way to the front of the crowd and read the edict with a sinking heart:

1. AS OF JANUARY 10, 1940, A GHETTO WILL BE ESTABLISHED FOR JEWS.
2. EVERY JEW IS REQUIRED TO WEAR A YELLOW ARMBAND BEARING THE "JEWISH STAR" (MOGEN DAVID).
3. EVERY JEW WHO EXPECTS TO RECEIVE BREAD HAS TO REGISTER WITH THE JEWISH CONGREGATION AND BE AVAILABLE FOR WORK.

I was filled with anger when I read this unbelievable heartless proclamation. Hadn't we suffered enough persecution from the Poles without this further abuse by the Germans? The order had a frenzied effect on the people. They sensed that these words had a far more sinister aspect than simply a means for identifying Jews. After studying the message, the crowd became crazed and ran about in all directions with one goal in mind: to get out of the city using any means—before being trapped in the Warsaw ghetto.

I told Malka the bad news. As we stood discussing what it really meant, German trucks full of soldiers and police dogs came down the street, causing more panic among the people.

I grabbed Malka's hand and led her into a house nearby. We ran downstairs to where an old nightclub used to be. From a window we watched in horror as the soldiers with their dogs descended on the Jews and shot people for no reason at all.

The Germans were launching a new phase in their campaign of terror. Before long, Jewish neighborhoods would become hell on earth. And all the while, some devoutly religious people kept praying for the Messiah to come, drive the Germans away, and reopen the gates of Jerusalem and the Promised Land. Some of us suspected that a different fate awaited those who stayed behind.

Once the German patrol had passed, we went back to the street. My knowledge of the many underground tunnels and cellars in Warsaw helped us to get safely to the railway station.

We approached the outer limits of the Warsaw-Gdansk railway line, walking through wild grass and brush weeds that seemed to grow despite war and winter. I guided Malka along a shallow ditch that led to the tracks. As we waited in the ditch, I made periodic trips to see whether there were any German patrols or a train coming our way. I put on a brave show, assuring Malka it was easy to get a train. I told her of an adventure I once had with some of my classmates when we had jumped a train moving out of the yards and then explored the outskirts of Warsaw in an empty freight car. But in those days all we had to fear were some hooligans or anti-Semitic students. And the worst that could have happened to us was a beating. Now, however, running into hostile Poles or the barbarous Germans could mean the end. "Don't worry, Malka," I said, "have faith in me. We'll make it."

The sun had set and the evening air was frosty when I heard a locomotive approaching. It rumbled down the tracks and away from the station, its bright headlamp gleaming in our direction. We remained hidden in the ditch while the locomotive passed, and I was glad to see that the train appeared unarmed with no Germans riding on it. Once the coal tender had passed by, I motioned for Malka to get ready. We moved closer to the track, until we were only a couple of meters away. Several freight cars passed, but the doors were all closed. Then came a series of flat cars loaded with goods packed beneath tarpaulins.

Boarding the train was easy. We both jogged alongside a flat car and Malka pulled herself up onto the car by grabbing a handle and stepping on a small metal rail that protruded from the side. I followed her and in a moment we were rolling north.

The night grew cold and we climbed beneath the tarpaulin while the train gathered speed. We huddled closely in the darkness, departing Warsaw for our uncertain future.

CHAPTER 6

Mularek

The rising sun treated us to a bright, crisp day, and for the first time in many weeks I felt free.

We tucked ourselves warmly into the folds of the giant tarpaulin and watched the countryside roll past in a panorama that seemed to have been little touched by the war. Peasants were up and about their morning chores as thin streams of smoke drifted lazily from their cottages. Malka and I shared a breakfast of bread and water as the scenery passed by.

Shortly after dawn, the train started to chug while going up a gentle grade. I was familiar with the terrain and knew we would soon be approaching Mlawa, which was near the border of East Prussia. Most of our journey was behind us.

As we moved into Mlawa, Malka and I slipped back beneath the tarpaulin and crawled to the west side of the car. I knew that if we stopped at Mlawa the Germans might search our train, and we would have to make a quick escape. If we jumped off the west side of the car, the Germans looking at the train from that angle would have the sun in their eyes. This would facilitate our slipping away unnoticed.

Fortunately we didn't have to use this plan. The train did stop, but only briefly to take on water for the engine, and then we were on our way again. Our car wasn't searched. Further north, we skirted the western edge of Masuria, the land of lakes and forests where the Teutonic Knights had started the long and bloody process of German militarism.

By midafternoon, after descending along the gentle grades toward Lubartow, we prepared to leave the train as it slowed to approach the station. We stepped down to the steel rail by the car's side and then tumbled off into tall grasses. The village of Brezezinka was a couple of miles away.

We walked through the woods and avoided the main road. Exhausted, we came to a grassy field and lay down to rest for several hours. A noise woke me up, but it was just a few boys playing games; they paid no attention to us.

When Malka awoke, she stared at the clear blue sky for a while, then said softly, "It's so peaceful here."

I stroked her hair, then withdrew my hand quickly, afraid that she might resent this familiarity. Instead, she looked into my eyes as if to ask, "Why did you stop?"

After a few moments, she said, "You're in love with Halina, aren't you? How did you two ever get together?"

I told her how Halina lived near me and used to watch me play soccer. "Now, it's all over between us."

She looked relieved, then asked, "Why?"

I told her what had happened only two nights before when I saw Halina and her mother. "That was one of the most painful moments of my life. I could never love her after the way she so selfishly betrayed me."

Malka shook her head and remained silent. She was distracted by a farmer in a nearby field playing with his dog. The man would toss a branch a few feet away and the pooch would charge after it ferociously. When he bounded back with the bark in his mouth, his master rewarded him with a pat on the head.

"That dog doesn't know how lucky he is," Malka said. "We'd be better off trading places with him. He's better treated in this country than a Jew. No one would kill him without reason, the way the Germans massacred those poor people yesterday."

"You're right. To them, we're scum—like rats or roaches. But we have other matters to think of right now. We have to concentrate on survival. I believe that if we use our wits, we can stay alive. Not only now—but throughout the war. If I hadn't jumped out of the window in that factory, I would have been killed the next morning."

"I know you are right."

"So what must we do now?"

"Mularek's cottage is nearby. I'm sure he'll take us in."

"And what if he doesn't?"

"Then we'll live in a tree like the squirrels."

Malka smiled, but I could tell she was worried.

"One thing I've learned," I said, "is that you can't worry

about anything in life until it happens. And even then, instead of worrying about it, you have to decide the best way out of your trouble. That's what we'll have to do from now on.''

I asked her to wait for me behind a tree while I knocked on Mularek's door. She didn't relish my leaving her alone, but she knew I would only be a few feet away.

I knocked on the cottage door, and some dogs started barking inside.

"Who's there?" a gruff male voice asked without opening the door.

"It's Maurice Shainberg from Warsaw. My father and uncle were friends of yours and used to buy fruits and vegetables from you.''

The door opened slowly, and Mularek peered at me. He had seen me a few times in my uncle's store, and he opened the door wider.

"Come in, come in," he said. "What can I do for you?"

I entered the cottage and noted that his wife, who was drying dishes in the kitchen, didn't seem happy at this intrusion.

"You must be seeking shelter," he said before I could speak. "Are things very bad in Warsaw?"

"Dismal," I replied. I told him about yesterday's massacre and the posting of the Warsaw Ghetto notice. He looked toward his wife, who motioned him into the kitchen. They argued in low tones for a while and I heard her say, "But he's a Jew." She seemed outraged that her husband would entertain the thought of taking me in. But then I heard Mularek mention my father's name, and that seemed to soften the lady.

"You can stay in the barn," he said when he returned. "But we have to be very careful. The Germans are all around us.''

I summoned the courage to tell him about Malka. "Please let her stay with me in the barn. We can help you and your wife with the chores.''

"You must bring the girl in immediately—before she's discovered. Our neighbors can't be trusted in these times.''

I thanked him and ran out to summon Malka. She had been watching the cottage and ran toward me with relief. When Mularek's wife saw how young and helpless Malka was, she took pity on us and served us some tea and biscuits. We spent the rest of the day telling them about the inhuman things that were happening in Warsaw. When I told him about my escape from the factory, the man's wife kept crossing herself.

After a sparse but welcome dinner, the couple showed us where we could sleep in the barn. They made us feel comfortable and secure. We promised to do all we could to help with the housekeeping and farm work. After talking several hours into the night, we went out to the barn where we would spend most of our time. The barn seemed ideal as a safe haven for it was set back from the road and full of hiding places.

Malka and I made our bedding from straw in the barn's loft. Below, dairy cattle shifted occasionally in their stalls, and above us, under the eaves, we heard a nest of birds settling down for the night. Malka and I stretched out in the straw and enjoyed the simplicity of country life. There were no bright street lamps or the sounds of marching soldiers to interrupt the night. There was only the murmur of animals, the caress of a light breeze and the ghostly glow of star light.

Although Malka and I slept near each other, I had always thought of her as almost a sister and did not attempt to take advantage of the situation. We both slept soundly through the night.

The next morning, Mularek's heavy footsteps and husky voice woke me. "Know how to milk a cow?" he asked.

"I don't know," I replied. "Does it give kosher milk?"

"As kosher as all the potatoes I supplied to your uncle's store," he replied.

"Come down here, I'll teach you how to earn your keep."

I stepped down the wooden ladder, tucking in my shirt and brushing the straw from my hair as I went toward my amiable host.

"Here, now," Mularek said. "Watch me." He sat himself on a three-legged stool beside the cow, slipped a wooden bucket beneath her, and started to pull at the swollen udder. Milk squirted out in long streams that quickly filled the bucket. It looked easy.

"It doesn't look like you need a university degree to do that," I said. "Let me try."

Mularek stood up and offered me his seat. "Go ahead. Maybe you don't need a university degree, but I think you'll need some instruction . . . Go ahead, let's see how you do."

I didn't do so well. The best I could manage was a few drops that didn't quite make it into the bucket. And then the cow started moving around, annoyed at my novice attempts.

While Malka crawled down the ladder, Mularek took back the milking stool and resumed his work with the animals. "I'll do this now, then you can do it in the evening when we have more time. We must take care of the animals before we have breakfast."

Mularek worked swiftly. He showed me how to feed and water the cows while he was milking them. After this was done, we went to the cottage and had the finest breakfast I had tasted in a long time. During the next few days we adapted to the farm routine, working mostly indoors, helping with chores in the barn and cottage. By the second day, I could even milk a cow, if not with practiced skill, at least adequately.

The work was tiring, but I enjoyed being kept busy all day. It helped to clear my mind of the memories of my suffering family. After the nightmare of Warsaw under German occupation, Mularek's cottage was a wonderful refuge for me—a place where I could do an honest day's work and receive a modest reward for it.

But our paradise didn't last long. We had only been at the cottage a few days when a neighbor stopped Mularek on the road and said, "Why are you harboring Jews in your house? Don't you realize you're endangering the whole village?"

"Who knows this?" Mularek asked.

"*I* know it and soon everyone else will. Didn't you read the poster at police headquarters? It's forbidden to hide Jews. If the Germans should find out, they will punish the villagers."

Mularek protested, but this neighbor reminded him that it was not only the Germans who were hostile to Jews, but the Polish National Armed Forces. "They will seek revenge if they find out you're hiding them. If you want to risk your life and your wife's, that's one thing, but what right have you to risk the lives of an entire community?"

Mularek told us about this when he came home. He seemed sad and couldn't look me in the eye.

"He's right," I said. "Malka and I have no right to risk your lives in order to save our own skins. We'll go back to Warsaw—there's no choice. But, I'd like to ask a favor of you. Let me go first. I think it would be safer for both of us if we travel separately. Let Malka stay just a few more days, then she can make her way back alone. I'll leave tonight."

Mularek agreed to this. "Don't worry about your friend. When I bring my vegetables to market in Warsaw, I'll take Malka along. If anyone questions us, I'll say she's my daughter. I have a married daughter, you know."

Now I was faced with the difficult task of giving Malka the bad news about our impending separation. I knew she would be very upset. Whenever I left her for just a few moments, she worried.

I found her in the barn, milking the cow. She threw her arms around me and handed me some fresh milk to drink.

"You look miserable," she said. "Has something gone wrong?"

"Yes. We have to leave. Poor Mularek is being criticized by his neighbors for harboring Jews. We can't risk their lives by staying here."

She looked crushed.

"Mularek and I have talked this over, and he agrees with me. I must leave first. It will be easier for me to get back to Warsaw by myself—."

She started to protest, but I put my hand over her mouth.

"Please let me finish. Mularek goes there every few weeks to bring his produce to market. He'll be going soon and he can take you with him. He's going to pass you off as his married daughter."

She nodded, but still looked glum. "I'm thankful to Mularek for his offer, but I feel safer with you. We had no trouble getting here together—why can't we go back that way?"

"Because some of the villagers know we're here together, and they'll easily spot us if we leave at the same time. We have two enemies: the Germans *and* the Poles. The Poles will gladly turn us in to the Germans to stay on their good side. It will be too risky unless we leave separately."

Malka seemed to understand. "You've been very kind to me since my mother died. If it weren't for you, I would probably have killed myself by now. I have complete trust in your judgment. We must do everything we can to stay alive—and your plan is sensible. You leave tonight; I'll leave with Mularek. We'll meet—God willing—in your apartment."

Malka helped me get my things together. Mularek's wife gave me some bread, fruit, and wine to take with me. She made a tasty farewell dinner, and we ended it with a wine toast to my safety and to Malka's as well.

I could see that Mularek and his wife both felt bad about our situation. In just a few days we had become close, and might have stayed close if only Jews had been recognized as human beings.

When it was dark, I kissed Malka goodbye, shook hands with my protectors, and started my perilous journey back to Warsaw. It was bitterly cold that night. The countryside was covered with snow and the wind was fierce and stinging. After walking for hours, I stopped for a moment in an open barn, where I ate some of the bread and drank the wine that was packed in my knapsack.

When the sun came up, I found shelter in a Catholic church. I sat in the back pew during morning Mass. Several worshippers looked curiously in my direction when they first entered the church, but once Mass started, they forgot about me. After the congregation had gone, I remained in my pew and dozed off. I stayed until sundown, eating a little more of the bread. I felt odd finding sanctuary there. But somehow, it was peaceful and mysterious, with candles flickering in red holders and an alien god eyeing me from the ceiling.

At sundown, I left my hiding place and headed toward the

railroad crossing. In about an hour, a freight train passed through, and I was able to hop aboard.

The car was filthy and appeared to have recently been used for hauling livestock. Nobody had bothered to clean it out. The best I could do was to kick a small area clear and cover it with a few bits of straw.

The night was extremely cold, and I shivered in my place. I found out why the door had been left open—there was nothing there to protect. Nor were the sides of the car solid—they were made of wooden slats to provide proper ventilation for the livestock transported to market.

I felt like Jonah in the belly of the whale. I was going to my Nineveh; I was going to the corruption of Warsaw. Then I thought of the holy rabbi who told my father to excuse me from Yeshiva. "I'll be a good Jew," I promised him on that beautiful day so long ago. I had made a vow.

Jonah had also made a vow to be a good Jew and follow the command of God. "But I will sacrifice unto thee with the voice of thanksgiving," Jonah said from the belly of Leviathan. "I will pay that that I have vowed. Salvation is of the Lord."

Jonah was spit from the belly of the whale and made his way to Assyrian Nineveh. I jumped from the train before it rolled into the station and found my way to the heart of Nazi Warsaw.

It was still dark when I reached Gesia Street, where I slipped into our courtyard and up the steps to our apartment. I knocked at the door, but there was no answer. I didn't want to pound on the door too loudly at that late hour; it would only frighten my family and wake Leah's children. So I settled down in the hallway and went to sleep.

Some time later, I awakened when my father opened the door to go out. He almost tripped over me and seemed startled by my presence.

"Oh, it's you!" he exclaimed. "What are you doing there? Have you lost your senses? Come in, son."

He didn't ask how I was. His first concern was Malka.

I explained that she would be returning with Mularek. That news pleased him. He told me he was on his way to his friend Rabbi Kolobier's synagogue at 5 Pawia Street and wanted to get there before daylight.

"Isn't it dangerous for you to go out alone?" I asked.

He dismissed that with a shake of the head. "No more dangerous than staying home. I must go now. Remember the Talmud, my son; whenever two men meet to study the Torah, there is holiness. The more Torah, the more life!"

My stepmother rushed out and embraced me. She seemed overjoyed to see me again. I assured her that Malka was in good hands, and she was happy to hear that.

Papa said goodbye and went downstairs. I sat at the table and drank some weak tea. I still had a little bread and fruit left, which I handed to my stepmother. She awoke Shloyma and Esther and shared the food with them. They were jubilant to see me. Even in the midst of tragedy, the young can be joyous. They were ravenously hungry, and it pained me to see how they devoured the pitiful scraps I gave them.

After I had washed and changed my clothes, I decided to go down to the Jewish Congregation and sign up for a work crew. I told my stepmother not to expect Malka for about a week.

Down at the Congregation, I got on one of the work groups assigned to cleaning the German officers' barracks. We worked hard, scrubbing floors, cleaning windows and latrines. All I heard from my co-workers were tales of misery. When one of them asked why I had only just started to work, I told him I'd been home in bed, sick. I feared that someone might pick me out as the man who had escaped from the factory, but no one connected me with that event.

Some of the men on the work detail with me were old friends from my Zionist days, now involved in the underground. They gave me the address of their hiding place, and I promised to attend their next meeting.

I got home safely that night, and so did Papa. In those days arriving home safely was an achievement. I managed to bring my family home a loaf of bread, courtesy of the underground, and that served as our entire supper. We were more fortunate than most, who had nothing to eat.

The German occupation was taking a heavy toll on the community. The Nazis had been in Warsaw for only two months, and already there was widespread killing, hunger, and depression. My father retreated to his Torah and Talmud, putting his faith in God and praying for mercy. Leah appeared to be doing well, but behind her cheerful smile was an intense sadness.

Every day I remembered my vow to be a good Jew, and one afternoon, while scrubbing floors in a German barracks, I decided what this meant. Like Jonah, I would have to go out into the pagan world on behalf of my people. I could not be content with only the word of God; I would have to take action. I finally resolved to visit the Jewish resistance group and offer my services to the cause.

Two weeks went by, and there was no sign of Malka. Just as we were beginning to lose hope for her, she walked into the apartment early one morning. She was dressed like a typical farm girl and looked healthy and rested. We were all relieved to see her and gathered around the table to hear her story.

The trip back to town had been uneventful. She easily passed for the farmer's daughter, and no one had stopped them. But she had experienced one bad moment at the farm after I left.

"One morning—quite early," she said, "I was half awake in the hay loft, when I suddenly heard a car approaching along the road. I looked out through a crack in the wall and saw some German soldiers talking to Mularek. They wanted milk, and he brought them into the barn. He milked one of his cows, and they snatched the pail from him and drank greedily. I was so terrified I could hardly breathe. One of the soldiers noticed Mularek's hay and said it would make fine feed for the horses in the German barracks. I was sure that they would climb up to the hay loft and find me, but fortunately they didn't. The soldiers said they would be back later with a truck for some hay. I watched them leave and saw them steal some of Mularek's chickens. The poor farmer called me down and said that we would have to find a new hiding place. He spent many hours digging a hole under the barn floor, which he covered with boards. He made the hiding place more comfortable by adding a mattress and a pillow. Mularek was so kind to me that I hated to leave."

Sitting at the table and listening to Malka's experiences seemed to bring us all closer together than we had ever been before. We talked about Mularek and agreed that he had a certain saintliness despite his gruff manner. He had helped us all he could and took a substantial risk in doing so. When his position became futile, he had the wisdom to acknowledge it.

I have heard how some Polish Gentiles had sheltered Jews throughout the war. These extremely rare people risked their lives to save others. Poland was not like such Western countries as Holland and Denmark, where much of the population sympathized with the Jews. Mularek had not only the Nazis to worry about, but also his fellow Poles.

I have always treasured his gestures of good will during those hours of desperation. He offered to help Jews at the most difficult time of the war; he assisted when Hitler seemed to have an invincible hold on Europe, when the Russians sat smugly behind their non-aggression pact, and England and France cowered behind the Maginot Line during their *Sitzkrieg,* when even those Jews who wanted to resist hadn't begun organizing an effective fighting force.

CHAPTER 7

The Ghetto

In November 1939, a group of Jews who had served as officers in the Polish Army formed an underground resistance organization called the Jewish Military Union. Their goal: to resist the Nazis.

Not everyone could join the Jewish Military Union or Z.Z.W., as it was called. Only members of the following organizations were allowed to participate: Betar, Brit Hachail, Akiba, Tel-Chai, and Hashmonea. To illustrate the selectivity of this group, only eight hundred members were accepted from the five thousand persons who qualified. I was honored to be able to join.

The Jewish Military Union occasionally had the support of the A.K. (Polish National Army), which, depending upon the commanding officer, supplied it with weapons and ammunition. High ranking officers of the A.K., such as Colonel A. Petrykowski (code name: Tarnawa) and Captain Henryk Iwanski (code name: Bystry), were especially helpful to the Z.Z.W. It was Bystry who supplied weapons, bullets, and grenades.

At this time, another underground unit, the F.P.I., otherwise known as Plan, was organized with a Captain Cezarny Kettling in charge. This group was composed mainly of members of the press who united to disseminate information and propaganda. The unit specialized in underground posters which publicized the group's activities, popularly called the "Revenge Unit."

We worked along with Plan in its early days; but later, we severed relations with the group after discovering that it had betrayed the underground by collaborating with the Nazis.

The Jewish Military Union's leaders were brilliant and courageous. President and chief, David Apfelbaum, who operated under such code names as Jablonski, Kuwal, and Mietek, was a former Polish Army lieutenant and an active member of Brit Hachail. Pawel Frankel, who was a student, acted as a liaison officer between the Z.Z.W. and Plan, the propaganda arm of the underground. When I joined the Jewish Military Union, I was appointed to act as Frankel's guard.

When the Jewish Military Union got going and began raiding German sites, our members always wore masks. To combat us, the Nazis organized a group called "The Jewish Star of Freedom," headed by a known Gestapo collaborator, Abram Gancewaich, a member of the Bund. This group was organized by the Gestapo and was composed of eighty-five desperate Jews who were Nazi collaborators. Its purpose was to spy on us and report our activities to the Nazis.

Also in November, 1939, the Germans began to close off the Jewish districts of Warsaw with barricades and military police guards. Strands of barbed wire signalled the first stage. A year later, the infamous wall created a final seal around the ghetto.

This was a mournful time for the Jewish population of the city. We watched the brick wall going up around our sector until it was nine feet high and topped with barbed wire. We felt that we were being buried alive. On the other side of the wall, at intervals of about one hundred feet, stood German guards.

The Ghetto was a complex labyrinth, divided by the Germans into four parts. Section One comprised the even-numbered houses and buildings on Leszno, Nowolpki, Smocza, and Karmelicka Streets. This came to be known as the Productive Ghetto, since it included the factories and business establishments of such German exploiters as Tobbens, Schultz, and Hallman, who enslaved not only Jewish adults, but children as well.

Section Two, adjacent to the Productive Ghetto was a smaller, semi-industrialized sector with Swietojanska, Walowa, and Franciszkanska Streets as its borders. A broom factory was located here along with some smaller business concerns.

Section Three, the central Ghetto, consisted of Zamenhof, Nalewki, Gesia, Muranowska, Niska, Mila, Wolynska, Stawki, and Kupiecka Streets. In this area were located the Jewish Police Headquarters and the infamous Wertenfassung Office of the German occupational forces that dealt with stolen or confiscated Jewish wealth.

The Fourth and last sector was known as "The Small Ghetto," where the only industry was a garment factory belonging to

Tobbens. Because one needed a special permit to enter this area, it also became known as "The Forbidden Zone."

To add to our misery, we had to wear those yellow armbands which identified us as Jews and made us walking targets for trigger-happy Germans. The hostility toward us intensified after the wall was completed.

One morning when I reported to the Congregation for work, I was astonished to see Dr. Manski, whom we had always thought to be Polish, lining up with us for a work assignment.

I managed to get behind him on line. "What are you doing here?" I asked.

He looked at me for a moment with a sad smile. "It seems, my dear Maurice, that I am, like you, Jewish."

"Since when?"

"Since the moment the Germans found out my grandfather was a Jew."

He then told me how he had been summoned one morning to the Gestapo Building at 7 Sucha Alley.

"I went to the second floor to see First Lieutenant Adolf Rinke, the Gestapo Commandant for Jewish Affairs. A sentry told me to wait, so I sat down on a bench. My hands were trembling. I had no idea why I had been ordered to appear. After a while, the sentry ordered me to go to Room 225, Second Lieutenant Brand's office. A guard escorted me to the room. Ordinarily, I'm a calm man, but now my knees were shaking.

"The lieutenant called me in brusquely. When I entered, he glared at me, wiped his glasses and stared at some papers on his desk.

" 'Dr. Manski!' he said. 'How do you have the audacity to continue living outside the Ghetto masquerading as a Pole? Have you no regard for our Fuehrer's orders?'

"I told him I was not disobeying any orders. I was doing everything according to the City Council's instructions.

" 'You are disobeying the Fuehrer's orders by not moving into the Ghetto!'

"I tried to explain to him that I was a Polish Catholic—not a Jew—so there was no reason for me to live in the Ghetto.

" 'You are a Jew!' he roared, pounding the desk and causing the papers on it to fly off. I tried to pick them up, but he shoved me aside.

"I took out my identification papers and put them on his desk. 'I am a Polish Catholic,' I repeated, 'and my pastor, Father Grzelak, will verify it.'

"The officer didn't even look at my papers. He said, in an ominous tone, 'According to our regulations and to the order issued by our supreme authorities, people of Jewish origin up to three generations are subject to regulation 132. They are regarded as Jews and must live in the Ghetto.'

"This came as a shock to me; I didn't know that my grandfather was a Jew. I repeated that to the lieutenant, but he ignored me. He pressed a button on his desk and a soldier entered. The officer then asked him to bring the folder on Dr. Manski.

"The soldier returned with a file and placed it on the desk. Lieutenant Brand looked it over, then rasped, 'Your grandfather's name was David Berman; your grandmother's first name was Sophie. We don't know if your grandmother was Jewish, but we know for certain that your grandfather was a Jew. And that's enough evidence for us to accord you the honor of moving your family to the Ghetto, where you deserve to live among your own people. Now, Dr. Manski, please listen carefully. You will move in twenty-four hours, or you and your family will be shot. I'm also fining you three thousand zlotys for having failed to move to the Ghetto on the date stated on our posted edict.'

"I had to go home and bring this tragic news to my family. My wife was horrified—and the children—how can you explain to children that because your great grandfather was a Jew, you must be punished? There were tears and lamentations, but we had no choice. Before nightfall, we had moved as much as we could from our apartment into this wretched Ghetto—and here I am, waiting for an assignment just like you."

Dr. Manski's troubles were just beginning. This was his first visit to the Jewish Committee for work. When some of the officials spotted him, they were furious. They refused to believe that his grandfather had been a Jew. They accused him of being sent here by the Gestapo to spy on the Jews. These people had known the doctor all their lives as a Pole; they could not suddenly accept him as a Jew.

Dr. Manski was ordered to step ahead of everyone on line. He was then questioned at length by the committee. He repeated the story he had told me and showed the men the new identification card the Germans had issued to him, which stated that his grandfather, David Berman, was a Jew.

After much discussion and doubt, the Committee finally believed him. He was assigned to a work detail. It saddened me to think that this man, a brilliant surgeon, could have been so demeaned by the Nazis.

That day I worked alongside the doctor on a clean-up squad.
We had to clear a vacant lot of debris, so the Germans could
build new barracks for their soldiers. During a break, the doctor
told me about another scene that had taken place at Gestapo
Headquarters. At one point during his meeting with Lieutenant
Brand, the door burst open and First Lieutenant Rinke stormed
into the room in a fury. Ignoring Dr. Manski's presence, he
ordered Lieutenant Brand to hold a meeting for all policemen the
following morning.

Dr. Manski quoted Lieutenant Rinke as saying, "Our Fuehrer's wishes are being disregarded by some of the Poles and
many of the Jews. We have discovered that the Poles are making
money by selling false identification cards to Jews. The flight of
this rabble from the Ghetto by this ruse is not to be tolerated. We
must warn the police that if they participate in this criminal act,
they will be dealt with in court. Any Jew caught outside the
Ghetto must be instantly shot. All Jews will have to be liquidated
eventually, be it in Warsaw or Moscow. A world without Jews—an
Aryan paradise—that is the Fuehrer's grand plan. Heil Hitler!"

Each day on work detail, I heard more and more gruesome
accounts. One day, the president of the Jewish Congregation
received a call from Gestapo chief Lieutenant Rinke, who demanded that the president supply him with 100,000 Jews of both
sexes in three days. The story was that they were needed for a
special work detail outside the Ghetto.

The Congregation's president timidly stated that he had already supplied Rinke with seventy-thousand Jewish workers,
none of whom had ever returned to their homes. Rinke replied
curtly that he must have the 100,000 or there would be serious
repercussions.

The Jewish Congregation had no choice. The organization's
president started rounding up 100,000 Jews with the certain
knowledge that he was sending them to their deaths.

Chief Rinke became a fanatic during these days. He established an agency inside the Ghetto to uncover the names of the
Jewish underground leaders. He organized another agency outside the Ghetto, composed of Jews coerced into spying on their
own people. These Jews were promised survival if they would
just turn in names of their fellow people who had managed to
escape from the Ghetto. They were stationed around restaurants
in Polish Warsaw, where the defectors might show up. In addition, the Jewish police, who could be just as cruel toward their

own people as the Germans, were ordered to provide evidence of any known Jews carrying false papers.

At this time, a massive Nazi propaganda program was launched. When the Gestapo was informed that an International Commission was arriving in Warsaw to inspect the Ghetto in two weeks' time, an intensive project was set up to seriously discredit Jews.

On orders from Adolf Eichmann, the Germans occupying Warsaw were to take incriminating photographs and movies to "prove" that the Jews were a decadent race. This evidence was to be presented to the commission as an argument for separating these corrupt people from other races.

As part of the project, Lieutenant Brand had his soldiers round up a group of Jews of both sexes—young, middle-aged, and even bearded old men. He ordered them taken to a bathhouse at 22 Dzielna Street. There, in one large room, the women were instructed to stand on the left, the men on the right. All were ordered to undress.

The men did so without protesting, but many of the women were ashamed to disrobe before the soldiers. Lieutenant Brand warned that any woman who did not undress would be shot. When the soldiers pointed their guns at the women, all of them undressed immediately.

Once this was accomplished, the women were told to get into the water in the next room. After they had done so, the men were ordered to join them. The group was photographed and filmed bathing together in a manner which suggested an orgy.

The diabolical mind of Lieutenant Brand also conceived another deception for this film that would discredit our people. He escorted a frightened group of Jews to one of Warsaw's finest restaurants, where a bountiful buffet was on display. Although the Jews were told to form an orderly line, the Germans knew that once these famished people, having been virtually starved by the Nazis, saw the food, they would behave like wild animals.

The hungry group rushed toward the buffet pushing and screaming to get at the food. Several old people fell down in the scramble and were trampled by the mob. The scene resembled a wild Roman feast, as the hungry crowd slobbered over the food like pigs in a sty. The photographers and cameramen were elated. They were getting precisely the sort of footage that the Gestapo wanted.

Next, Brand and Chief Rinke called a meeting of the Nazi-controlled Jewish policemen, and cheerfully told them there was to be a Carnival Ball to which they should invite the most

beautiful and promiscuous women in the Ghetto. The police
were not to wear their uniforms at the ball, but were to come in
their best civilian clothes. At the dance, they had permission to
take any liberties they wished with the women. Any woman who
resisted them would be killed on the spot.

The collaborating Jewish policemen, as has already been noted,
could be just as harsh toward the Jews as the Nazis. The sadistic
nature of some of them fell in perfectly with the Nazi plan. Also,
the police knew that their only hope of continued survival was to
do the bidding of their conquerers. They invited their female
friends and acquaintances to the dance, knowing very well why
it was being staged.

A majority of the women invited by the police were known
prostitutes with criminal records, but some were respectable
women who only came to the dance because they had been
warned that a refusal would mean death to them and their family
members. A few who were actively hostile toward the police had
been forced to attend.

When the guests arrived at the so-called dance, they were
purposely plied with liquor before any food was served. Although many of the women refused to drink, the police, not
accustomed to all that free liquor, speedily got drunk and started
taking advantage of the situation.

The prostitutes went along with the action, giving in to the
men with relish. Before the evening was half over, many couples
were sexually engaged on tables and couches. This entire scene
was being filmed by the Nazis' cameramen.

One outraged woman slapped her date when he tried to tear
off her dress. A German officer standing nearby coolly took out
his revolver and shot her. The body was dragged off the dance
floor. After that incident, there were no more refusals on the part
of women guests.

Most of the police satiated themselves on food, drink and sex.
A few were appalled by the shocking spectacle, but knew that
they had to accept it. Some tried to turn their faces away from
the cameras so they wouldn't be recognized in the film.

The Germans added to the shock value of the movie by putting
on a lewd nightclub show featuring lesbians and transvestites.
Soon the stage was covered with writhing bodies engaged in all
aspects of sex, which the cameramen duly recorded.

When I heard about this sickening event, I was grateful for
one thing: no one had invited Malka. She was still living with

us, and other than going to work in the sewing factory, she remained secluded.

On the day that the International Commission arrived, I was placed on a work detail at a restaurant where the members were taken to dinner. The Germans obviously thought that I made a good appearance and asked me to work as a waiter.

I was in the dining room when Adolf Eichmann rose to speak. He said he was happy to welcome the commission to Warsaw, because it gave the Germans an opportunity to show how fraudulent the Jewish accusations against them were. He claimed that Jewish propagandists were planting lies on the radio and in the world press. Hitler's goal, he said, was to raise the standard of culture, to stamp out backwardness and inferiority, and to create a superior race. The film they were about to see would persuade them that the Germans were right to consider the Jews an inferior race.

The lights dimmed and the movie began with a written preface stating that the documentary footage about to be shown was taken clandestinely at various Jewish gatherings in Warsaw. These were not staged situations but actual happenings, photographed without the knowledge of the participants.

I couldn't believe what I saw on the screen.

Several commission members gasped when they saw the men and women bathing together naked. But this was only the beginning. Next came the revolting restaurant scene, which appalled them even more. The final outrage, of course, came with the orgiastic scenes at the carnival ball. I watched some of the commission members turn their heads from the screen in disgust.

Of course, *I* knew that the people in the movies had to have been drunk or drugged to perform such shocking acts, but I wondered what the commission members were thinking.

As soon as the film was over, I ducked through the kitchen door before the lights came on. I was the only waiter who had remained in the room during the showing, and I feared that I would be punished or killed if the Germans knew I had seen it.

The commission members were obviously shocked by what they had seen. When I returned to the dining room with the other waiters, I overheard a delegate from Switzerland say to one of his colleagues that he did not trust the Germans. "These unfortunate people may have been forced to appear in this disgraceful film. I think we should demand to be taken on a tour of the Ghetto."

His friends agreed with him and said that it would be ideal if they could talk directly to some Jews, without having the conversations monitored by the Nazis.

"That will never happen," the Swiss man said.

A request was put to Eichmann for a tour of the Ghetto.

"But of course," Eichmann said. "We have already planned such a tour for tomorrow."

The following day, the entire Ghetto received orders about the coming inspection. We were warned not to criticize the German occupation, or we would be killed and our families would be made to suffer. "Do not volunteer any information to the visitors," a German officer cautioned. "All questions must be answered in our presence."

When Malka came home from the factory that day, she told us how the Germans had put on a false front for the inspectors. "They gave us clean new uniforms to wear, cooked delicious food, and pretended it was the workers' rations. They even joked with us to show how congenial they were to the help. It was unbelievable. I never knew such hypocrisy could exist."

The unfortunate part of it all was that most members of the commission were taken in by these shenanigans.

That evening, as a final proof of the animalistic nature of the Jews, the visitors were taken to a nightclub, where, once again, the commission members observed a live performance of drunken Jewish policemen raping and beating women. They were all Nazi collaborators, out of their police uniforms. Some of the girls from a local brothel propositioned the visitors on orders from the Nazis, but were insulted and slapped by the accompanying Germans when they did so.

Before the commission left Warsaw, I overheard their leader remark that the tour had been a revelation to him. "What you have shown us," he said to Eichmann, "is disheartening. We will make a full report to our countries on the immorality and grossness of these people."

Later, the Warsaw paper *New World* reported that the commission had registered its disgust at the "gross immorality" of the Jews.

Eichmann was obviously elated when the commission left. His project had achieved its purpose and all who had helped to make it a success would soon be rewarded.

About a week later, I was put on duty as a waiter at a special dance that Eichmann staged to reward his men. This time it wasn't filmed. I witnessed a most tragic scene at this ball. It was mainly for German officers and their girls. Rinke was seated at

the main table with a beautiful woman who kept glancing at me
while I served them drinks. I dared not return the looks of
course, for the officer would kill me in an instant.

Lieutenant Brand was also seated at this table. He had a good,
strong voice and led the singing of martial songs and of the
German anthem, *Deutschland Ueber Alles*. When the singing
was over, Brand said, "What we need is a Jewish violinist to
serenade us."

"Excellent notion," the drunken Rinke agreed. "I commission you to find one, Lieutenant Brand."

Brand got up with some difficulty, walked unsteadily to the
bandstand, and stopped the music. He ordered the violinist to
play at the chief's table.

I happened to know this man. His name was Zomerstein and
he was one of the most respected musicians in Warsaw. He also
was strong-willed and loathed the Germans.

"Over here, Judas!" Rinke yelled.

I saw the violinist wince. He seemed pained to see me in that
room, but then he must have realized that I was ordered to work
there. I could tell that he was furious at being summoned by
these pigs in such a coarse manner.

Brand saluted Rinke and blurted, "Mission accomplished—
one plump Jewish violinist."

Rinke scrutinized the musician with disdain and detected a
proud look on Zomerstein's face. The Chief took out his pistol
and waved it at him. "Do you know what this is?" he threatened, pointing the gun at his face.

"Yes, I do," Zomerstein answered in a strong voice. "It's
used to kill innocent people like us."

Rinke's eyes opened wide at this retort. "And you consider
yourself innocent, Jude?"

"I consider myself innocent of enslaving and slaughtering
people who have done no wrong."

Rinke rose and struck the man's face with his gun. "Now,
Jude, play the German national anthem."

"That's one tune I don't know," the violinist replied calmly,
"Whistle it."

"Before you die, you'll learn how it goes."

"Make him play the Jews' holy song—*Kol Nidre*—for us,"
Brand demanded.

"You heard him," Rinke barked at the old man.

I had to control myself as I watched this scene. I had a violent
desire to stick a knife in Rinke's chest.

Zomerstein stood there without playing. Brand leaped at him and pounded the old man's face.

"Please," I whispered to the old man. "You'd better play."

Rinke shoved me aside. Zomerstein put the violin under his chin and started to play *Kol Nidre*. He grinned as he played and tears rolled down his cheeks.

His smile infuriated the officers. They began to insult him. This so incensed the violinist that he switched to playing the *Hatikvah*, the national anthem of today's Israel. The ringing song seemed to give him courage and he played with fervor.

One of the officers recognized the song and became furious. "He's defying us!" he shouted.

Brand snatched his Chief's pistol, and before anyone realized what was happening, he shot the violinist in the head. The old man fell toward me, repeating, *"Am Yisrael Chai"*— the Jewish people live. And with his dying voice he whispered, *"Shema. . ."*

At that moment I didn't care if they shot me too. I held the man in my arms. He started to say something, "Maurice . . . Maurice . . ." but the sentence was never finished.

"Yisrael," I murmured, finishing the prayer—the final statement that a good Jew utters when leaving the burden of life.

The room fell into a deathly silence.

"Music!" Rinke ordered, and the band resumed playing, halfheartedly. Two German officers dragged the violinist's body away, and the officers continued with their party.

We were a captive nation. The Vistula was our Euphrates, Warsaw our Babylon. And there we were intimidated, tortured, and murdered. And there we learned a new intimacy with our Holy Scripture.

> "By the rivers of Babylon there we sat down; yea, we wept, when we remembered Zion.
>
> "We hanged our harps upon the willows in the midst thereof. For there they that carried us away captive required of us a song; and they that wasted us required of us mirth, saying, 'Sing us one of the songs of Zion.' "
>
> (*Psalm 137:1-3*).

All through my youth, I had avoided Scripture. It was a weight about my neck, the voice of an ancient past that could obscure the present, a talisman waved to dispel the Zionist atheists.

But once the Germans had occupied our streets, beginning their incessant murders, Scripture took a new meaning. We learned it was timeless.

Another tragic event occurred that typified the bestial nature of our enemy. I was in the Jewish Military Union basement headquarters at number 5 Karmelicka, when one of our men burst in with a young girl who seemed to be in a state of shock. He had found her wandering in a field, and from her mumblings had determined that she was a sixteen-year-old named Sarah from the Ghetto. Something horrible had happened to her twelve-year-old sister, Laya, and the incident had sent Sarah into shock.

We gave the unfortunate girl some sedatives and put her to bed. She remained in our headquarters for several days, still rambling on and on about what had happened to her sister.

I finally decided that I might be able to help the girl by taking her to see Dr. Mendelson, who lived in our building.

I managed to get Sarah to our apartment through underground tunnels. But bringing her to the doctor turned out to be a mistake. As soon as the girl saw the doctor's white uniform, she screamed and tried to jump out the nearest window. We had to pin her down and calm her with an injection.

When the girl came to, the doctor's mother, who shared his apartment, began talking to her in soothing tones. It took several days of gentle reassurance to convince the girl that she was among friends.

A few nights later, while we were sitting in the doctor's living room, trying to cheer Sarah up, she suddenly came out of her trance and told us her horror story.

Her ordeal had begun some weeks before, when two Germans had knocked on her parents' apartment door and ordered them to turn over their daughters, Laya and Sarah.

The parents protested, but the soldiers, who were armed, showed them a document signed by Eichmann and Lieutenant Rinke, stating that fifty young girls, from twelve to fifteen years old, were to be recruited for a research project. When the survey was completed, the girls would be returned to their parents.

The girls became hysterical when they heard they were being taken from their parents, but nothing could be done to prevent it. They were not even given time to pack any clothes. The parents were told that the children would be provided with clothes and fine food, and that they would be far better off than they were here in the Ghetto.

Sarah and Laya were forcibly taken down to a huge van. The

back doors were opened, and the sisters found themselves packed in with a crowd of terrified young girls. When the doors were closed, it became dark inside, and young Laya started to cry. Her sister put her arms around her, but that did little to reassure the young girl. "Crying won't help," one of the other girls said.

Sarah said the van stopped several more times in the Ghetto. Each time the back doors opened, more girls were squeezed in by the Nazis, and the same tearful scenes ensued. By the time the last pick-up was made, the rear of the van was so congested that panic set in. The girls started beating on the walls of the vehicle and forced the soldiers to stop along the road.

She said the Nazis told them to be quiet; otherwise they would be shot.

The girls sat in terrified silence for the rest of the journey.

The van finally came to a stop, and the back doors were opened. The girls were ordered to get out. Sarah realized that they were outside the Ghetto and on the grounds of what appeared to be a hospital in the country. She took Laya by the hand and followed the soldiers to a waiting room. Here, sandwiches, milk, and candy were served to the newcomers, which appeased the older girls, but did not quiet the young ones, who still wept for their mothers.

Shortly afterward, Sarah said, a beak-nosed doctor entered the room, followed by his assistant. "Good afternoon," the doctor said, "I'm Dr. Hoheneiser. This is my assistant, Dr. Krauss."

Dr. Hoheneiser said, "Don't be frightened, little girls. No harm will come to you. You will be well fed and well treated here. You should all be proud to be part of a medical experiment that the German nation is conducting for the betterment of the human race."

While he spoke, Dr. Hoheneiser kept staring at Laya, who thought him so ugly that she hid behind her sister.

"You may go to your rooms now," the doctor reportedly told them, "where you can play and have some supper. Our experiments won't begin until tomorrow."

The girls were then taken upstairs to what appeared to be a hospital ward. It was a large, clean room with a bed for each girl. A severe-looking nurse asked the girls to disrobe and handed them white outfits to wear. After announcing that supper would be served in about an hour, she left.

Although there were toys and games in the ward, Sarah said, none of the girls felt like playing. They continued discussing their plight until the nurse and some attendants entered with dinner trays. The food was plentiful and tasty and it served to cheer the girls up a bit.

After they had eaten, the girls were allowed to play with the games, and the atmosphere became a bit more relaxed. But at 9:00, when lights-out was called, the younger girls again started crying for their mothers. It was a long time before any could sleep.

Next morning, after an ample breakfast, the girls were assembled in the waiting room and Dr. Hoheneiser entered, followed by his assistant.

"Now, aren't we all in better spirits this morning, girls?" the doctor reportedly asked. "We are going to start with our experiments this morning, but we will take only one girl at a time. I'm going to start with the youngest first." He pointed to Laya and smiled. "Come here—you with the pigtails—what's your name?"

Laya hid behind her sister.

"What's her name?" the doctor asked Sarah.

"Laya," she replied.

"Pretty name," he said. "I want her in my office."

"May I come in with her?" Sarah begged. "She's very young—and she's very frightened."

"Nonsense—I'm not going to hurt her. I don't permit spectators during my medical work."

"Please don't hurt her," Sarah pleaded.

Laya started crying, and Sarah put her arm around her.

"Don't cry," she whispered. "He won't hurt you. And I'll be right outside the door. Don't worry."

Laya put up a struggle, kicking her feet and refusing to be taken through the door. But the doctor and his assistant grabbed her and carried her into the other room.

The nurses then announced that this was a free period and the girls could return to the ward and play.

Sarah told us that she tried to remain behind, but a nurse ordered her upstairs with the other girls. As soon as the nurse left the ward, the girls stopped playing and crowded around her. "If I were you," an older girl said, "I'd try to sneak down there and see what's going on."

After almost an hour had passed, Sarah opened the door slowly and peered out. No one was in the corridor, so she tiptoed down to the waiting room and heard a commotion in the doctor's office.

She hid behind one of the curtains and the door opened. She

saw the doctor and his assistant carrying Laya out on a stretcher. She almost screamed. Her little sister's body was covered with blood, and she looked dead.

"We must burn the body immediately," she heard the doctor say to his assistant. "The other girls must not find out—especially the sister. We'll take care of her next."

Sarah told us that she knew she had to get away from there before they went searching for her. She waited until the two men left the building, then decided to try escaping through the doctor's office. As she passed through the room, she was petrified at the sight of blood splattered on the couch and the operating table.

She opened a rear window and jumped out. Fortunately, there was no one in the area and she was able to run into the nearby forest without being detected.

Sarah managed to cover a long distance before stopping to rest. She told us that a few days had elapsed and she was too tired to continue wandering. By then she was in a stupor and would not speak. It was in this condition that my friend from the underground had found her.

We all agreed that Sarah must stay in the doctor's apartment for a few more days. When Dr. Hoheneiser discovered her escape, he would undoubtedly notify Rinke, who might send soldiers to the girl's apartment to check if she had returned there.

Dr. Mendelson and his mother said they would shelter Sarah as long as they could. But they felt that her parents should be notified of her safe return and also of Laya's murder.

The man who had found Sarah volunteered to undertake this unpleasant mission. Sarah begged him to explain to them that she could not possibly have saved Laya without being killed herself.

"Just think that not far from here," Dr. Mendelson said quietly, so that Sarah couldn't hear him, "there are forty-eight girls who are going to be mutilated and slaughtered like this poor child's sister—and there's nothing we can do to stop it."

Sarah remained in Dr. Mendelson's apartment for several weeks. No Germans had gone to her parents' apartment, so, after a month, it was decided that the girl could go home.

My underground friend had notified her parents about Laya's death and they were stricken with grief over the atrocity. But Sarah's return lifted their spirits. Their happiness was not to continue. Sarah and her parents later perished in a concentration camp.

It did not take long for the Jews of Warsaw to comprehend the Germans' intentions. Many of us had smelled blood long before the first shot was fired. Some held back from accepting the inevitable conclusion, perhaps until they were starving to death or herded to the gas chamber. But eventually, everyone understood.

Through the thousands of years of Jewish history, we learned there were but two ways to end oppression: to fight or take flight.

Warsaw was not our promised land, so many Jews believed that the answer to the oppression lay in flight. To fight, they argued, would be disastrous. Rising up against the Nazis could only result in a new Masada, and we would all die in the end. Considering the extremely remote chance of beating back the Germans, where would all the bloodshed have gotten us?

My friend Tod Mazur believed in flight. His father had amassed a fortune by cornering a trade monopoly with Great Britain.

Tod looked so happy that it made him stand out in the grim atmosphere of the Ghetto.

"Why are you so cheerful?" I asked.

"I'm happy because soon I'll be leaving here forever."

"Where are you going?" I asked.

He led me to a secluded spot where no one could overhear him and told me his plan—an incredible story that I found difficult to believe. "My family and I have purchased a plane for a few million zlotys. We are going to fly it to England or the United States. There are sixteen of us in the group. We will settle wherever we're welcome."

"But how will you ever get out of Warsaw without the Germans trapping you?"

"It's all arranged. We've paid a fortune to make this flight."

I wished him the best and envied his good luck. But my envy was misspent. Three weeks later I reported to the Jewish Congregation for work, and there, to my amazement, stood Tod.

"What happened?" I asked.

He started to speak, but his voice broke. After a few moments, he said, "Nobody wanted us. They ejected us from England. When we landed in New York, they arrested us and turned us over to some officials who ordered us to fly back to Poland. Those countries have no idea what's going on over here. They turned their backs on us. We even appealed to Jews, but none would have us. I'd rather be dead than be here again."

Tod was a broken man, and he got his preference. Soon, he and his entire family would die in the Warsaw Ghetto.

He found escape possible, but refuge impossible. The world did not want any of Hitler's Jews.

At this time, Papa also had troubles. The Germans not only took over his factory, but removed machines that were worth hundreds of thousands of dollars. The equipment was shipped to Germany, where it was installed to help the war effort. Father resigned himself to the theft. "What does it really matter," he said, "as long as we're still alive?"

It had been made quite clear to the Jews of Warsaw that they could not avoid oppression by passively accepting Nazi abuses. It was also understood that escaping from the present situation was impossible. We had only one alternative.

By the rivers of our Babylon, we could no longer sit, we could not weep for Zion. Those who held us captive, calling for a Jewish song, would finally be defied in a well organized way.

> "O daughter of Babylon, who art to be destroyed; happy shall he be, that rewardeth thee as thou hast served us." (*Psalm 137:8*)

CHAPTER 8

A Time To Kill

"To every thing there is a season, and a time to every purpose under the heavens . . . A time to kill . . . a time to tear down . . . a time to hate; a time of war. . . ."

(Ecclesiastes 3:1-8)

The underground tunnel system in Warsaw had not been discovered by the Germans. I only found out its actual capabilities after joining the underground fighters.

One night, while hurrying through one of these tunnels, I was pleasantly surprised to run into my friend Leo, Malka's brother. He had attempted to find refuge in Russia, just before the German invasion. For a time, the Russians had invited Polish Jews to come to their country and settle, but Leo had arrived too late. The Russians had a change of heart and were welcoming no more Jews. He was sent back to Warsaw.

Leo was staying with a relative of his inside the Ghetto. He was so relieved to hear that Malka was living with us that he wept. He and Malka had a joyous reunion at our apartment that evening. Leo spent the night with us and became a frequent visitor to our home.

In the spring of 1940, my family was in dire need of food, as were all the Jews in the Ghetto. I swore that I would do anything—even kill—to appease their hunger.

One afternoon, I, along with some friends from Betar, spied two German soldiers guarding a wagon that was full of food. We were armed and decided to attack them before they could distribute the provisions to the German soldiers in the Ghetto. We waited until no other Germans were in sight, then quickly approached the soldiers and shot them. I was so preoccupied with getting the wagon laden with food out of there that I felt absolutely no regret about having just killed someone.

I had never imagined that I could kill a man without remorse, but hunger and hatred for a murderous enemy overrode any feelings of guilt.

One of my former soccer teammates lived nearby at 11 Muranowska Street. His father was the super in that building, and he let us hide the wagon in a shed there. We helped ourselves to some of the provisions. I took a small sack of flour and a small sack of sugar and brought them to 5 Muranowska Street, where the Lubavitcher rabbi lived with his wife. I had heard that they were desperately in need of food, so I made my way to their third-floor apartment and knocked on the door.

No one answered. I listened for a moment, then heard soft footsteps inside. Still, the door remained closed. I put my lips close to the door and spoke in Yiddish.

"Please open the door. It's Maurice Shainberg from Gesia Street. I have some food for the rabbi."

Finally, the rabbi's wife, a small woman of sixty, opened the door slightly. When she saw who it was, she opened the door further.

"This is for the rabbi and you," I said. She took the food and patted my hand in thanks. The rabbi, a distinguished-looking man with a white beard, came to the door. He looked at what I had brought, and his eyes filled with tears. "Thank you, my son," he said, "and may God go with you."

"I'll be back later with some potatoes," I promised.

"No, no. It's almost curfew, and the Germans will shoot you. Please don't risk your young life for an old man like me."

I showed him my gun and said, "Don't worry about me. I can take care of myself."

Later that evening Leo and I were able to return to the rabbi's apartment with a sack of potatoes. The rabbi and his wife were overwhelmed with gratitude. They invited us in, but we had to leave before the Germans discovered us. The rabbi blessed us and wished us a safe return.

I brought ample supplies home to my family. They had been living on bread and water for so long that the sight of my provisions delighted them. For a change, the apartment seemed full of life.

•   •   •

In the spring of 1941, the German Reich was secure along all its borders, from the Atlantic in the west to Stalin's grinning face in the east, from the Arctic Ocean to the Sahara Desert.

Only England and America were left to fight the Nazis, but we in the Ghetto had little hope that they would come to our rescue. We would fight on our own, as Eliezer Ben Yair did at Masada. If we were doomed, so be it, but we would not die without a fight.

The Germans had been executing Jews for more than a year, and by 1941, they had even given up the pretext of serving some sort of justice. They simply meant to kill every Jew within their reach. Our retribution was simple: kill every German we could.

During those days, I devoted myself to the underground, working alongside resistance leaders such as David Apfelbaum and Pawel Frankel. As our resistance to the Germans increased, new parties and factions were formed to combat the Nazis.

By 1942, a powerful new leftist group of Bund-Communists, the Z.O.B., would be formed. In its headquarters would hang no Jewish flags, only portraits of Lenin, Marx, Stalin, Trotsky, Engels, Tellemann, Torres—and lots of red flags.

The Jewish Military Union didn't trust the budding Z.O.B.'s Communist foundations, but as the war continued in the Nazis' favor, the two organizations would merge and fight together against the German enemy.

In the spring of 1941, we were informed that the Nazis planned a conference followed by a drinking party in a nightclub at 13 Rymarska Street where Halina and I used to go dancing. Pawel, myself, and six other resistance fighters formulated a plan of attack. We dressed as farmers and hid bombs and grenades in bushel baskets covered with rags. We waited until after the 6:00 p.m. curfew, then made our way through the underground tunnels to a hiding place at 2 Krulewska Street.

When it was dark at 10:00, we stealthily made our way to the nightclub, once again using tunnels that the Nazis did not know about. At a prearranged signal, we tossed the bombs and grenades through the windows. The building was an instant mass of flames. The explosion was so powerful and immediate that I was thrown to the ground and injured my leg. As we ran from the scene, we sprinkled a special chemical powder to cover our scent so that the Gestapo's dogs would have a hard time tracking us.

The following day, we were exhilarated to hear that thirty-eight German police had perished in the fire. As was to be expected, the Nazis retaliated by killing twice as many Jewish hostages. They posted notices all over Warsaw, offering huge rewards for our capture, but we had worked so secretly and silently that no one knew we were responsible.

Doctor Mendelson treated my wounds. I knew he could be trusted and told him about the attack. He responded by offering his services to the underground and was of great help to our sick and wounded. In fact, he was so helpful to the resistance movement that he became one of the unsung heroes of the Ghetto.

Not long after this incident, the Gestapo began making frequent roundups of men, women, and children. Ostensibly, these persons were going to be put to work on some vague German project, but they never returned. As we learned later, they were instead transported to Wawer, near Warsaw, and shot.

Simon Grossman, a neighbor of mine and former owner of a soap factory at 27 Okopowa Street, was picked up in the Gestapo's most recent kidnapping and taken to Wawer. From what we learned of his fate afterward, it seems that he recognized a Polish policeman there who had once been his factory employee. This was his only hope, Grossman thought. At least the policeman was not a German, so he went to him and begged for help.

The policeman, whose name was Zymaniak, said that he had no sympathy for Grossman, that he had always hated him because he was a Jew and had only worked for him to support his family. He would, however, do what he could to spare his life if Grossman would tell him where his money and other valuables were kept. Grossman told him that they were all hidden over a doorsill in his aparment. Zymaniak, never intending to keep his end of the bargain, then lifted his gun to Grossman's head and pulled the trigger.

Later, we found out, when the policeman was off duty, he went to Grossman's apartment and told the distraught wife that her husband was being held by the Germans but his release was being negotiated. He needed their money and jewels to save her husband's life. The wife led him to the hiding place. He gathered up the valuables and then shot her in the head.

The Grossman children, who had been playing in another part of the apartment, dashed into the room to see what had happened. When they saw their mother on the floor, covered with blood, they started shrieking. The policeman fled.

Dr. Mendelson, who lived in the apartment next door, heard the children's cries and rushed in.

Mrs. Grossman was still breathing, but the doctor knew she was dying.

"The children," the dying woman whispered. "Please watch over them. They . . . have my husband . . ." She tried to say something further, but the words froze on her dead lips.

The children burst into tears and held onto their mother. Isaac, who was six, said to the doctor, "I saw the man who shot her. He used to work for my Papa. He's a policeman now." But he could not remember the man's name.

The doctor led the children to his apartment, where his mother did her best to calm them. Then he came down to our apartment to tell me what had happened. I had heard the shot, but thought it better not to investigate.

I went upstairs with him and was sickened by the sight of Mrs. Grossman lying dead on the couch.

"Don't worry," I said to the shaken doctor. "We'll find out who that policeman is, and my friends in the underground will take care of him. All we have to do is ask one of the Jews who worked in Grossman's factory. This murder will be avenged."

I helped the doctor wrap Mrs. Grossman in a sheet. "What will happen to these children now that their parents are dead?" I asked.

"My mother and I will take them in." The doctor and his mother were known for their kindness long before the swastika fluttered over Poland.

"How unbelievable our lives have become," I said. "In half a minute, these unfortunate children have lost both parents."

"Nothing surprises me these days," the doctor said. "I wish we could all get out of here. I have plenty of money, but I don't know who to approach."

"Would you take the children with you?"

"Of course—unless some relative claims them."

"I can show you the way out of the ghetto—through the underground. That's easy. But how to get out of Poland—out of Europe—that's difficult."

I told the doctor what had happened to my friend Tod and his family. That really shocked him.

"Foreigners can't be expected to believe what's going on here," the doctor said. "You have to be here to fathom the horror. Still, there must be a way out. I refuse to be destroyed by these animals. You and I must do everything we can to save our loved ones."

I called the Jewish Congregation from the Grossman apartment and informed them of what had happened. They promised to help give the woman a decent burial. Dr. Mendelson gave his name and the apartment number. The man on the phone said the funeral would have to wait until the next morning.

We wrapped Mrs. Grossman in another sheet and placed her on the couch. There was nothing more we could do.

Word about the Grossman incident spread rapidly in our sector. Soon we had the information we wanted. The policeman's name was Zymaniak and he had boasted to friends about the valuable cache he had stolen from the Jewish family.

Pawel was infuriated when I told him about the incident. "We must take care of this rotten bastard," he said. One of our underground colleagues pointed the man out to us, and we bided our time.

It is unfortunate but true that a war, especially one motivated by racial prejudice, can imbue a man with the pleasure of killing. We carefully planned our revenge on the policeman. Several truly macabre deaths were suggested for him, but we finally settled for a simple, speedy solution. We learned how Zymaniak had brutally killed Mr. Grossman, and that added to the fervor of our vendetta.

Three of us kidnapped him as he was returning from work. We dragged him over to a sewer and held his head under the filthy water until he was dead. Justice had been served. The members of our resistance group felt that the aggrieved family had been avenged—something that did not usually happen in this war against the Jews.

Even Dr. Mendelson was happy when I told him what we had done. "An eye for an eye," he said, "that's the only way in this war."

Since no relatives of the Grossmans came forward to claim the children, they continued to live with the Mendelsons. Meanwhile, the doctor explored every avenue he could for an escape from the Ghetto and Poland.

At the Jewish Congregation, things were getting progressively worse. When officials complained that Jews recruited by the Germans for "special projects" never returned to Warsaw, they stopped supplying people. This enraged the Nazis, and they repaid the Congregation by randomly shooting down Jews in the street.

Our resistance leader, David Apfelbaum, appeared before the Congregation and pleaded for help in organizing Jewish resistance groups. The Congregation ignored him. "How can we fight the Germans without boots, without bread, without ammunition?" one member demanded. "What can we possibly achieve with our empty hands?"

Apfelbaum was not discouraged by this rebuff. "We young people wlll fight the enemy with our bare hands if necessary. Hitler described in *Mein Kampf* what was in store for all Jews. We may not win, but at least we won't be slain like sheep. If you won't help us organize a Jewish fighting group, then we'll do it alone."

We walked out of the Jewish Congregation's headquarters with more faith than ever in our cause.

At the next meeting of the Jewish Military Union, we discussed how we could secure additional arms for our fight. David Apfelbaum suggested that we go to the underground group known as the Polish Liberation Staff and buy arms from them. "We have sufficient funds to pay for more ammunition," he said.

Other members were skeptical that the Poles, who always had been extremely anti-Semitic, would change their attitudes toward Jews now.

One of our leaders, Dr. Widowinski, disagreed. "I think they might help us. I'm willing to contact them and take a chance."

We all agreed that the doctor would be a good spokesman for us. Pawel and I volunteered to go along with him.

A few days later, we made our way underground to a Polish church on Jan Kilinski Street, which we knew was a front for the Polish Liberation Staff. We entered the vestry and introduced ourselves to a startled priest.

The doctor handed the priest a letter and asked him to give it to the head of the Polish resistance group.

The priest appeared frightened. "I'm sorry," he stammered, "but I have no connection with the underground."

"Father," the doctor said, "you're supposed to be a holy man. Surely you wouldn't lie? We know all about your connections, and we also believe that you would not deny us help at this crucial time. We are all brothers—even if we practice different religions—and we must help one another. We urge you to show our letter to Major Grezlak."

At the mention of the major's name, the priest changed his attitude. He stared at the envelope without opening it. Finally, he said, "Yes—please wait. I'll see what I can do."

"Remember," the doctor warned, "that we represent the

Jewish Military Union. If you turn us over to the Nazis, our group will retaliate.''

The priest made no comment, but left the room hastily. In about ten minutes, he returned with the major. The officer scrutinized us carefully, then coldly nodded to our group.

I immediately distrusted him.

"Have you read our request?" the doctor asked.

"Yes. I think your cause is admirable. But before I can sell arms to you, I must have the permission of my organization's leadership. I cannot do this on my own."

"This is not the time for delay; one day may mean our total destruction. Our people are being slaughtered like animals. We can't wait for meetings, red tape, and double talk. I have a sizable amount of money with me. I beg you to sell us arms."

"Out of the question," the major said. "You will have to follow *my* procedures. When our leadership has reached a decision, we will contact you. Where can you be reached?"

The doctor glared at him. "That is our secret. We will contact you."

"Whatever you wish," the major said with a tinge of disappointment. It was becoming increasingly clear that this officer had no intention of helping us.

"I have the feeling, major," the doctor said heatedly, "that just as always, you Poles have no intention of helping us Jews. It is the history of your bigoted upbringing."

"Insults, my dear man," shouted the major, "will delay the sale of arms even further."

Doctor Widowinski was livid. As we walked out of the church he said to me, "All we can expect from those bastards are bullets in our backs."

We never went back to the church and later discovered that the major had told the Germans about our visit. In any case, after that meeting we were especially careful to limit our contact with the Polish underground organizations. Even without much ammunition, we had some major successes. Within a few weeks in 1941, the Jewish Military Union liquidated three pro-German Polish groups called Zagniew. About six hundred members of these anti-Semitic organizations were killed as a result of our activities.

For security reasons, we operated from several different locations. One of our secret meeting places was in an underground tunnel that led from the Eastern Railroad Station to Targowa Street. In this passageway we had a special room for storing arms and conducting planning sessions. Another secret meeting place was located at 5 Karmelicka Street, between the non-Jewish sector and the Ghetto.

Our headquarters at 7 Muranowska Street had a tunnel underneath, leading out of the Ghetto. Whenever we successfully negotiated arms purchases, this was where the materials were delivered.

During the first two years of the Ghetto's existence, the Jewish and Catholic underground forces were divided, unable to act as a united front for the anti-Fascist cause. In 1942, however, representatives from all the major resistance groups held a significant meeting.

The assembly was called by *Der Ruff*, an organization composed of both Jewish and Christian members of the press. The purpose of this conclave was to establish one strong organization—the Jewish Fighting Brigade (Z.O.B.)—to combat the Nazis. The strongest block of the Jewish Fighting Brigade was composed of members of such leftist organizations as P.P.S. (Polish Socialist Party), Gwardia Ludowa (People's Guard), P.P.R. (Polish Workers Party), all under the leadership of Ignacy Narbut. These organizations finally decided to collaborate with Jewish resistance groups to more effectively fight the Germans.

The Jewish underground groups were represented by Isaac Cukierman (code name Antek) and Miss Cywia Lubetkin (code name Celina). They jointly represented approximately five hundred members of the Jewish resistance groups: Hashomer Hatzair, Poaley Zion, Hechalutz, and Dror.

The Jewish Fighting Brigade was officially founded in July 1942, with Mordechai Anielewicz as its commander. Its purpose was to fight the Nazis and protect Jews against deportation and liquidation. The organization was financed by local citizens. Its leaders kept in close contact with representatives of other groups and political parties, which supplied them with arms.

The summer of 1942 was the beginning of the end for the Jews of the Warsaw Ghetto. Liquidation of our people was being accelerated, with thousands of Jews rounded up, again supposedly for work projects. We soon learned, however, they were being shipped to the dreaded Treblinka concentration camp.

The first major transport of Jews from Warsaw left on July 22, 1942. It was a tragic scene. Many of our friends were taken. There was a steady stream of Jews to the gas chambers of Treblinka and elsewhere. By September 1942, more than 300,000 of our people had been removed from the Ghetto.

One of my most poignant memories of 1942 was the faithful observance of Yom Kippur, despite the fact that our people knew there was no escape, no hope, no consolation. Yet, the Jews of Warsaw continued praying, "Out of distress, I called to you, O Lord." There were no night services that September.

How could a Jew on this Yom Kippur attend the autumnal lamentations prescribed by the Torah? The Germans had turned most of the synagogues into piles of rubbish. We dared not surface on the streets. Going out was tantamount to death. Day and night, the Germans patrolled the streets in their armored cars and trucks. Strident voices barked orders over loudspeaker systems. When Jews were shot down in the streets, they were eventually dumped into pits which were then covered with chemical lime to quicken their decomposition. The city was terror-stricken.

The only safe hiding places, for a while, were basements, sewers, and secret tunnels that the Germans hadn't discovered. Some of the Jews managed to escape to the forests and mountains. But most trusted their underground hideouts, chimneys, or church lofts. A few even staked out in treetops.

The Poles were often motivated by greed and watched our every step, keeping the Germans informed about our activities and hiding places. In general, they and the Germans had a mutual interest: the acquisition of Jewish property and valuables. Despite the German invasion and destruction of their country, the Poles still preferred the Kraut to the Jew.

Mistakenly, Jews sometimes confided in their Polish neighbors, revealing their plans to escape, and worse yet, turning their possessions over to them for safekeeping. In innumerable cases, soon after their valuables had been transferred, the Nazis would arrive and drag the Jewish families off to certain death.

Some Poles contemptuously considered us cowards; others laughed at our hopeless will to survive. The majority felt no guilt in turning over Jews to the Gestapo, the Polish occupation police, or the Ukrainian fascists.

In churches, sextons with candles searched the choir lofts after vespers for Jews. And when they succeeded in ferreting one out, the terror in the eyes of the hunted amused them. Crowds would gather to watch with delight the apprehension of a person they had been taught to hate. That hostility had been transferred from father to son as a continuing heritage.

The Poles took a hunter's pleasure in tracking down an escaped Jew. No fox ever experienced a more elaborate chase than did a fugitive Jew from the Ghetto. They pursued us through back alleys and in canals, sewers, and coal cellars—in places that the Nazis would never have found. They felt the thrill of trapping their quarry and riddling the body with bullets until it was still. The hunt rid the world of one more Jew.

On that Yom Kippur in 1942, the Germans were making one of their sweeping roundups on Mila, Kupiecka, and Karmelicka Streets. Ignoring the jeers of their captors, the Jews put on their *kittlach*—white cloaks bordered with silver embroidery—and their *tallesim*— prayer shawls—as they were shoved into open trucks with the butt ends of rifles.

When the trucks started to move, a wonderful thing happened. The Jews raised their hands towards the sky and chanted, "From the bottom of my heart I called out to you. O Lord! Lord! Listen to my voice. May your ears be receptive to the voice of my prayer."

The more the German guards struck them with rifles, the stronger the psalm rang from their lips.

Their sonorous Hebrew chant filled the Ghetto, making the informers, spectators, and guards uneasy. Some of them must have realized that the captives were pleading with their God to liberate them from their certain fate.

The trucks entered Zoliborz, opposite the Warsaw citadel, where the Czar had once jailed Polish patriots. The German guards of the convoy were silent. On the sidewalk, German soldiers lowered their heads and looked away. Could it be that they understood the significance of the lifted hands? Did they sense the guilt that was theirs? The mobile *Bet Ha'Midrash* filled the streets, the back alleys, the squares, and the churches with prayer: "Out of distress, I called to you, O Lord."

The voices grew stronger and stronger. When one Jew began singing *Kol Nidre,* all the captives joined in. For once, there was no distinction between the Orthodox and the nonobservant Jew.

From my basement hiding place, I observed the children, huddled at the feet of the singers, and the women squatting alongside the wooden boards of the trucks. They were all crying. They knew that this was to be their last glimpse of their birthplace. Along these streets, they had escorted the funeral corteges of their parents. Here were their synagogues, one on every street corner of the Ghetto.

They also must have known that this was to be their last Day of Atonement. Their mournful chanting was their death song. It lingered in the city long after they were gone.

The trucks stopped once more before they left Zoliborz. From a hilltop, the people inside could view the city where they had been born, raised, and schooled, where they had loved and married, where they had rejoiced and shed their tears. For the last time, they looked at the tower of St. Mary's Church and Bonifraterska Street—where the Ghetto started. Beyond this marker were their homes, workshops, stores, houses of worship—their lives.

CHAPTER 9

Stefan

By November 1942, Nazi pressure on the Warsaw Ghetto seemed to have slackened. The Nazi attack on Russia was bogged down, the Allies had landed in North Africa, and resistance movements were growing throughout Europe.

The first snow flurries blew over Warsaw.

On November 29, 1942, the underground learned that the Germans were planning even larger transports of Jews to Treblinka and other death camps. When I mentioned this fact at home, Papa became very upset—not for himself, but for me.

"Maurice," he advised, "save yourself. Try to flee from here. You are young and must save yourself."

I knew he was right. He had repeatedly told me this, and now it was even more urgent. Every day was a Jew hunt. Drunken Germans turned the activity into a sport: how many Jews did you kill last night? It was a sadistic, brutal game, ending with the slaughter of an entire family at the whim of some bloodthirsty, drunken Nazi.

There was no alternative. Once again, I made a knapsack and bade my family goodbye. Malka realized that she couldn't burden me with her presence, so she resigned herself to watching over my family for me. They were all depressed to see me leave, but the hope that I might possibly survive this certain genocide gave them strength.

I tenderly kissed them all goodbye. If nothing else, I was thankful that there was now warmth and love among us instead of the sanctimonious coldness of my early family life.

I had no trouble escaping from the Ghetto through one of the tunnels. As an underground fighter, I was armed, and this gave

me added courage. Of course, if the Germans were to catch me
with a gun, they would shoot me immediately. But they were
randomly shooting Jews anyway, so what was the difference?

Once again, I hopped a freight car, making my way to the
resort town of Michalin, where my father had a hotel. My
father's caretaker before the war, Stefan Rudnicki, lived there
and immediately offered me refuge in the cellar of his cottage.
He had been commuting between his house and Warsaw, bringing my family food whenever he could. His connections with the
underground were invaluable in getting him in and out of the
Ghetto.

I soon observed that Stefan's home was a meeting place for
Polish members of the P.P.S. (Polish Socialist Party), who were
fighting the Nazis in alliance with other partisan groups. The
meetings took place during the night, and I could overhear the
conversations from my hiding place under the floorboards.

One night, just before New Year's Eve in 1942, I was sitting
in Stefan's rustic kitchen, reading a Polish classic, *Pan Tadeusz
(Sir Thadeus)* by Adam Mickiewicz, which had been suppressed
by the Germans. I was particularly struck by one sentence which
I thought about in the days to come: "The wind does not bring
freedom; one has to fight for it." That night when I was reading,
I suddenly realized how lucky I was. I had been born with "a hat
on," and a child born with "a hat on" is supposed to be fortunate all his life. I had often ridiculed this old wives' tale, but
now as I was sitting snugly in this warm cottage, away from the
dangers of Warsaw and the Nazis, I began to think that perhaps
there was something to it.

I kept looking up from my book at the snow flurries outside
and thanked God that I had a friend like Stefan. Although he was
taking a serious risk, he had regularly urged me to come out of
my hiding place at night and breathe some fresh air.

There were eight in Stefan's family, but they never resented
my stay. My father had always treated the Rudnicki family
fairly, and now they were repaying his kindness.

I especially enjoyed sitting in the kitchen with Stefan's six
children, who always brought me the news of the day. Sometimes it was cheerful—the Soviets had demolished hundreds of
Germans; sometimes it was heartbreaking—twenty thousand Jews
had been killed in the towns of Falencia and Otwock, where my
sister Hena lived.

One night, around 11:00, I was sitting at the kitchen table with

Stefan and his wife, when we heard a knock. Stefan was petrified. The knock persisted.

"It's Conrad," a voice said. "Open up."

Stefan and his wife relaxed. It was obviously a friend.

Stefan opened the door quickly and admitted a stout, balding
man with a kind face.

"Stefan," the man said, "you're needed tonight." He turned
to greet Mrs. Rudnicki and looked frightened when he spied me.
"Oh, I'm so sorry. I didn't know you had company."

"He's all right," Stefan assured him. "His father owns the
hotel nearby. He's hiding out here. Let's go in the other room
and talk."

They stayed in the other room for about twenty minutes.
Stefan's wife made no comment about the visitor. She was a
friendly but tight-lipped lady who allowed her husband to do all
the talking. We sat there in silence, and I continued to read my
book.

When the two men returned, they sat down with us. Mrs.
Rudnicki served us coffee and I noticed Conrad was staring at
me. Finally, he asked, "How do you like staying here with the
Rudnickis?"

"I like it fine. When one is with friends in these times, one
doesn't analyze the situation."

Conrad was curious about the Ghetto and inundated me with
questions. I told him about the daily atrocities. I also expressed
great fear for my family and friends, and mentioned that I had a
sister and sister-in-law living in nearby Otwock. Conrad and
Stefan looked grimly at each other, but said nothing.

In a few moments, they left together. Stefan didn't return until
dawn.

During the next few weeks, Conrad returned frequently to the
cottage and seemed more and more interested in me. I soon
learned that he was the leader of the Polish partisans who were
hidden in the woods surrounding Lublin. I was pleased to learn
that Stefan was one of them. It made me feel more secure to be
protected by this valiant Pole.

It soon became apparent that Conrad was eager to make use of
me in his resistance activities. One night, he noticed my handwriting and commented on its fine quality. He asked me how my
printing was, and I gave him a sample.

"We can use you in our cause," he said.

"Good. I'm with you."

The opportunity presented itself shortly. Around 10:00 p.m.

one night, Conrad burst into the cottage. ''I have something for you to do,'' he commanded in a military tone, which irked me a bit. He was usually gentle in his speech.

''I need one hundred posters printed immediately, in an hour. Can you do it?''

''Since you're ordering me to do it,'' I replied in an annoyed tone, ''I have no choice.''

He was not pleased by my answer. ''We are engaged in a cause that seeks to make Poland free for people like you,'' he said sternly. ''If you're not interested in that goal, then don't bother to help us.''

I apologized. ''Of course I'm interested. What do you want printed?''

He smiled and handed me a sample poster which bore this message:

POLES AND BROTHERS!
Don't help the Krauts, the killers of the Polish
nation. Come out and battle fascism.
The Germans lost at Stalingrad. Over 200,000
German soldiers and their leader, Field Marshal
Paulus, were taken prisoners. Freedom is just
around the corner. Don't let up, Brothers, and
don't lose courage.

P.P.S. (Polish Socialist Party)

After I read that message, I was even more eager to help Conrad's cause. I wanted to show him that I was entirely with him in his fight, not only for my people, but for all mankind.

Stefan supplied me with ink and pens. I worked very quickly and neatly, finishing the posters in an hour, as promised. Conrad returned at 11:00 p.m. and was pleased with my work.

''Excellent!'' he exclaimed. ''Now please pack them in bundles of ten each, and I'll distribute them to my men.'' He shook my hand. ''You've worked quickly and well, and I plan to use your talents again.''

''Any time,'' I said, hoping that next time he would include me in more active work than printing posters.

But as the weeks went by, Conrad kept me busy with secretarial chores. I printed hundreds of posters, wrote letters, composed announcements. He admired my work so much that he appointed me his aide and secretary. But Conrad would not permit me to engage in guerrilla attacks. When he discovered that I had studied military tactics with the underground, he was overjoyed. I was soon helping his group plan its raids.

"As my administrative aide," he said one night, "you're worth fifty fighting soldiers to me." He treated me like a brother, and since I had never felt this kind of trust and love from my own brother, I became very close to him.

During this time, I constantly worried about my family. It had been some time since Stefan had been able to get to the Warsaw Ghetto to bring them food. Finally, I could bear the worry no longer and asked Stefan to let me return through the tunnels just to see how they were. He agreed to let me go on one condition: he would go with me.

Stefan's wife was not at all happy to see him venture into that zone again, and Conrad resented our absence when we were needed in the underground. But we promised to return in a few days, and they reluctantly let us go.

Stefan's family had not yet suffered the pangs of hunger. They were Poles and had little trouble getting provisions. Therefore, we were able to bring sacks of bread, potatoes, flour, and vegetables with us on our perilous journey.

God was with us. With the help of partisans and with our knowledge of underground passages, we were able to arrive at my apartment without incident.

I knocked on the door and said, "It's Maurice—open up!" My half brother, Shloyma, started screaming, "Mama, Mama, it's Maurice."

My stepmother flung open the door and pulled me in. Stefan followed quickly, and we bolted the door. Leah was in a state of hysteria. She threw her arms around me, but it was something about my father that she kept babbling.

"What's the matter with Papa? Tell me!"

"Your father," she finally spilled out, "went to the rabbi's house at 5 Pawia Street two days ago and he's never returned. The Germans have killed him. I know it. I've had terrible dreams."

My half-sister Esther tried to soothe her, but she only grew more hysterical.

"Don't worry," Stefan said. "Maurice and I will go there and investigate. Perhaps he decided to stay there because it's safer."

Leah shook her head violently. She appeared to be losing her mind. "I've seen his blood in my nightmares. I know he's dead."

"Here," I said. "Eat something. All these sacks of food are for you. You'll feel better after you have some food in your stomach."

The children fell on the food like vultures, but my stepmother had no appetite. She looked pitiful, with sunken eyes and a drawn face. All she could do was pace up and down, moving her lips in prayer.

"Don't kill yourself with anxiety," I said. "You must stay healthy for the children's sake. Stefan and I will go to the rabbi's apartment and investigate. We won't be long."

The distraught woman merely kept pacing as if we weren't there.

Stefan and I resumed our underground journey and emerged from a sewer at Pawia Street. We stood a moment before the apartment house where Rabbi Kolobier lived. My heart sank when I saw that his windows had been broken.

We dashed up the stairs and found his apartment door ajar. When we entered the flat, my body froze. Everything was askew. There was dried blood all over the floor and walls; the room had the appearance of a slaughterhouse. Holy objects and vestments had been slashed and desecrated. There was no sign of life.

I knocked on the apartment next door. No one answered. "It's Maurice Shainberg," I said. "I'm looking for my father. Please let me in."

The door opened quickly and the rabbi's wife took my hand. Stefan and I stepped inside; I introduced him.

"My stepmother is beside herself with worry about my Papa," I said. "Do you know what's happened to him?"

"Maurice—how can I tell you what happened to him? You saw our apartment, didn't you? The Germans broke in during a prayer meeting. They tore down the *Aron Ha-Kodesh*, the *Torah*, everything in the room. . . ." Her voice faltered. "They killed them. They killed everyone in the room. It was a bloodbath. If I had been there, they would surely have killed me too."

I managed to ask, "Where was Papa's body taken?"

"Members of the Jewish Congregation came for the bodies. They couldn't notify any of the families. They are too frightened to go anywhere these days. It was a horrendous thing. Even children were killed."

The woman was so overcome with grief that she couldn't go on. I took her hand and offered my condolences. She thanked me. When we left, she was crying softly.

I was distraught, but could think only of Leah and how the news would affect her. "How can I ever tell my stepmother?" I asked Stefan. "It will unhinge her completely. You saw the condition she's in."

"Don't tell her. Just say that no one was in the apartment, and you could not learn anything. In her condition it's better to have a little hope."

We were making our way through a cellar when we noticed that the entire block was jammed with German soldiers. We had to stay undercover for hours until the street had cleared.

In the hallway of our apartment building we ran into Dr. Mendelson. We were overjoyed to see each other. I asked him how his mother was and how the Grossman children were adjusting.

"Theyre fine, but we must all get away from here before it's too late."

I introduced Stefan to him and told him about the Polish Partisans' underground accomplishments. The doctor shook Stefan's hand and thanked him for helping our people.

I told the doctor about my father's murder, but asked him to keep it quiet, since I didn't want my stepmother to know. He agreed that I was doing the right thing.

"Such a wonderful man to come to such an undeserved death," the doctor said. "If this continues, we'll all lose our minds."

We shook hands with Dr. Mendelson and returned to my family's apartment. My stepmother shrieked on seeing us. She was in a crazed state. "I told you, didn't I?" She began wailing. "I told you he was dead!"

What could I say? It was so difficult to lie to her. "We couldn't find out anything," I managed to say, but she clearly disbelieved me.

"Liar!" she said, pointing a bony finger at me. "How can you lie about such a thing? He was your father, and he'll never come back. And I hope I join him soon. How can I live without him?"

Before we could stop her, she ran down the stairs into the street. Stefan and I chased her, but every time we saw some Germans, we had to hide. We saw her run into a synagogue, but had to wait five minutes before it was safe to run across the street.

She was inside, had opened the *Aron Ha Kodesh* and was yelling, "Where are you, God—where? Why do you inflict such suffering on us? These German beasts are slaughtering fathers, mothers, children—and you keep quiet and let it happen. Why don't you send an earthquake or a flood that will destroy us all at once and have it over with?''

The old rabbi came out to see who was desecrating this holy place. When he saw my stepmother, he bowed his head in grief. He obviously knew that my father had been killed.

''Please, Mrs. Shainberg,'' he said. ''I know that you have much trouble. We are all suffering now. But what you're doing is a sacrilege. Close the Holy Ark.''

''A sacrilege!'' my stepmother cried. ''They killed my husband—that's a sacrilege.'' She seemed to be addressing God instead of the rabbi. ''What kind of God are you who lets the heartless Nazis live while honest fathers are slain?''

The shocked rabbi covered his ears. He had never heard such blasphemy. My mother kept shouting to God with accusations and curses until Stefan and I were finally able to lead her out of the synagogue. We safely made our way home through the tunnels.

In the apartment, we tried to comfort her. But I feared that she was beyond help. All the horrors she had viewed in the Ghetto in the last few weeks had unbalanced her, and her husband's death had been the final turn of the screw. We forced her to eat, but she couldn't keep the food down.

I ran up to Dr. Mendelson's apartment and asked if he could help her.

He came down immediately with his black bag to give Leah an injection. This calmed her, and soon she was asleep. The doctor said my stepmother was in bad shape.

After Leah was settled, Dr. Mendelson told us that he had made contact with a Polish underground fighter named Kaniak. The man had promised to smuggle him, his mother, and the children out of Poland, but at a very high price. He was to meet the man and pay him in a sewer tunnel at the corner of Senna Street the following day.

Stefan and I wished him luck and predicted that we would run into each other again. I was sorry for our sake to see the doctor leave, but I knew that it was the best thing he could do.

Since my stepmother seemed to be resting comfortably, I decided to take Stefan to our underground headquarters to meet the main leaders of the Warsaw resistance, David and Pawel. I felt certain that they could collaborate somehow in their anti-Nazi maneuvers.

My friends were pleased to meet Stefan and to see that I was well. David and Pawel were very interested in the work that Stefan and I were doing with the Polish Liberation group. In the days that followed, Stefan was able to coordinate activities between the two groups and to conduct several successful night raids.

Stefan told us that he must get back to his cottage, but he promised to keep in contact with our group. I decided to stay in the Ghetto a little while longer. My stepmother was in no condition to take care of the children.

CHAPTER 10

Uprising

During the next few days, the Germans intensified their round-ups of Jews. It was no longer safe to go out, even during the day. Staying at home was no guarantee of safety, either, for the Germans periodically broke into apartments and dragged the occupants out for shipment to concentration camps.

The Nazis were aware that Warsaw was full of hiding places. One day, it occurred to them to flush people out of their secret havens by starting a gigantic fire in the Ghetto. The blaze had precisely the effect the Germans wished. Jews came pouring out of cellars, roofs, and lofts by the hundreds and were quickly shoved into trucks.

We were in our apartment that day, and a German soldier kicked our door in. He grabbed me and started pulling me down the stairs. Fortunately, I didn't have my gun on me, or he would have used it to shoot me on the spot. Still, I thought, this is the end. They finally got me, too.

Then a dreadful thing happened. My half-brother Shloyma ran after me and tried to pull me away from the German. The soldier shot the little boy in the face, killing him instantly. My step-mother stood at the top of the stairs screaming. Esther tried to stop her mother but Leah pushed her aside and ran to the dying boy screaming, "You're not dead, little Shloyma. I'll just wash off the blood—you'll be all right."

"He's dead, Mama," Esther said, crying. "He's dead."

"Don't say that," her mother snapped. "I tell you he's alive. I'll revive him. Quick, get some hot water."

I wanted to run back upstairs and comfort my distraught

family, but the German threw me down the stairs, then forced me into a van at gunpoint.

There was a window in the van and through it I saw Esther running down the stairs looking for me. I called to her to run upstairs and hide before she was caught, too.

"Mama's gone mad," she cried. "I don't know what to do."

"Run up to Dr. Mendelson's apartment—he hasn't left yet. He'll help you. It's your only chance. Please go."

She looked tenderly at me. We both sensed that we would never see each other again. She sadly waved goodbye.

Soon the van was packed with Jews. The panic-stricken captives were shaking with fear and saying that we would all be gassed right in this truck. I kept control and assured them that was not the case. "We're going to the railroad station—I heard one of the soldiers say so."

"That means Treblinka—or some other death camp. Our fate is sealed," said a weeping old man.

The van started to move, and I pressed my face near the open window to get some air. Some of the men passed out and an older man suffered a heart attack and died en route.

We finally reached the railway station, where a cattle train was waiting. We were pushed into a cattle car, but at least this was roomier than the van. It was old and creaky, and I decided that I would try to find a way to break out. This train was surely headed for a concentration camp. Once it arrived there, that was the end. There was no escaping those death camps, unless you wanted to throw yourself against electrified barbed wire.

The others in the car scoffed when I said there must be a way to escape. "Are you a simpleton?" one of the younger men sneered. "Do you think the Gestapo's so dumb? How can you possibly get out? I dare you to try."

I started searching the car for some instrument and finally found a metal pipe in a dark corner. I tried to lift it, but it was too heavy. The others laughed and made no attempt to help me. I couldn't understand their attitude. It seemed far better to attempt escape than be led to slaughter like lambs.

I kept straining to lift the metal. Finally, the young man who had dared me to escape came over and said he would help. Together we raised the pipe to the window, which was barred. After much exertion and cursing, we managed to bend the bars enough for a body to fit through. We smashed the window behind the bars and removed the splintered glass.

Our detractors stopped laughing. Only my helper and I, however, had the courage to squeeze through that window and jump off the train while it was going full speed.

As far as I know, the others stayed aboard and were taken to the ovens of Treblinka.

I never saw my helper again. We were separated when we jumped. But I like to think that he, too, succeeded in surviving the Nazi holocaust.

I don't remember how many days I walked. It must have been about a week, a week of sloshing through the melting snow of the first days of spring, 1943.

I moved mostly at night. The night brought the security of darkness. It also brought its sunless chill, and walking helped keep me from freezing. I rested during the day, usually in a crudely thrown-together shelter of tree branches and bushes, within sight of a road.

The others on the train were probably dead by now, I thought. I wondered what had become of those left behind in Warsaw? David and Esther and Pawel? The Germans had cut the Jews in half, and consumed one half. Then they cut the remainder in half, and consumed that half. And they were cutting what was left in half again.

The nights were long as I walked along the lonely roads toward the south. The farms and barns reached out from the night, beckoning to me. The farms seemed to offer food, warmth, and rest. They were a great temptation. But I knew the risk was too high. Most Polish farmers would either turn me over to the Germans or kill me themselves.

The only thing that kept me going was the thought of revenge. I was determined to fight against those who would do my people further harm.

I do not remember finally arriving at Stefan's cottage. I only remember waking up there.

Stefan said I had arrived late in the night, exhausted. He put me to bed, and I slept through until the next night.

When I awoke, we had a celebration. Stefan learned that the Germans had taken me prisoner, and every one of my comrades in Warsaw was sure that I had been sent to Treblinka. Conrad came that evening and was surprised to see me. After a slap on the shoulder and a warm welcome, he said that he had many assignments waiting for me.

He was a bit premature. Although the sleep had refreshed me a little, I was suffering from exhaustion, physical and emotional. I had seen too much, felt too much, walked too far, and shivered too long. I needed rest. Indeed, the simple climb from my cellar hiding place tired me. I felt as if I were an old man. I was not yet recovered enough to resume my underground activities.

Stefan recognized this and predicted it would be at least a month until I regained my strength. He made me comfortable and promised to keep me informed of partisan activity and the progress of the war.

The war was going well, he told me. The Germans were falling back all along the Eastern Front. He had recent copies of *Free Poland,* a newspaper put out by the Union of Polish Patriots in Moscow, which detailed the great encirclement of the Nazis. To the east, Marshal Zhukov and General Rokosovsky were following up their victory at Stalingrad by relentlessly pushing the Germans west. The Americans and British had taken most of North Africa and had Rommel's divisions bottled up in Tunisia. Allied bombings were pummeling Berlin, Hamburg, Cologne, Frankfurt, and the Ruhr on a daily basis. The Germans were on the defensive everywhere. The great Third Reich was in retreat. When I finally resumed my work as aide and secretary to Conrad, resistance fighting was gathering momentum as the war progressed, but reports from the Ghetto were growing more and more grim.

One day Stefan returned from the Ghetto with some satisfying news for a change. A Jewish barber, Idel Waksman, had been collaborating with the Germans, supplying them with the names of Jewish and Polish underground fighters. When the underground learned of his traitorous activities, three men were sent to his shop with a written statement that said:

> You, Idel Waksman, born in Warsaw in 1906 of a Jewish family, are a traitor to the Jewish nation. After a long period of observation, the underground resistance, which operates in the Ghetto, has discovered that you have been in collaboration with the Gestapo. You have delivered our members over to the Nazis, have revealed their addresses, their places of work, and their activities.
>
> You have presented this evidence in handwriting under the pseudonym "ROM." You have supplied this information twice a week.
>
> Furthermore, you possess a pass, issued to you by the Gestapo, which enables you to leave the Ghetto at any time.

You, Idel Waksman, have caused the death of innumerable Jews by your treachery. The court of the
underground resistance therefore regards your activities
as inimical toward the resistance movement.

RESOLVED: THAT YOU SHALL BE SHOT AS A
TRAITOR—THE ORDER TO BE CARRIED OUT
IMMEDIATELY.

Signed,
Court Of The Underground Resistance

As the barber finished reading the edict, he was shot by the
three men.

But there was bad news as well. Stefan reported that Chief
Rinke was speeding up the liquidation of the remaining Jews in
the Ghetto. At this time, there were about 200,000 left. The
underground reported that Eichmann had now ordered Rinke and
Brand to dispose of all of the Warsaw Ghetto Jews by May
1943. The order decreed that 100,000 should go to Treblinka;
the remaining 100,000 were to be sent to Maidanek, near Lublin,
and shot. Forty trucks would roll twenty-four hours a day, so
that 100,000 could be transported to Treblinka in ten days. Some
trains would also be available to move the massive shipments of
humans to the furnaces and lime pits.

Stefan was now working closely with David and Pawel, who
had access to secret German information. His sorties into the
Ghetto were our major source of news. In April of 1943, he
made one of these trips to bring food to friends and run errands
for the underground. When he returned, he kept us spellbound
with his account of the events of April 18. Here I have reconstructed the story he told us:

"I entered the Ghetto through the sewer on Grzybowska Street,"
he said, "and what I saw astonished me. I had been away for
only a week, but in that short time, the Germans had reduced the
area to rubble. I heard motors, so I hid in a cellar. I caught a
glimpse of the men through a window, but they were not Germans. They looked like Jews. How could that be, I wondered?
These men were not wearing yellow armbands. And where had
they gotten their vehicles? I was very puzzled by this scene.

"Then, I went to the corner of Gesia and Zamenhof Streets
and saw many people gathered there. I hid and observed them,
and again I was puzzled. These were definitely Jews, and each
had a rifle in his hand. One of the men spotted me and called in
Yiddish, 'You there—who are you? What do you want?'

"In Polish I said, 'I'm from Lekar. I'm with the resistance there.'

"I heard a guard say to another guard, 'It's okay. He's one of us. He's with the People's Guard.'

"The first guard asked me what business I had here. I told him that I wanted to help the underground troops fight the Germans. He gave me permission to pass on.

"I went to the Jewish Military Union's bunker at 5 Karmelicka, but I found a group of strangers. They were all speaking Yiddish, and they ignored me. Then, I heard an announcement that all were to assemble at the square where David Apfelbaum would speak. I followed the others; no one asked me who I was.

"At the square, David was standing on a mound of debris. When he saw me, he waved and welcomed me to the meeting. He turned to the crowd and made this announcement:

> Brothers, this is an historic moment for us. It may not be like *Erev Pesach*, when Moses led the Jews out of Egyptian slavery, and the Jews regained their complete freedom. But today is historic in a different way. On this *Erev Pesach*, Jews are fighting, not just for our rights, but to prolong our lives a little longer. Only 100,000 Jews are left out of half a million who formerly lived here. The German barbarians murdered 400,000 of us in various brutal ways. Neither children nor old people have been spared. Now they're coming to liquidate us.
>
> It's unfortunate that we didn't offer stronger resistance until now. We should have acted according to the *Torah*—an eye for an eye and a tooth for a tooth. That's the way it had been before. A burned child dreads the fire. We know that we probably won't win. But our lives will cost them a lot, too. We cannot allow them to murder us without resistance. Let's not wait in vain for help from friends. We Jews have no friends. We are alone in the fight for our lives.
>
> Our position is more perilous than ever. The Gestapo has surrounded the Ghetto with soldiers, police, and guards. They are much better mobilized than we are. But they can't kill us all. I have faith that some of us will survive—and to those I make an appeal on behalf of the Jewish Military Union. Do not let the world forget our tortures, our murders. I ask you at this

moment to say a *Kaddish* for our murdered brothers,
sisters, fathers, and mothers.

"It was one of the most moving moments I have ever witnessed," Stefan said to us. "All those men stood there with their
guns in hand, praying for the dead. When they had finished,
David said, 'Brothers—go to your assigned positions—and
please—be thrifty with your ammunition.'

"I realized then that I was part of an historic uprising. As the
Ghetto fighters spread out, the German tanks started moving in
on Zelazna Street; then they rolled into the heart of the Ghetto.
The Nazis didn't know what hit them when the Jews started
hurling grenades and flaming bottles full of fuel at their tanks.
Some of the tanks started to retreat; others burned with their
occupants inside.

"I joined the fighters, and they gave me ammunition. I had
never witnessed such gallant resistance. The Jews hurled themselves at the Germans with an inspired force, throwing them
completely off balance. The Nazis lost most of their men
involved in this attack. Finally, German planes were ordered in
to bombard us.

"Several times during the battle, David asked me to act as a
courier to take messages to other fighting leaders of the underground. Everything was going well for us until the planes roared
overhead and started dropping bombs. Then it was chaos. The
little that was left of the Ghetto was leveled. I saw Jews being
blown up on all sides of me, and if I hadn't been near a sewer
that I could drop into, I wouldn't have survived.

"I was near David when I saw a bullet strike him. Pawel and I
rushed over to him, but there was nothing we could do. Pawel
lifted David's head to comfort him. His heart soon stopped and
Pawel covered him with a coat. Pawel then assumed command
of the battle, but there was hardly anyone left to give orders to.

"'We were supposed to have help from the Russians,' Pawel
said to me. 'Stalin promised he would back up our uprising.
Where are the Russian planes? Where are the Russian tanks?
Where are the Russian troops? We have been betrayed once
again.'

"The bombs kept dropping all around us, and I ducked back
into the sewer. I was glad to see that other Jews knew about this
escape route, and I ran into several underground friends."

"What happened to Pawel?" I asked Stefan.

"I lost sight of him. I hope he was able to escape as I did. We need gallant men like him for our cause."

We stayed up half the night asking Stefan questions about the uprising.

I wondered what sort of end the remaining members of my family had come to. For my stepmother, the afterlife could only have been an improvement. Judging by her recent state of mind she would have surely spent the rest of her days in a mental institution—if she survived the holocaust. But my half-sister Esther was a different matter. She was young and sweet. It sickened me to think that she might have died in the ovens of Treblinka. I never found out what fate befell any of them.

We all wondered why the Russians had not bombed the death camps. Why didn't the Americans and the Allies bomb the gas chambers and the ovens? Surely Treblinka was within range of Soviet bombers. Stefan did not know the answer to this. Neither did I. But we kept hoping.

During the first week of May, it became evident that further resistance was futile. The Jews had made their point. The Warsaw Ghetto tried to stand its ground against impossible odds. It was time for those who remained to attempt escape so they could follow Apfelbaum's command to tell the truth of the Holocaust.

They did their job, and the records of Nuremberg are a testament in blood to the sufferings and valor of the last Jews in the Warsaw Ghetto. Stroop, the commander of the Nazi legion that liquidated the Ghetto, met his end on September 8, 1951. He had been sentenced to death by an American court at Dachau, but was then extradited to Poland, where he was tried and sentenced to death again. He was hanged in the ruins of the Warsaw Ghetto.

Stefan's story of the uprising raised a great swell of emotion within me. It was as if my previous life had been erased. All that I knew, all that I was, all that defined me as a person had perished.

CHAPTER 11

Mieczyslaw Pruzanski

In the rubble of the Warsaw Ghetto rested all my past. It was to remain buried there for more than a decade.

I credit my survival in the war to a remarkable deception which I was able to pull off with the help of my two friends and protectors, Stefan and Conrad. Conrad was able to provide me with a false identification card that described me as Mieczyslaw Pruzanski, a full-fledged Polish Christian. Before the war I had been able to court a Polish girl without any trouble, and now I was able to palm myself off as a Polish Christian with my false papers. Only Conrad, Stefan, and his family knew my secret and they were to keep it throughout the war. They had taken to calling me by my new Polish name, so that I would get accustomed to it.

During the next month, as I continued my recovery, I worked at developing my new identity. I had to suppress what came to me spontaneously. A simple exclamation such as "Oy veh!" or "Meshugeneh!" could betray me. The thousands of folkways of my Yiddish culture had to be locked away in the far recesses of my mind.

At first, I felt guilty about changing my identity. I kept thinking of what my Papa would have said if he had known. But when I realized that posing as a Pole would enable me to continue fighting with the underground, my guilt vanished.

One evening in July 1943, Conrad came to the cottage and asked where I was. Stefan took him to the other room, removed a rug from the floor, lifted two planks, and showed him where I was hiding. Conrad had never seen the secret room before and was very impressed with it.

I was lying on my cot when Conrad came down the ladder. There was barely enough room for two bodies in that small space.

"Mieczyslaw," he said briskly, "get dressed and come upstairs. We're going to Lublin."

Without asking any questions, I got dressed and climbed the ladder.

"I have good news for you," Conrad whispered. "The Polish Committee for National Liberation in Lublin is planning an uprising. I'm one of the organizers, and I'm going to need your help."

I was pleased, proud to be allied with him in any project. I might be posing as a Pole, but the cause these men were fighting for would benefit my people too.

My farewell to Stefan and his wonderful family was very emotional. The children didn't want me to leave, and even Mrs. Rudnicki, who wasn't the warmest woman, was sorry to see me go. By now she regarded me as a member of the family, and she hugged me tightly when I said goodbye.

Our journey was uneventful. We passed through the villages of Falencia and Wawer without coming across any Germans. Finally, outside Lublin, we encountered the new Polish Army and the Soviet Army, which had combined forces. All over the city, posters announced the mobilization of every man under fifty years of age. Naturally, that included me.

July 22, 1943, was eventful in many ways. On this date, labeled the Day of Poland's Liberation, the Polish Committee for National Liberation commenced its operations, and Conrad was elected Secretary of this new Polish government. He was given the rank of colonel, and I finally found out his real name: Jan Janasek. The other notable event that day was that I received my formal letter of induction into the army.

I thought I had better inform Conrad about my draft notice, but it was difficult even for close friends to get through to him in his new position. A special permit was needed from the Citizens' Militia, and this wasn't easy to secure. Finally, by protesting loudly that I was the colonel's aide and secretary, I was allowed to see him in his new offices.

Conrad was jubilant to see me. His new rank and impressive uniform did not alter his affection for me. I told him about my draft notice, but he wouldn't hear of it.

"You—a foot soldier—with your intelligence and experience?"

he exclaimed, waving his arms. "Nonsense. Let me take care of this. Would you wait in the other room for a moment?"

From the other room I could hear him speaking on the telephone. In about ten minutes he called me back and handed me a sealed envelope. There was an address written on it, and he instructed me to go there immediately. He shook my hand and said he had big plans for me. "Don't worry—I'll put you to the proper use in our army."

The building I was sent to turned out to be the local headquarters for the new army intelligence unit. I handed a receptionist the envelope. He opened it, then left with the enclosed letter for a few moments. He returned and asked me to follow him to Colonel Szydkowski's office.

The colonel rose, shook my hand and greeted me cordially. "Colonel Janasek certainly thinks very highly of you," he said. "We need men like you."

He then handed me a forty-two page questionnaire. "The Colonel has something special in mind for you. In order to qualify for the assignment, you must complete this document. It's quite long, but you can take your time with it. There's a room next door where you can work in peace."

He escorted me to another office and wished me luck.

I sat down and looked at the pages of questions. I would have to completely fabricate a Polish background for myself. Thank God both Stefan and Conrad had briefed me on a false family background, education, and job experience.

It took me three hours to complete the form, and I felt confident with my replies. I returned to the Colonel's office with the papers, but he made no attempt to read them in my presence. Instead, he engaged in a long conversation about the war and about my former work with Conrad. He seemed impressed with my experience.

"The Colonel has recommended you for a course that would lead to a commission in intelligence work. I will read your questionnaire and notify you of our decision in a few days."

"Colonel," I said. "I've already received my draft notice. I'm supposed to report to this army unit by the end of the week." I handed him my notice.

"I'll take care of this. It's a small matter." He jotted down the name of the unit.

We shook hands, and he wished me luck.

That night, I couldn't fall asleep. I kept reviewing the questions on that form, worrying that perhaps somewhere I had slipped up and had given myself away. I wondered what they would do to me if they found out I had falsified my entire background? I would have to fall back on Conrad's kindness. After all, he was the one who gave me the phony I.D. card.

All my doubts were squelched the next morning when I received a top secret letter, hand-delivered by Colonel Szydkowski's secretary, informing me that my questionnaire had been most satisfactory and that I was to start my training program at the military intelligence unit the following morning. This unit was the Polish equivalent of the American intelligence division that later would become known as the Central Intelligence Agency.

The first thing I did was to call Conrad and thank him. "Don't be ridiculous," he said. "We need people like you. I didn't do this because you're my friend; I did it because you're indispensable. I know you will repay my trust with a brilliant career."

Early the next morning, I arrived at the intelligence agency and was assigned to classes for Polish officers' military training. The course turned out to be even more grueling than my classes at Yeshiva had been. We had to attend classes every day for twelve hours. But what a difference from Yeshiva! Here the lectures were completely dominated by top Soviet officers, and their talks were both fascinating and frightening.

A typical day at school might include lectures by several high-ranking Soviet officers: Colonel Vozniskensky on "Work with Intelligence Agencies"; Colonel Fayguin on "Laws of the Penal Code"; Colonel Zaitzev on "General Intelligence Work"; Lieutenant Colonel Frolov on "Political Problems"; and Colonel Svetlik on "Economic Matters."

As a matter of course, they would inform us of sensitive military secrets. We learned, for example, that the popular Russian chief of the Polish army, Zygmunt Berling, had been yanked from the Polish front line and recalled to Moscow because he had displeased his Russian superiors. Berling, without consulting the Russians, had attempted to collaborate with General Bor-Komorowski, commander of the Warsaw uprising, and had sent the general two battalions to aid his insurgents. These troops had arrived via the Vistula River in the middle of the night. However, they never engaged in any combat. Apparently there were countermanding orders from the Russian high command preventing any assistance.

When I heard this information, I recalled what Stefan had told me about the 1943 Warsaw Ghetto uprising. The Russians had promised full support: planes, army units, and ammunition. Obviously, they had had no intention of coming to our aid; otherwise they would not have recalled Berling to Moscow for attempting to send troops to Warsaw.

Berling was very popular with the Polish soldiers and they resented his recall. To appease them, the Russians announced that they had recalled him to send him to a military academy in preparation for an even higher post.

My six months in the officers' training program passed quickly, and at the end of the course I not only passed my exams, but came out the highest in my class. I was awarded the rank of Second Lieutenant and assigned to the Fourth Pioneer Brigade, stationed in the woods near the village of Brezezowice, District of Lubartow, Province of Lublin. There I served under Captain Kochetov, head of intelligence for this brigade.

Our duties were varied and full of intrigue. My section was responsible for discovering persons or groups who were hostile to the new Polish government or to the Soviets. We arrested Gestapo collaborators like members of the Polish Fascist Home Army, and we uncovered the names of individuals who had worked with the Nazis.

Our brigade numbered four thousand men, including the security platoon of the intelligence section. We were divided into four battalions bearing the code numbers 28, 29, 30, and 31. In turn, each battalion was divided into four companies.

I was a permanent officer of the intelligence staff.

Although Captain Kochetov was my superior in order of rank, I was actually working as adjutant to Colonel Gregory Zaitzev, who was the overall head of Soviet military intelligence for the Polish Second Army. He worked directly for Larenti Beria in Moscow, head of the NKVD, later to be called the KGB. This was the beginning of my military life under Russian tutelage.

My duties included overseeing the work of the staff, supervising their reports, evaluating the records of people with disreputable backgrounds, and briefing intelligence officers on new assignments.

The intelligence system employed by the Polish Army was then, as it is now, based on the system of the Soviet Academy of Counterespionage in Leningrad, as established by Professor General Yarmoolov. Among many other activities, the Academy issued monthly bulletins on military counterespionage, intended for the exclusive use of intelligence officers.

According to the Soviet system, intelligence was derived from three components: the agent, the undercover agent, and the informer. The agent in each section employed informers that kept him abreast of all activities in his section.

The recruiting of informers was done by the head of intelligence for each platoon. A platoon consisted of four squads, and each was required to have two informers. The intelligence agent would find these men by having informal conversations with soldiers about their family life, education, sex life, and their opinions on the war. These conversations usually determined whether a soldier qualified to be an informer working directly with an intelligence agent.

Since most agents had more than one platoon under their jurisdiction, they often had more than forty informers working for them. According to regulations, the agent was supposed to meet directly with his informers or receive a report from them at least once a week.

Undercover agents assisted agents by meeting with specified informers and editing their reports. These were forwarded to the agent for his analysis. These undercover agents had to be strong supporters of the new Polish government and outstanding members of their units. In most cases, platoon leaders, squad leaders, or medics were ideal candidates for undercover agents because they could approach informers without arousing suspicion. Also, they had the necessary permits to leave restricted areas whenever necessary.

Informers wrote their reports by hand, providing exact details of incriminating conversations with suspected parties, and listing the names of all persons present during subversive dialogues. When informers presented their reports, they would be instructed by their undercover agents on how to further proceed with an investigation.

Of special interest to an intelligence agent were:

1. Details of utterances against the Russian political system or against Soviet officers (95% of the officers in the Polish Army were Russian).
2. Reports on any instances of terrorism.
3. Names of armed deserters who had joined underground groups.
4. Reports on any instances of espionage.
5. Reports on any matter of interest to the agent.

Information involving terrorism, desertion, and espionage had to be in the agent's hands within 24 hours. The informer was then instructed on how to proceed with his investigation and how he should contact the agent with future updates.

In Poland's military hierarchy, the officers of each unit were under close surveillance by intelligence agents. The higher your rank, the more closely you were watched. You could be a Russian, Beria's brother, or an intelligence agent's father, and you would still not escape close scrutiny. According to the Soviet intelligence system, persons who had a family member in a high position were considered more susceptible to betrayal.

To qualify as an agent, a man had to be educated, cunning, and courageous. The agent received his orders from high-ranking intelligence officers, and was often sent to infiltrate underground organizations.

All agents working for the Polish military intelligence department had to remain neutral in their remarks during political discussions. They were trained not to praise the ruling regime, nor to express hostility towards it. By being noncommittal, they were more likely to gain the confidence of prospective victims.

Even agents themselves were closely watched. Devious traps were set for them by superiors to test their loyalty and truthful reporting of information. Informers were also constantly tested for loyalty. If they were suspected of failing to turn over subversive material, other informers were used to trap them. Typically, a set-up informer would make inflammatory remarks about the Soviet or Polish regimes in the suspected informer's presence. If the treasonous remarks went unreported, the informer was accused of withholding valuable information, sent to Russia, and condemned to a forced labor camp.

It was a labyrinth of suspicion. Your best friend could be spying on you and reporting your every move, while he, in turn, was being watched by another informer. I found myself keeping as silent as possible and restricting my social life to a few tried and true friends whom I felt reasonably certain could be trusted. It was a system that instilled needless fear, but it was brutally effective.

I wasn't bothered much by it, because I was too absorbed with the challenge of my job. I dedicated myself to my work, seeking out Nazi collaborators and Polish Fascists wherever I could find them. Whoever was assigned to watching me must have quickly found this out, and I suspect that no one spent much effort shadowing Mieczyslaw Pruzanski.

CHAPTER 12

The Road to Liberation

By the end of 1943, the Red Army had dislodged the Germans from almost every significant Soviet city. On New Year's Day, 1944, the Russians were about 150 miles east of Lublin, approaching the Polish border. The expected liberation was great cause for celebration.

At the conclusion of fighting in Russia in 1944, the Polish Kosciuszko Division was formed to aid the Soviet armies in their march against Hitler's forces. This Polish Army, together with detachments of the Soviet Red Army, entered Poland in the summer of 1944. The combined forces met with their first success when they freed Lublin. Soon after that, they captured the infamous torture camp of Maidanek, and people from outside Poland had their first opportunity for a close-up look at a Nazi death factory.

During those days, beginning in the summer of 1944, I was ordered to assist Polish partisan groups in their intelligence gathering activities. When I was not busy with the partisans, I taught signals and codes to men of the armored tank divisions. I was also sent to a special officers' school and learned to reconnoiter. Graduating with the rank of Lieutenant, I was appointed head of the 28th Reconnoitering Battalion of the Kosciuszko Division.

I was, of course, still masquerading as Mieczyslaw Pruzanski, a disguise which allowed me to see more than ever the depths of Polish bigotry against the Jews. Since none of my fellow officers suspected my origins, they often made anti-Semitic comments in my presence, which I had to bear with a smile.

Moving between Soviet and Polish units, I had the opportunity

to compare attitudes on this issue. All things considered, I found
the Poles vastly more hostile to Jews than the Russians. Soviet
troops were generally ambivalent about Jews. They had no great
compassion for Jewish suffering, but they generally did not go
out of their way to injure Jews. Their one burning desire was to
drive onward to Berlin. Anything else was peripheral.

But the Poles had a tradition of deep anti-Semitism. Perhaps it
was their Catholic Church that fostered this or maybe it was a
flaw in their culture. I hoped that the massive Soviet influence
on postwar Poland might actually change their vicious bigotry. I
hoped that the Communist doctrine about international brother-
hood and toleration would re-educate Poles and make Poland a
place where a Jew could live in peace.

The problem bothered me, but I didn't have much time to
come to any final conclusions. I sympathized with the Russian
philosophy: finish off the Germans, and then move on to other
problems.

Through June, July, and August, there was a euphoric rush
across Poland. We felt invincible. By the end of summer, we
were halted along the Vistula, catching our breath and looking
across the river at the bridge that the retreating Wehrmacht had
yet to destroy. An intact bridge waiting for the Polish and Red
Armies meant a quick crossing and easier pursuit of the half-
beaten Nazis. Our forces maintained pressure on the German
units, preventing them from reorganizing to attack the bridge.

By the time our units crossed the Vistula, Warsaw was in
ruins. The Jewish Ghetto had been destroyed in the uprising of
1943 and the rest of the city was dismembered as the Russians
approached.

The people of Warsaw revolted against the Nazis when the
Red Army approached the city. There was a fierce struggle, and
many Poles fell. There has been great criticism against Moscow
for not pushing the Red Army into the struggle to liberate
Warsaw while the Polish insurrection was still going on. To
some extent, this is a valid complaint. But there were other
considerations at the time. Most importantly, we were tired. The
Russians had just finished a grueling summer advance that liberated hundreds of thousands of square miles of Eastern Europe. In
addition, the Germans had mustered their top forces at Warsaw,
and attacking them prematurely would have meant a costly river
crossing. Furthermore, the Warsaw uprising was staged by groups
sympathetic to the Polish government-in-exile, located in Lon-

don. They were a group of reactionaries, highly critical of the
Soviet Union, who wanted to restore Poland's prewar status quo.
The Russians were reluctant to sacrifice thousands of lives to
directly help these anti-Soviet elements.

Before opening a new offensive, the Russians had waited for
their old ally, winter. By December, all available German reserve units had been sent to the Western Front, trying to breach
the American lines in the Battle of the Bulge. Within a few
weeks, the German attack had been shattered, and while the
German generals were trying to decide how to prevent an American counter-attack, the Russians acted. On January 12, 1945,
Soviet Marshal Ivan Konev broke through the German lines at
Baranov, along the Vistula south of Warsaw. Then Zhukov
divided his army and crossed the Vistula both north and south of
Warsaw. Two other Russian armies opened yet another attack
near the Baltic. Altogether, we numbered nearly two hundred
divisions, and the Germans soon felt the weight of the greatest
offensive of the war.

Warsaw fell in a few days. I walked the streets of that ancient
capital on January 17, 1945, the day of its liberation. But there
was little left to liberate. I could not believe what I saw. The
entire city was practically gone. The Central Railroad Station
was demolished, except for a skeletal wall or two; most houses
were destroyed or charred by fires. It was truly, as Arthur Bliss
Lane, U.S. Ambassador to Poland in 1944, described it, ''a city
of the dead.''

When I walked down Gesia Street, I shuddered. Only rubble
and ashes were left of our neighborhood. The apartment house
where I had lived with my family was completely leveled, as
were all the other houses on that block.

There was not a familiar face on Gesia Street. I felt as if I
were in a foreign country or on another planet, instead of the
city where I grew up. Among the few buildings left intact were
the Hotel Polonia, near the railroad station, and Gestapo Headquarters at Chelbinski 7, which we appropriated for our own
headquarters.

I asked Major Czarley of the intelligence department if I could
be excused for an hour, and he replied, ''Sure—but I can't
imagine where you want to go in this graveyard.''

The major didn't know how clairvoyant he was. That was
precisely where I wanted to go—to the Jewish cemetery on Gesia
Street.

It was a bleak, wintry day, and the cemetery was deserted, but at least it was intact. Most of the graves and tombstones were undamaged. I found my mother's grave and removed some rubbish from the plot. I had no flowers to leave there, but I stood before the tombstone and said *Kaddish*, the prayer for the dead. I also prayed for all the members of my family who had most likely perished at the hands of the Germans.

I left the cemetery and walked about the destroyed capital. People followed me and begged for food. There was no use giving them money; there was no place to spend it. It was impossible to walk on the sidewalks. They were covered with mortar and debris from bombed and gutted buildings.

I returned to our new headquarters and the activity there caused me to become extremely apprehensive. Our intelligence men were poring over documents found in the building which contained names of former Zionists, including mine. My activities with the Jewish Military Union were recorded and so were my various code names. The Gestapo had known my real name, and that too was recorded. I was most afraid that there could also be a picture of me which would identify me, as my former name would not.

These records which focused on non-leftists who were active in the early days of the Zionist movement, were sent to the Soviet archives in Russia.

We found a sickening batch of papers that contained detailed facts about that medical project that had taken Laya's life in the Warsaw borough of Praga. I discovered that Dr. Hoheneiser and his assistants had attempted different techniques for sterilizing the children, and most of them had died. It was a vile, inhuman project, and it sickened all who had to read the documents.

During the afternoon, I went across the river to Praga on an errand and ran into a familar face at last. Standing in front of the Jewish Committee was Dr. Mendelson.

"David! Is it really you?" I said. After all we had been through, I felt I could call him by his first name.

"Maurice!" he exclaimed, throwing his arms around me. Then I noticed at his side a strikingly beautiful Polish woman.

"Oh, I'm sorry," he said, "this is my wife Danka. This is a dear friend, Maurice Shainberg," he said to her, "who lived in the same house with me."

It was alarming to hear my real name. I winced when he said it, and he noticed my fear.

"What's the matter, Maurice?"

"I can't tell you now—I'll fill you in. At the moment, please don't call me by that name. As far as anyone knows, I'm Mieczyslaw Pruzanski."

They looked somewhat startled.

"That's a Polish name," Danka said. "I'm Polish."

"So I've noticed," I said a trifle icily.

"You obviously have no love for Poles," she said softly,"although you bear a Polish name."

"That was a necessity."

"I only see a person, not his origins," she replied calmly. "I love my husband. His life is my life, his God is my God, his religion is my religion."

"I do not hate Poles," I replied, admiring her courage. "In fact, I was once in love with a beautiful Polish girl. But when the Germans arrived, her true feelings came out and she renounced me. I wish you and David the greatest happiness. We certainly all deserve something good after the hell we've been through."

She smiled and turned away.

"Please," I begged David, "let's get together tonight. I'm sure you have a lot to tell me, as I have to tell you. There's hardly any place to meet in this area, so why don't you come to our headquarters at 7 Chelbinski at eight. I'll have some food and wine for you. And please bring your beautiful wife."

They both shook my hand and promised to meet me. It was so good to see a friend in this wasteland that I was in a cheerful mood for the rest of the day. If only I could have found other familiar faces—but that pleasure was not to be mine.

I wandered back through the broken city toward our headquarters. Along the way, I looked at the people who drifted through the rubble. They seemed to be part of the rubble, broken people among broken buildings, trying to comprehend what had happened. The cold January air seemed to numb everybody. Here in this rubble most of my life lay buried. Beneath these shattered walls and scattered bricks were my youth, my world, and the world of my father.

For a while I searched the faces of the refugees, trying to find another link to my past. But all I saw was a foreign blankness that refused acknowledgment. They weren't brothers and sisters; they were starving strangers. They weren't cousins and uncles; they were homeless orphans. They weren't mothers or fathers; they were petrified relics of a former existence.

There was a temptation to join them. I wondered, why was I spared their fate—or worse? Why was I wearing this Polish officer's uniform when my rightful place was with them? Why was I spared their suffering? The world was verifiably insane, and there didn't seem to be much reason to remain part of it. Reason could only be found in one's fantasies. Seeking out my parents, my brother and sisters, my old friends could only result in frustration. No mad hallucinations of mine could be worse than the effects of this war and the raving lunacy in the world around me.

I stopped for a moment and looked at myself. I was not like these lost people. I was not the young man who watched German bombers destroy occupied buildings along Gesia Street five years ago. I had undergone a metamorphosis. I had a new identity, and this identity was alive and productive. Mieczyslaw Pruzanski had a purpose: to return to headquarters and continue working to destroy the Nazi war machine. Maurice Shainberg was hibernating, awakened briefly by a meeting with Dr. Mendelson, but passing most of the Holocaust in a protected state of slumber.

Schizophrenia? Perhaps. But it was a mechanism of sheer survival. I was destined to be Mieczyslaw Pruzanski for nearly another decade, but I was grateful. I fared better than most of Europe's Jews.

Back at headquarters, the officers were still engrossed in the captured records the Nazis had left behind. I was almost amused to think that they were reading about me, never suspecting that I was Maurice Shainberg.

I hoped some of them were learning about the Nazis' methodical destruction of the Jews and how Jewish resistance had been a cornerstone of the war effort. I hoped that after discovering these facts, my comrade Slavs would begin to see Jews as people; that the anti-Semitism they had been weaned on would finally be offset by understanding. This could be the first step toward rapprochement.

That evening, precisely at eight, David and Danka arrived. They hungrily ate the food I served them, and drank wine with gusto. While we enjoyed dinner, we exchanged incredible stories about what had happened to us since we last met.

My friends were astounded when I told them how I was successfully masquerading as a Pole. When I explained how I had escaped from the freight car, they were even more amazed.

"Will you ever reveal that you're Jewish?" David asked.

"Yes, when I feel that the time is right. I'm proud to be Jewish, and it will please me to make the fact known at the proper moment."

"What do you think will happen when your superiors find out?"

"I have no idea. I've thought about it. They surely won't react favorably. After all, I did make false statements on my intelligence application. I'll have to bide my time and see."

David asked about my family. "I'm afraid they're all dead," I replied. "The only survivor may be my brother, the rabbi. And I'll probably never know where he ended up."

I asked David what had happened to him after he left the Ghetto with his mother and the Grossman children. His story was as tragic and horrible as mine. His underground contact, Kaniak, had arranged, for a very high price, to transport him and his party to a forest in the Kieleckie Province. They got there safely, but then their troubles began.

They were captured by some nasty Polish guerrillas who took them to their headquarters in the mountains. The only reason David was spared was that they badly needed a doctor, and he fit the bill. Nevertheless, they were so anti-Semitic that they wouldn't spare his mother or the Grossman children. They told him they were sending them to another province where they would be taken care of by the underground.

It was not easy for him to tell the gruesome details that followed.

"It wasn't until I met Danka that I learned the bitter truth of what had been done to them. They had taken them out to the woods, tied my mother to one tree and the children to another. They left them there to starve. Months later, their ravaged bodies were still tied to those trees."

He couldn't continue; his grief robbed him of his voice.

I didn't know what to say. It was still another example of man's inhumanity to man. Every Jew who survived the war had similar or worse horror stories to tell.

"And how did you two meet?" I asked, trying to lighten the atmosphere in the room.

"My brother, Lieutenant Zawadzki," Danka said, "was one of the guerrilla leaders. When he discovered David was a doctor, he asked me if I would like to be his assistant. I declined. The sight of blood had always made me sick, and I couldn't imagine myself in the role of a doctor's aide."

"Fortunately," David said, "she got ill herself—and that's how we first met. She had a terrible cold—no, it was the flu."

"Yes," Danka said, laughing, "and he wanted to examine me. He asked me to take off my blouse and I flatly refused. He ended up prescribing pills for me. I got over the flu, but not over him. I was attracted to him from the moment we met. I guess that's why I was so embarrassed that I wouldn't remove my blouse. I couldn't get him out of my mind. So one day, not long afterwards, I said to my brother that I had changed my mind. It would be charitable of me to help the doctor with his work. My brother got angry and told me it was too late. He had already assigned a corporal to the job.

"I thought for a moment and then told him I was furious at the idea that they would use a fighting man as a hospital orderly when a woman could do the job. He saw my point and sent the corporal back to active duty."

"How was she as your assistant?" I asked David.

"Beautiful, but clumsy—at first. And very loyal. One day, I had bandaged a soldier and I inquired if the bandages were too tight. 'You just try to do a bad job on me, Jew-boy,' he said, 'and I'll finish your doctoring days.' Danka heard him and really let him have it. 'You rotten bastard,' she yelled at him, 'he's trying to save your life. You'd better keep a civil tongue in your stupid mouth, or I'll finish you—you ungrateful animal.' "

We laughed heartily.

"I could afford to be brave," Danka said. "My brother was a big shot in the resistance—and the soldier knew that. He kept his mouth shut after that."

"It was at that moment that I realized Danka loved me." David said. "When you're surrounded by hatred, moments like that are especially meaningful."

"And how did your brother react to all of this?" I asked Danka.

"He was livid. One of his close friends, Captain Stankiewicz, was in love with me and wouldn't leave me alone. I couldn't stand him and I told my brother this many times. He said I was a Jew-lover, and I told him, 'If it wasn't for this Jew, half your men would be dead.' He realized I was right and never said another word against David."

We continued talking for hours, recalling some of the people on Gesia Street who had died or disappeared and exchanging stories about our war experiences.

"And what are your plans now?" I asked.

"We're going to stay in Warsaw," David said, "They'll need doctors and nurses badly here, and who knows, maybe there will be less prejudice now that the Poles have had a taste of the Nazis."

I disagreed. "I don't believe that prejudice against Jews will be at all changed by the war. As soon as the city rises again, the same old bigotry will rise with it. I plan to go elsewhere, eventually—possibly to Palestine. I couldn't bear to stay in this land that has always hated us so."

Danka said that she understood my feelings. "I have seen David insulted and rebuffed by my people, and it makes me ashamed to be Polish. Prejudice is ignorance—and ignorance is often incurable."

"Yet," David said to me, "you and I both owe our survival to Poland."

"How do you mean that?"

"You have taken a Polish identity, which saved you from liquidation; I have also assumed a Polish identity." He handed me his I.D. card which identified him as Stanislaw Zawadzki.

"But that's your brother!" I said to Danka.

"Yes," she said. "When David and I decided to marry, we knew my brother would never approve, so we decided to run away from the partisan camp together. I stole my brother's I.D. card one night and substituted David's picture, and we've traveled everywhere with it. It really saved our lives."

"Well, now," I said to David, "are you going to continue as a Pole?"

"No," he said. "When you ran into me today, I was about to go to the Jewish Congregation to sign their register of those who had survived. I signed it as David Mendelson."

"I can't make that revelation yet," I said. "I want to continue fighting for our cause, and the best way for me to do it right now is as a Pole. I could probably comfortably stay Mieczyslaw Pruzanski the rest of my life and never experience prejudice and hatred again."

"Not really," Danka said. "Don't forget there are places where the Pole is hated."

"True," I said. "Anyhow, I couldn't deny my Jewish heritage for the rest of my life. My greatest happiness would be to go to Israel someday to help build our new nation there."

"Then that's what you must do," David said. "And perhaps, if things don't go well here, we'll join you there."

We bade each other goodnight and promised to meet as often as we could. I explained that I would probably not be in Warsaw more than a few days, since there were many other places that had to be liberated.

We agreed to meet again someday, in the Jewish state that was bound to be born. They disappeared into the ruins of Warsaw, and I prepared to return to the road of liberation.

CHAPTER 13

Berlin Is Burning

The following morning, I was told that General Swierczewski wished to see me. I went to his office, and he wasted no words. "We're going to take Radom. Come outside in the wagon with me so we can talk."

"Yes, Sir. Just let me tell my boss where I am. I'll be right there."

He excused me, and I dashed to Colonel Zaitzev's office. I told him that the general wanted me to accompany him to Radom.

"Yes, I know," Zaitzev said. "That's fine."

I thanked him, saluted, and left. I was eager to hear the general's plan. I walked quickly outside and joined him in his horse-drawn military wagon. He gave instructions to his driver, then settled back to talk with me. I had always liked the general, and he had a rather paternal attitude toward me. I was certain that he had something good in mind for me at Radom.

His first question surprised me a bit. "Have you seen the documents that we found in Gestapo Headquarters?"

"Yes," I replied warily, "but as a member of the intelligence department, I cannot discuss them. Please ask Major Czarley or Major Kochetov about them. They will give you the information you want."

He looked at me for a moment, and I was certain that he would dress me down for my refusal. Instead, he said, "You're right. You must abide by the regulations."

He changed the subject quite radically. "Do you have a girl friend? Are you sleeping with anyone?"

I started to laugh. Sex was a private thing to me and I never

discussed it, not even with my closest friends. I also had no
interest in hearing about other people's affairs. Unfortunately, in
the army, that was the one topic that no one ever tired of
discussing.

"No, not at the moment," I said. "I had a wonderful girlfriend but like most Ghetto people, she vanished."

"What was she doing in the Ghetto?" he asked.

I had almost betrayed myself. "Her father was a postman," I
said truthfully, "and he had to live near his place of work."

"And how did you meet this creature?"

"I played on a soccer team—and she used to watch me all the
time. That's how we met."

"Oh, yes. Girls love athletes. Their sexual fantasies revolve
around them. They envision them as the epitome of virility, and
very often they have less in their pants than other men." The
general slapped my thigh and laughed uproariously. I tried to
laugh along with him, although I didn't find his remark particularly amusing.

"You're much too serious," he said, "and you have no sense
of humor. With your good looks and youth, you should be
raising hell."

"I find it difficult to raise hell when I've lost my entire
family. I intend to keep searching for them. Maybe if I find
them, I'll have time for affairs."

I had the uneasy feeling that the general was checking up on
me. He knew that I was the only Polish officer in the Russian-
dominated Intelligence Corps. That made him a little suspicious.
It was an ironic situation. As an intelligence officer, I knew so
much more about him than he knew about me.

I knew, for instance, that he was an old Communist Party
member who had fought in the underground against Franco in
Spain. I also knew that for a general, he was remarkably devoid
of arrogance.

The rest of our conversation was merely small talk. The
general liked gossip about his colleagues. I could have given him
reams of it, but once again, as an intelligence agent, my lips
were sealed. I was hoping that he would turn the conversation to
Radom and what was expected of me there. But he never did.

The next day, Colonel Zaitzev, General Swierczewski, and I
were driving in the general's horse-drawn carriage on the way to
Radom when we came upon a field strewn with the bodies of
fallen Polish soldiers. It looked like a massacre. We stopped to
take a closer look.

"What happened? Why so many dead?" Zaitzev asked.

The general said, "What did you expect? The Russian headquarters sent so many untrained men to the front line—they were really nothing more than cannon fodder."

From across the field, we saw two mutilated human forms move and we heard them cry, *"She'ma Yisrael!"* They obviously hadn't seen us. Then the two men, crawling on the ground, lifted their rifles and fired at each other simultaneously. Both fell dead. We approached them and saw that they had both lost their legs from a mine on the battlefield.

"What was it they said?" Colonel Zaitzev asked. "It didn't sound like Polish to me." Although the colonel's wife was Jewish, he did not understand Yiddish or Hebrew. But the general did, apparently, for he offered an explanation: "It was a prayer they said—the prayer of a Jew before he faces death. These two wanted to die. They were badly hurt, and they had nowhere to go and nobody to help them."

We returned to our wagon and rushed to catch up with the head column. I learned later that some seventy percent of the soldiers in the ten divisions in the area were Jewish. Many of them were killed because they lacked any proper military training. Many died because Jewish soldiers were commonly used by the Russians as human mine sweepers, clearing suspected mine fields by detonating the explosives with their bodies so that Russian troops could march on with fewer casualties. They were also positioned in the front lines, taking the brunt of German attacks away from the Russian troops who would march behind them.

Our journey after this incident was uneventful until the general decided to stop at a farmer's hut some miles from Radom. The hut was filled with Russian officers and a dramatic scene was unfolding before us. We learned that Captain Kochetov had received a confidential letter from Colonel Zaitzev, Chief of the Second Polish Army, ordering him to supply the colonel with the names of officers with a "B" classification, those who opposed the Communist regime and the People's Poland. These were marked men. Here in this hut, officers were turning over their lists of the doomed to the captain.

The actual roundup occurred at a local schoolhouse. The captain surrounded the building with his intelligence platoon, composed mainly of Soviet soldiers posing as Poles. Soon, trucks arrived bearing about two thousand frightened men with "B" classifications.

"Where are we going?" they kept asking in their limited Russian.

"Nowhere," the Soviet soldiers in Polish uniforms replied. "The front is near."

But the Polish officers didn't believe them. They knew well that the front wasn't near because there was no artillery bombardment going on nearby.

The general and I were put up for the night, but I couldn't sleep. Even though I had little love for the Poles, I hated seeing these soldiers and officers led to slaughter.

Before daybreak, these unfortunates were awakened, piled onto trucks, and taken away. At 7:00 a.m., Captain Kochetov reported to his Russian superiors that the order had been completed. The men were never heard from again.

The general and I continued on our journey. Six miles from Radom, we stopped in an abandoned building which was being used as headquarters for Marshal Konev's forces. We were asked to join the officers assembled in the next room for an important meeting. I noted as we entered that the men looked somewhat curiously at me. What was such a young officer doing in the company of the general, they must have wondered.

Colonel Borzov arrived and briefed us on our target. "Radom is a vital industrial center," he told us. "There are many important factories here which the Germans have been using to manufacture arms. We want those plants intact, so there must be no action taken that could destroy them."

He spread out a map of the city and pointed to areas which should not be disturbed. "There is to be as little destruction as possible. Our objective is to take this town using minimal force."

The eight officers in the room were assigned to draw up attack plans. "The plan that seems the most sensible for our purposes will be used," the colonel announced.

This is going to be ticklish, I thought. I was probably the lowest-ranking officer in the room. If my plan were somehow chosen, it would probably trigger deep resentment. But I didn't care. I was more interested in devising a plan to regain one of our cities from the Nazis.

We worked diligently and silently. I studied the map carefully and noted that there were trees on one side of the city and marshes on the other. The remaining sides were occupied by German forces.

I devised a plan whereby the Germans would be duped into

believing that we were all in the wooded area. I would have my men start shooting small artillery in that section to distract the Germans from the marshlands. While the Germans concentrated their firepower and attention on the woods, the majority of our men would surprise them by advancing through the open side in the marshes and surrounding them.

The colonel studied our plans carefully, asking each of us detailed questions about our campaign. There was much tension in the room, with each officer praying that his plan would be chosen. A successful maneuver might lead to a highly desirable promotion.

After an hour's deliberation, the colonel asked, "Who is Lieutenant Pruzanski?"

There was silence as I stood up.

"Please come here," the colonel said. Every other officer in the room looked as if he would like to slit my throat. It must have humiliated them to be upstaged by a babe in arms like me.

"How long have you been in the army?" the Colonel asked.

"Two years," I answered, "and before that, three years in the underground."

"Excellent. I'm going to use your plan. It seems the simplest and most logical."

I dared not look at the other officers. I could feel waves of resentment inundating the room.

The colonel and the general went over my plan in detail, instructing each officer on the maneuvers assigned to his division. When all instruction and orders were dispensed, General Swierczewski came over and shook my hand. "An excellent plan, Lieutenant," he said. "I'm certain that it will work."

The general, colonel, and Marshal Konev had a short conference, after which they announced we would attack in two hours. The officers were dismissed to alert their divisions, but I was requested to remain.

In two hours, we were ready to strike. I was ordered to accompany the Signal Corps men who were to serve as communications for all divisions during the attack.

General Swierczewski and Colonel Borzov were in command, and I watched their maneuvers through my binoculars. One division patrolled the area first, searching for mines and snipers; after their reconnaissance, the attacking divisions moved in.

The ruse I had concocted worked well. As soon as our men began firing into the wooded area, the Germans concentrated their efforts and men in that section, leaving the marshes wide open for our penetration. Soon they were surrounded and defeated. More than eight thousand German soldiers were captured. The town of Radom was ours without damage and with only a few casualties.

On January 21, General Swierczewski commended me before all the divisions and promoted me to captain and head of the Operations Group. The older officers resented this bitterly. They made malicious remarks about my relationship with the general and said I only made my rank because of nepotism. That really amused me. If only they knew I was a Jew masquerading as a Pole to survive, they would have changed their tune.

That night, I couldn't sleep. I was elated over my promotion, but I was upset over my colleagues' hostility. As a Jew, all my life I had been exposed to resentment. Ironically, even as a Pole, I was still not immune.

My orderly, Tadeusz Spakowski, was a good man. He heard me tossing and turning and came to see if I was ill. I had to confide in someone. I told him why I was upset.

"They're jealous of you because you're younger than they are and have achieved more recognition. But the soldiers are all for you. I know. I was in the mess hall before, and I heard nothing but praise for you and your promotion. Don't pay any attention to the officers. Your soldiers are more important. There are *more* of them."

That made me feel better. "I'm not doing any of this for promotions," I said to my orderly. "I'm in this war to help defeat the Nazis. I want to fight Nazis more than anything else. I care nothing for this new rank and the distracting politics associated with it."

"The men know that," Tadeusz replied, "and they're proud to serve under you."

The next day there was another roundup of officers who were in the "B" classification. Captain Kochetov called the personnel chief of the brigade, Captain Voytkin, and read him a list of fourteen officers who had been transferred to Warsaw so that their commissions, issued by prewar military authorities, could be examined. The officers were crowded into a van with Captain Voytkin as their escort. Among them was First Lieutenant Caruk, head of the 20th Battalion. He, unlike the others, had not received a prewar commission. He had graduated from officers' training school in Rayzan, two hundred miles southeast of Mos-

cow, a school which had been founded by the Soviets for the
Polish Communist Army. This officer, a native of Lodz, was
highly intelligent and beloved by his soldiers. I believed him to
be of Jewish origin. I asked Captain Kochetov why Lieutenant
Caruk was included among these men.

"Because he is the same sort of troublemaking reactionary as
these others," the captain said. "He must die with them to
purify our new army."

Once again, the men vanished, never to be heard from again.

Near the end of January 1945, I was ordered to lead a reconnaissance mission to the infamous extermination camp at Auschwitz. We had reports that the Gestapo was so terrified of the
Russian advance in Poland that they had evacuated as many
inmates of the camp as could be transported. The last of these
transports departed on January 18. The only remaining prisoners
were too emaciated to be moved.

I suggested that we attack the camp at night. All of us were so
eager to liberate the victims of that despicable horror that we set
off on our mission four and a half hours early.

We entered the camp through the main gate on the left side.
The first of many things to disgust us was the sweet, sickening
smell of burnt flesh. Although the gas chambers and ovens were
no longer in operation, the stench of their victims lingered on.

Then we saw scenes that were to plague me in vivid nightmares for the rest of my life. The living dead who were left
behind were huddled in piles, their faces and bodies so hideously
wasted that it was impossible to tell men from women. But no
matter how wretched their condition, they still clung to life and
feebly stretched their arms toward us in thanks. Smiles stretched
across their bony, emaciated faces as they waved while we
marched into the camp.

The few SS troops on hand were stunned to see the Polish
army taking over the camp. They started shooting, but we out-
numbered them so heavily that they quickly surrendered. Had we
been as merciless as the Germans, we would have shoved them
into the ovens alive.

As we moved about the camp, the unbelievable horrors increased with every step. I shuddered to think that most of my
family had probably died in one of these places.

One group of prisoners refused to believe the reality of our
arrival. They were convinced that this was still another German
torture. They crept closer and closer. When they were finally

persuaded that we weren't the Gestapo, they began kissing our uniforms. They had no idea that I was Jewish—like them.

This handful of bones and parched skin was all that remained of millions of Europe's innocent Jews who had been incarcerated, sterilized, and incinerated in this man-made hell. Their only crime: being Jewish.

The most pathetic sight of all was the children who looked old and hopelessly deformed. Some had bloated stomachs; others had lost their hair and were covered with sores. The most shocking of all were those with scars from sadistic Nazi experiments. Their grateful looks, in spite of their misery, have haunted me since that day.

When I returned to headquarters and described what we had witnessed, my superiors were stupefied. They knew that the Germans were heartless murderers, but they never dreamed that any race could be so sadistic and bestial toward its prisoners. Whatever medical aid could be mustered—and it wasn't much—was dispatched to the camp. We rounded up a van of food and supplies for these survivors.

With the camp liberated, we probed its grounds. We were looking for stray Germans, but we found only the dying survivors. They stared out at us cautiously, in disbelief.

My emotions about this experience are too painful to put into words. I'm left with images only. The sad face of a frail woman, a face that expressed all the torture of more than five years of war. The pleading expression of a little boy wrapped in rags, the face of incomprehension. I wondered how he would grow up after the unbelievable experience of that place.

Who was a Jew? Who was a Russian? a Gypsy? a Pole? One could not tell. I could identify only one group on sight—a small band of Catholic women who tied two pieces of wood together in the shape of a cross, set it in the earth, and kneeled down before it in prayer.

I came across a Jewish man who was standing with a blanket draped about him, staring into one of the fires that had been built in the yards. "Berlin is burning," he kept saying in Yiddish as he peered into the flames. "Berlin is burning. Berlin is burning."

Throughout that night, we worked with quiet efficiency. Voices were muffled. The usually boisterous Russian troops maintained a solemn reverence. We were in the most infamous depths of the Third Reich. Our eyes saw sights unimaginable to civilized humans. We were among the first non-German witnesses of mass-production death factories. I doubted that any of us would voluntarily discuss this mission. It was an error in history, something that could not have happened. Yet it had. We were witness to crimes of unprecedented evil.

As soon as a communications squad was brought up, I handed them a message to be transmitted to Warsaw.

Would Doctor and Mrs. David Mendelson please come to Auschwitz as quickly as possible? There was much work for them.

CHAPTER 14

Reichstod

With the fall of Silesia, we knew victory was ours because we had captured the last of the Nazi coal reserves. Without coal, their war machine would grind to a halt.

As we started to swing north again, three elements merged to prime us for the final death blow to Nazi Germany. First, the experience of Auschwitz demanded immediate vengeance. Soviet examinations of the death camp immediately after the liberation estimated that four million people had been exterminated there. Justice had to be served.

Next, there was the capture of Silesia, Hitler's fuel bin. No more coal for armaments factories. None for troop trains. None to be synthesized for tank and aircraft fuel.

Third, Zhukov's armies had cut off Prussia from the rest of Germany, crossing the Oder River into Mecklenburg. They were within a hundred miles of Berlin!

We had the momentum to carry us to victory. The assault that was launched on the banks of the Vistula would not stop until the German Reich was dead.

Soviet armies rolled through Poznan toward the German border, and we prepared to move in behind them.

Poznan was the fourth largest city in Poland. It was an industrial center for the manufacture of metal and farm equipment. My Russian superiors had enough faith in me by this time to appoint me Military Commandant of the city for a five-day period.

One afternoon, I was riding in an American jeep with my orderly, Sergeant Spakowski, and a corporal, who was driving. My orderly spied a man walking along the road.

"Look!" he said, "that must be a German soldier."

I looked at the man, who seemed hungry and dirty, and said, "I don't think so. But let's stop and find out."

When my orderly spoke to the man, a touching thing happened. The man put his hand on my orderly's uniform with a grateful look. "Thank God," he said in Polish, "to see you instead of the Germans."

I asked him to get in the jeep, and assured him that we would help. When he told me his name—Lichtenstein—I realized that he was a Jew.

"Come to my office," I said. "You can wash and shave there, and have a meal. We can even find some better clothes for you."

"Oh my God," he said, clutching my hand. "Can this really be happening?"

"Yes, I think your worries are over. We're moving on to Berlin in a few days, but you'll be safe here. Nobody will terrorize you anymore."

At headquarters, he told me that there were about eight Jewish people left alive in the area. They had been sheltered through the war by a Catholic priest, a Father Kwiatowski, but now they hoped for places of their own, along with food and medicine.

I recalled that there were some empty apartments in town where the Gestapo had lived during their occupation. "I think I can find places for you and your friends."

Lichtenstein looked as if he would pass out. "We would be so grateful," he managed to say.

I instructed my orderly to take the man and his friends to the empty apartments and to see that the group was supplied with food and medicine that the Germans had left behind.

Lichtenstein showered and shaved, put on the new clothes we gave him, ate a meal, and looked like a different man when he left with my orderly. I felt deeply satisfied to be able to help him and his friends.

That evening, he returned to my office and thanked me on behalf of his friends. "Your orderly found us four excellent apartments at Matejko Street. We have only one worry. Do you think anyone will try to evict us from there?"

"I'll fix it so that no one does," I said. "We're leaving here in a few days; then the civil administration will take over. They might try to throw you out."

I scribbled a note. "Take this to Captain Ognev's office down the corridor. He will issue you proper papers with a military stamp on them. These documents will establish you and your friends as the proper residents of the apartments, and no one will dare evict you.''

The man was so overcome that I was tempted to tell him that I too was Jewish. But I checked myself.

Lichtenstein took the note and went to see the Captain. Just as he left, my orderly burst in, grinning, his face all flushed.

''What's happened to you?'' I asked, laughing.

''I saw the most beautiful girl I've ever seen in my life today. You have to meet her! She's a blonde with big blue eyes and she plays the piano beautifully. Everybody was sitting on the floor listening to her.''

''Where?'' I asked.

''Over at those apartments where I took the group. She was one of them. Her mother has asked about you and said she would like to thank you in person for all you've done for them.''

''Well, let's go. After what we've been through, I'd like to see this beauty.''

My orderly drove me to Matejko Street and escorted me to the apartment. I asked him to wait downstairs for me.

I knocked on the door and it was opened by an attractive woman. I introduced myself, and she almost burst into tears. ''We are so grateful to you, Captain. You have saved us from despair.''

''Please don't thank me. We have all been through enough hell the last few years. The least we can do now is help one another.'' I astounded her by saying this in perfect Yiddish.

She was quite moved. ''Where are your parents?'' she asked.

''All dead, I believe. And my sisters and a half-brother, too. The only one who may have survived is my brother Nathan, who's a rabbi. But let's not talk about that now. I don't wish anyone to know that I'm Jewish until the war's over. It must remain secret. My orderly doesn't even know. That's why I asked him to wait downstairs.''

''Of course. You can trust me. Come tomorrow night at six. We will celebrate our first Sabbath together. Then you can meet all the others—including my daughter, Sabina.''

Sabina, I thought. What a lovely name. I was so happy that I almost felt as if I had found my family again. I kissed the gracious lady's hand and said I would be honored to spend the Sabbath with her and her friends.

My orderly teased me a bit when he heard I hadn't met the

girl. But I silenced him when I told him I was invited to meet her the following evening.

The next day dragged slowly on as I pushed through a sea of paperwork. Much of what I had to do meant a lot to the people of the city—orders for food delivery and distribution, emergency water supply, preliminary lists of suspected Nazi collaborators, the analysis of captured German documents to be forwarded to Army headquarters. Important work, but it was all paper to me. I couldn't concentrate on anything. I thought only of my meeting that night with a blonde, blue-eyed beauty named Sabina. I suppose that in the back of my mind I was associating her with another blonde I had been in love with—Halina.

Finally, we concluded our workday and I ran back to my quarters for a clean uniform and a shave. I even managed to find a bottle of kosher wine for the evening and polished it until the bottle glistened. I hid the wine in a closet in case one of my military colleagues should drop in on me for a chat.

When I had finished my preparations, I rushed out the door, jumped into my jeep, and roared off. I arrived just before sunset.

"Welcome, Captain Pruzanski," Sabina's mother said. "Everyone's so eager to meet you."

She escorted me to the other room where a *Kiddush* table had been prepared, complete with a white linen tablecloth and two candles. My new friend Lichtenstein introduced me to everyone as their savior, and I felt embarrassed at their effusiveness.

Suddenly, I saw Sabina. She was standing a little away from the others, and the first thing I noticed was her stately appearance. Even though she was young, she held herself like a member of royalty. And she was far more beautiful than I had imagined. She had a fine porcelain face, with haunting, sapphire blue eyes, a slender, yet fully developed body, and soft blonde hair that cascaded to her shoulders. She was the most stunning girl I had ever seen.

Lichtenstein stood up and prepared to say *Kiddush*, the prayer welcoming the Sabbath, traditionally intoned over wine or challah. But in my absent-minded state, I had forgotton to bring my bottle of kosher wine. I jumped up and said, "Please wait a moment. There's something I forgot. It will only take me a moment to get it."

Before anyone could protest, I was out the door, down the stairs, and back at headquarters in my jeep to pick up the wine bottle. On the way back to the apartment, I realized how insane I must have seemed to those people. They were surely wondering where I had gone, and probably thought it was rude of me to take off like a madman just before *Kiddush*. All along the way, I kept peeking at the sky, watching for the appearance of stars that would signal the start of the Sabbath. By the time I returned to the group, the dusk was just yielding to an evening sky. I had raced the beginning of Sabbath and won.

When I once again arrived, this time feeling like a triumphant warrior with my prized trophy, they all laughed with relief.

"We couldn't imagine where you went," Sabina's mother said. "You needn't have gone to all this trouble."

"It's nothing," I said. "But you can't have *Kiddush* without wine. How stupid of me to forget it."

"You are here," Lichtenstein said, "and that's enough for us. We are honored to have you at our first Sabbath celebration in our new surroundings."

The group applauded and I blushed. Lichtenstein conducted the ritual of blessing the wine and greeting the Sabbath. Everyone was on the brink of tears as we joined in the first joyful *Kiddush* that any of us had experienced for many years. And for me, it was the first joyful greeting of the Sabbath in my life.

Before the war, I had tried to avoid such ceremonies. They smacked of the forbidding Orthodoxy that had repelled me throughout my youth. I only began to comprehend their deeper significance after the war started, but greeting Sabbath in the Warsaw Ghetto was always without the openness and joy it deserved. *Kiddush* in the Ghetto was more of a defiance, a statement of being Jewish, than a statement of joy.

After dinner, I went over to Sabina and said, "My orderly tells me that you play the piano very well. Would you play something for me?"

"What shall I play?" she asked in a timid voice.

"A nice Jewish song—the kind we would sing on Friday nights."

"I don't know any Jewish songs. But, if you hum a melody for me, I can play it."

I went to the piano with her and hummed "Shir Hashirim," the "Shepherd's Song." She picked it up immediately and played it perfectly.

Sitting on the piano bench with Sabina filled me with the greatest happiness I had known in years. Being here with these warm people in a family-type gathering made me feel alive again. It also made me remember—more than ever—the loss of my own family.

I had little chance to talk with Sabina that night. There were too many people in the room, and they seemed to be listening to my every word. They were in awe of my ability to survive by palming myself off as a Pole. I got the impression that somehow they looked upon me as their talisman and felt that, from now on, everything was going to go well for them.

At 10:00, I announced that I had to leave. They begged me to stay, but I explained that I was still in the army and had to observe the military curfew. They all shook my hand and made me promise to return. Before I left, I asked Sabina's mother if I could return the following day to see her daughter.

"Yes, of course," she said.

I was so grateful that I kissed her on both cheeks.

The following morning at 11:00, I went back to their apartment. I was welcomed by Sabina's mother and invited into the living room to talk with her daughter. Sabina seemed to enjoy my company as much as I relished hers, and we chatted for over an hour.

She asked me many questions about myself, and I answered them honestly, including discreet mention of my romance with Halina. Sabina had such a soothing, musical voice, that I could have listened to it for hours. She also seemed wise for her age, with none of the adolescent giggling one might expect of a sixteen-year-old.

I gave her my address and begged her to write.

"Will you answer, if I do?"

"Of course. I'm a very good writer."

"Then I'll write."

"Good. I will be leaving shortly. We're heading toward Berlin. But my mail will be forwarded. Don't get nervous if my letters are delayed for a few days."

"I'm sorry you're leaving," she said in her lilting voice. "I'll miss you."

She had no idea how happy she made me feel with those words. For the last few years, I had had no one to write to, no one to wait for me. Now I had found this most entrancing creature who seemed, from her looks and her conversation, to care for me as much as I did for her.

I kissed her lightly on the lips before I left. She prolonged the kiss, and I knew that she would be thinking of me while I was gone.

I bade her mother goodbye and promised to come by as soon as I returned from our campaign.

The following day, we turned over control of Poznan to a civil administration and moved west. I went with tender memories of my new-found love. It made the last days of the war in Europe all the more golden.

This was an exhilarating time, but hectic and confused, as we went from town to town freeing the populace from Nazi bondage. The German divisions collapsed before us like rows of dominoes; they seemed to sense that the war was already lost and additional resistance would only bring them more suffering. This was not the case at Nissa, in Rotenburg, where we ran into some fierce panzer divisions.

The Germans were staging a tough defense. We had become used to easy victory. The mere presence of hundreds of battle-hardened Soviet divisions was usually enough to make the Germans either surrender or retreat.

During the battle I was in the headquarters of our commander, General Komar, coordinating reconnaissance reports. For a moment, it looked as if the German tanks had stalled our offensive. Suddenly, General Komar sank to his knees, raised both hands skyward, and intoned, *"Shema Yisrael."*

I was in a state of shock. I waited a moment until he regained his composure and returned to the tactics of dislodging the German defenders. *"Aluf sheli,"*—my general—I said to him in Hebrew during a moment we would not be overheard.

He was startled and stared at me. "Don't worry," I said. "Your secret is as safe with me as is my own secret." We shook hands on it. "And next year in Jerusalem," I said.

"Yes," he replied. "Next year in Jerusalem, comrade."

The German lines broke, and we pushed through. We had hoped to drive hard enough so we could take up positions along the Oder River south of Marshal Zhukov's main forces before the final assault on Berlin. But we ran into some trouble that was to bring me the greatest challenge of the war.

In the rush to the Oder, the Russians had broken through German lines but had not really stopped to clean up the panzers they had passed through. This turned out to be a trap. The Germans had deliberately left a gap open, and once three of the Red Army regiments had rushed in, the German tanks closed it again, surrounding nearly 3,000 of our men.

I mustered every available reconnaissance officer and explained our situation. I assigned each of them a sector to scout and gave them two hours to return with a report of German strength, support weapons, mobility, and terrain factors. While they were gone, I labored furiously over my maps and the most recent aerial reconnaissance photos. By the time the first of the reconnaissance officers returned, I had a good idea of what to expect and how we might work our way out of this trap. Within three hours, I had a report for General Komar, as well as a suggestion on how to handle our serious situation.

I had expected that the Germans would position their greatest forces to the north in order to block the trapped regiments from any attempt to link up with Konev's units. Reconnaissance reports confirmed this. But there was higher ground to the south, so I suggested the stranded regiments move a few kilometers south, behind the German lines, and dig in. Once they had good defensive positions, they were to stage a mock attempt at breaking out. This would draw the bulk of the panzers out of their existing positions to thwart the escape. Once they were on the move, we could attack the German northern defenses, break through, and swing south to link up with our stranded units.

Komar agreed and the plan worked better than I had expected. Not only did we link up with the lost regiments, but we also cut the panzers off. They were totally surrounded by the end of the day and surrendered the next.

A few weeks later, when Marshal Konev arrived at our headquarters at the German-Polish border, he asked, ''Who is this man who helped our three divisions escape from the Nazi encirclement?''

My superiors supplied him with background information on me, which he promptly sent to Stalin with a commendation for my heroism on the battlefield. Stalin awarded me a medal of high distinction plus the prestigious Stalin Gold Medal, conferred for acts of outstanding heroism or achievement. I was also promoted to the rank of major.

We then opened the final assault.

The Russian armies rarely mounted major offensives in the spring. Roads were muddy, making advances difficult for an army comprised essentially of infantry and heavy weapons. The Germans, with their light tanks, could race across sodden fields and along mud-encrusted roads. The Russian armies, however, needed a harder surface. Traditionally, the frozen earth of winter and the dry ground of summer had been the best terrain for Russian battlefield success.

But we were too close to victory. Our momentum from the Vistula would help push us through the melting snows and slippery mud of late March and early April. Although most of our troops were weary from their two-month blitzkrieg, capturing almost five hundred kilometers along the German front, we sensed that victory was around the corner and this gave us the spirit to carry on. On April 16, Zhukov led the attack across the Oder and within five days, we were shelling Berlin. On April 25, our 58th Guards Division met the Americans at Torgau on the Elbe River.

With each hour, the noose around Berlin tightened. Zhukov pounded hard from the east, destroying each German counterattack and following it with another advance. He was bent on reducing the Reich's capital to rubble. Through the end of April reports came filtering back. One sector of the city fell after the other: Buch, Pankow, Weissensee, and Lichtenberg.

Then we noticed that the worst of the Nazis, the Schutzstaffel units, seemed to disappear. They were running west, hoping to surrender to the British and Americans. These butchers anticipated retaliation from the victims of their atrocities and were fleeing in terror.

The *Reichstod* was achieved on May 7. The remaining German units surrendered unconditionally. Berlin was ours. The Third Reich was finally dead.

Rabbi Mikhail Osher Shainberg, Warsaw 1939.

Maurice Shainberg with William Pick, the first appointed leader of East Germany in East Berlin, 1945.

Captain Ogniev in Germany sometime in 1945 before the German surrender. Captain Ogniev participated in the Katyn Forest Massacre and also served under Shainberg in the Polish army.

Jan Konrad Janasek. In 1942, he was a leader of the Polish underground and later became the First Secretary of the Polish postwar provisional government. Janasek was one of two people who knew Maurice Shainberg's true Jewish identity.

High ranking Polish military officers at the ceremony
which formally marked the German surrender at the
conclusion of World War II. Bonn, Germany, May 9,
1945. From right: Col. Sokolow, Gen. Zawacki, Major
Pruzanski (Shainberg), Gen. Komar, Gen. Doszynski,
Gen. Jaroszewiz, Dr. Kenski (who was in charge of the
Katyn massacre).

Colonel Kondrashchev, extreme right, on an
outing with the Shainberg family and friends
in Sopot, Poland in 1947. Colonel Kondrashchev
was one of a handful of military officers who
were responsible for the Katyn Forest Massacre.

(From the left, in the middle row.)
Captain Kasprzak, Major Czaley, Captain Dworaninov,
and other high-level KGB officers in Sopot, Poland in
1947. In 1959, Captain Kasprzak was sent to Cuba to
organize Soviet intelligence operations there.

International Conference of Journalists. Sopot, Poland 1954.
Maurice Shainberg is seated at the extreme right next to future
Secretary General Gomulka's wife. Boris Pasternak, author of
Dr. Zhivago, is seated fifth from the left, under the letter "Z."

**Maurice Shainberg and his wife
in Gdansk, Poland 1947.**

**High-ranking Russian officers in the Polish army in Sopot,
Poland in 1947. Maurice Shainberg is at extreme left.**

RZECZPOSPOLITA POLSKA
MINISTER OBRONY NARODOWEJ

DYPLOM

NA PODSTAWIE DEKRETU

PREZYDIUM KRAJOWEJ RADY NARODOWEJ

Z DNIA 26. X. 1945 R.
O USTANOWIENIU
MEDALU ZWYCIĘSTWA I WOLNOŚCI 1945 R.

W UZNANIU ZASŁUG POŁOŻONYCH W WOJNIE Z NIEMCAMI

DLA SPRAWY

ZWYCIĘSTWA NARODU POLSKIEGO

NAD BARBARZYŃSTWEM FASZYSTOWSKIM

I TRIUMFU

IDEI WOLNOŚCI DEMOKRATYCZNEJ

N A D A J Ę

Podporucznik Truszewski

Mieczysław

„MEDAL ZWYCIĘSTWA I WOLNOŚCI"

WARSZAWA, DNIA 9 MAJA 1946 R.

MINISTER OBRONY NARODOWEJ
MICHAŁ ŻYMIERSKI
(MARSZAŁEK POLSKI)

№ 000590 ✱

**A certificate for the Medal
of Victory and Freedom
awarded to Maurice Shainberg.**

DYPLOM UZNANIA

NADANY

OB. *Pruzańskiemu Mieczysławowi*

PRACOWNIKOWI (ZESPOŁOWI)

C.S.T. Woj. Oddz. Gdynia

ZA WYDAJNĄ PRACĘ PRZY
WYKONYWANIU ZADAŃ NARODOWEGO
PLANU GOSPODARCZEGO.

PRZEWODNICZĄCY
RADY ZAKŁADOWEJ

PREZES ZARZĄDU

Gdynia , DN. *1.1* 19 *52* R.

An award for Shainberg's
efforts in fulfillment of the
Polish National Economic Plan.

An award for Maurice Shainberg's participation in the war effort.

CHAPTER 15

Return to Poznan

Immediately after the collapse of Nazi Germany, our Polish military units set up a headquarters in Bonn. There was much jubilation, but I was depressed that Sabina couldn't be there to help me celebrate this great event. We had exchanged several letters, and we were frank in admitting our feelings for each other.

In May 1945, I was chosen to be part of a five-man delegation of Polish officers that would go to Reims to accept the Agreement of Unconditional Surrender on behalf of our country.

After the ceremony, I found myself in one of the strangest situations of my life. I was twenty-three years old, I was carrying out this charade of being a Catholic Polish officer, and I was socializing with several of the highest-ranking military officers in the world—the men who had guided the Allied effort to its successful conclusion. One of these officers, a tall, bald man with a constellation of stars on his shoulders, shook hands with me. He spoke to me in English, but I didn't understand a word.

General Komar came to my rescue, saying, "Major Pruzanski, you have just been honored by shaking hands with General Eisenhower." I was stunned. This was the man who had led the combined armies of America, Britain, France, Canada, and others across the face of Europe.

Eisenhower said something to General Komar, who turned to me. "The General thinks twenty-three is a rather young age for an officer to reach the rank of major," Komar said. "But I told him you deserved it. Five years of war can age a man much more quickly than a calendar. The general congratulates you and wishes you continued success in the military service."

I beamed at Eisenhower, extended my hand, and thanked him. General Komar translated my words for Eisenhower, who smiled and tossed me a casual salute.

During the ensuing days, my fellow officers did nothing but speculate on whether the United States, France, and Great Britain would ally themselves against Russia and declare war on the Reds. Most Poles desperately wanted this to happen.

I found myself in a quandary. I had fought alongside Russians, and looked up to them. Colonel Zaitzev continued to treat me like a personal friend. The Russians were friendly toward everyone, whatever their rank or education. Also, they did not seem to harbor prejudices—except, of course, against the Germans. They treated the Jewish officers in the Polish Army as brothers, and I saw them as our possible salvation. True, they had arrested some Polish nationalists. But I really didn't care what happened to them.

One day, at the end of June, my mind was taken off political matters by an upsetting letter from Sabina. She wrote that the civil administrators were doing everything they could to evict them from their apartment, insisting that five rooms were too many for only two persons. Sabina's mother had pretended that her husband was expected back, although she and Sabina were certain he had died with the rest of their family in a concentration camp. But this didn't convince the officials, who were demanding that the two women find a smaller apartment.

I immediately dispatched Captain Ognev to Poznan to alert General Swierczewski of the matter. The general assured the captain that since friends of mine were involved he would personally see that the women were not evicted and that there should be no further concern on my part.

I trusted the general and calmed myself. Two weeks later, I received another distressing letter from Sabina informing me that she and her mother had been evicted and moved to a small room in a dilapidated building.

This infuriated me. I went to Major Czarley, the Russian officer in authority, and received his permission to drive to Poznan to straighten out the mess. I took two soldiers and my orderly along.

When we got to Poznan, we went directly to the address on Sabina's last letter. My entourage remained in the jeep and I knocked on the door of the apartment. When her mother opened it, I couldn't believe my eyes. They were living in a stifling, tiny room, about nine feet wide and too small for even one person.

Both were in tears when they saw me. I had trouble controlling myself. I told Sabina, "Don't worry—you'll be out of this place today. I'll take care of this mistake. I'll be back soon." I embraced the two women and charged down to the jeep.

We drove to Sabina's former apartment at Matejko Street. I asked the super who was occupying the flat. He replied, "Captain Olshewski and his wife." The Captain was an officer in the Polish army.

I went upstairs and banged on the door. The captain's wife opened it, seeming somewhat startled.

I introduced myself in an icy tone and said, "This apartment was allocated to someone else by military order. You and your husband had no right to have those two women evicted. You will be out of here today, or I will personally throw you out."

"Ridiculous!" she said. "I'll call General Swierczewski."

"Please do. In fact, I'll get him for you." I pushed past her, grabbed the phone, and dialed the general's number.

"I prefer to call my husband first," she said, snatching the phone from me.

"Do that," I said.

She spoke to her husband and told me he would be right over. I waited outside with my men for his arrival. In about twenty minutes, his car pulled up. I was surrounded by my three men. When he saw that I was a major and his superior, he spoke in a guarded and polite manner.

"We were granted this apartment by Military Headquarters. The women who occupied it were not connected with the army and had no need of such a large flat."

"That may be, Captain," I said "but the general himself signed the papers that made the apartment theirs. You will kindly come to headquarters with me, and we'll settle this matter with the general. Meanwhile, you can tell your wife to pack her things."

"Are you implying that I'm under arrest?" the captain said.

"I'm implying no such thing. I'm merely asking you to come to headquarters to settle this deplorable situation."

His wife rushed down to get into the squabble. When she heard we were going to headquarters, she announced she would accompany her husband. The captain seemed happy to have her along. She obviously ran the show in that family.

By the time we got to headquarters, the captain had cold feet. "Please, you can take the apartment. I'm certain you're telling the truth," he said, as his wife glared at him.

"Yes, of course I'm taking the apartment—I never doubted

that—but first I want you to tell your story to Colonel Zaitzev, head of Military Intelligence. You took this apartment away from two defenseless women who are now suffocating in one tiny room.''

''But they're Jews,'' he spat out.

''You don't like Jews!'' I exploded. ''What makes you think you're better than they are? I had hoped the defeat of the Gestapo had ended all this nonsense. Is there anything else that you have in common with the Nazis?''

The captain and his wife exchanged glances. They were obviously wondering why a Pole would be so concerned with fair treatment of Jews.

Although Colonel Zaitzev spent most of his time in Bonn, he was in Poznan that day on one of his scheduled weekly visits. We appeared before Zaitzev against the captain's wishes. I showed him the military document which permitted Sabina and her mother to occupy that apartment.

The colonel reprimanded the captain and his wife and ordered them out of the apartment immediately. Then, when I told the colonel the disparaging remarks the captain had made about the women because they were Jewish, he got so angry that even I was surprised. I knew that Colonel Zaitzev had no strong sympathy for the Jews. His reaction to this incident, however, seemed almost like an example that he wanted other Polish officers to heed. Or perhaps he was merely being protective of my feelings for Sabina. In any case, the captain not only lost the apartment but also landed in jail.

I returned in triumph to my friends with a legal document signed by the mayor of the city, granting them full rights to the apartment. Sabina and her mother very happily moved back into their spacious flat.

While still in Poznan, I looked into the background of the cowardly Polish captain. It took me four days of investigation, but I succeeded in uncovering that he belonged to the Fascist underground in Poland, which had over three hundred members in that town. I also found out that the chairman of the Polish Workers' Party was a member of that group.

I brought this information to Colonel Zaitzev, so that his staff could conduct further investigations. He thanked me for my investigative work and implored me to finish my job in Germany quickly and return to him. ''You're still my assistant,'' he reminded me, ''and I need you badly.''

Sabina and her mother were sad to see me leave, but they

perked up when I promised to be back soon—for good. It pained me to think of their plight had I not been a high-ranking officer who could help them.

When I returned to my division in Germany, I was assigned to track down a Polish officer named Joseph Cigankiewitz, who had operated as a secret agent for the Gestapo at Auschwitz. We finally caught him trying to cross over into the American zone in Germany. We brought him to Major Borchook, chief of the second section of counterintelligence. Instead of shooting Cigankiewitz or sending him to Siberia to a forced labor camp, the major struck a deal with him creating a false war record that masked his involvement and cooperation with the Gestapo. This ficticious war history claimed that while appearing to collaborate with the Nazis, Cigankiewitz was working for the Soviet military counterintelligence. All the evidence we had accumulated on this notorious rodent was sent to the archives in Moscow to be buried, and he was named First Secretary of the Polish Socialist Party. This was a sickening political deal where in exchange for not going to jail, Cigankiewitz would act as a Polish Communist puppet for the Soviets.

I was astonished at his appointment. My investigations had revealed that he had been a bloodthirsty monster at Auschwitz. His official position had been that of pimp for the sadistic German officers at the camp. He was in charge of providing Jewish women as prostitutes and had treated them brutally, condemning to the gas chambers and ovens those refusing to service the Nazis. Now, the Russians not only gave this traitor a high post, but promoted him in newspaper articles as a hero, and the ablest leader of the leftist movement in the Polish underground. What was even more shocking was his appointment as Prime Minister of Poland, after the war.

Finally, I had to admit to myself that if this devious political appointment was necessary to build the Communist Party in Poland, then there was something seriously wrong with the people running this system. This was obviously part of the Soviet plan—to have agents planted in all parties, united under the communist system. Anyone who criticized the placement of this man was told that it was an essential decision to gain the confidence of the postwar Poles.

In 1945, the demobilization of soldiers who had served for two or more years was proclaimed by General Zymierski. This meant that more than sixty percent of the Polish troops were eligible for discharge.

During the demobilization, I observed the antipathy between Soviet soldiers and certain Polish soldiers. For example, the majority of the Fourth Brigade hated the entire Soviet regime. They particularly disliked the Soviet officers who acted as their self-proclaimed liberators. Disregarding the danger involved, many spoke up and protested the treatment of some of their fellow soldiers by the Russians. These men were immediately arrested.

The Soviets found it impossible, however, to keep arresting large numbers of soldiers and deporting them to Russia. To deal with this problem, the Soviet officers in Polish uniforms utilized the odious method of "A" and "B" classifications I mentioned earlier. Arrested soldiers were classified either "A" or "B," and their status was sent to battalion chiefs and brigade leaders by various intelligence units. Those with an "A" classification were sent home to their families, either because they had become secret informers or because they were willing to play ball with the Russians and had learned how to suppress political opinions, even before their best friends. In those times, no one could be trusted.

Those with a "B" classification, known to be violently anti-Communist, were most assuredly deported to Russia.

The deportation procedure resembled the Nazi transports that had carried Jews to concentration camps. The chiefs of staff would escort the soldiers to a railway station, where cattle cars awaited them. These movements were always conducted in the middle of the night or in the early morning, when no hostile citizens could witness and interfere with the soldieres' forced relocation.

At the station, the "A's" were deftly separated from the "B's." An officer would call the roll and tell each man which railroad car he was to enter to receive his discharge papers. The "A's" were given their papers, but the "B's" found themselves locked in a car and taken to the city of Brezescz on the Russian border.

So, it was not unusual for two men who had grown up as friends in the same village, had lived through the German occupation, had fought together in the Polish Army, and had each survived, to be traveling in two different directions when they were discharged—one returning home; the other ending up in an obscure Russian labor-death camp. Nothing could help the marked men—not their families' pleas nor the best lawyers in Poland.

These unjust acts upset me tremendously. I was also shocked by the abominable behavior of the Russian soldiers who were robbing and raping Polish women of all ages. Our headquarters was inundated with complaints and charges by women who had been molested by the Soviets. Colonel Zaitzev's stock reply to these complainants was just as brutal as his soldiers' behavior. He would say officiously, ''We don't complain about our blood being spilled to defend you, but you complain about a loss of virtue?''

In September 1945, the Fourth Brigade of Engineers was sent to Poznan, and, happily, I was able to go with them. I had a joyful reunion with Sabina and her mother and spent all of my off-duty hours at their apartment. Soon I moved in with them. I truly felt that they were my family now.

Still serving as Colonel Zaitzev's personal aide, I was promoted to lieutenant colonel. The colonel valued my knowledge of Polish, Russian, and German, as well as my obedient, inconspicuous personality. My new duties included overseeing all matters concerning the affairs of the district chief, writing up internal instructions, receiving official visitors, taking care of the colonel's correspondence, and looking after some of his personal matters.

During my first day at this new assignment, I learned that my initial investigation of Captain Olshewski had mushroomed, implicating several hundred Poles still living in the Poznan area. They had all been involved with Fascist groups before the war and served the Germans as informers and undercover agents during the occupation. When it became evident that the Germans were going to lose the war, they tried to escape detection by volunteering for service in the new Polish Army.

My close association with the Russians was giving me a stark lesson in comparative brutality. While the Germans had quickly liquidated their enemies in ovens and gas chambers, the Russians preferred to send them to their version of the concentration camp—Siberia. Here, sustained by meals consisting only of soup and a piece of black bread, they would do hard labor throughout the summer months. After being sapped of their strength and hope, these weary laborers were ready for death, saving the Russians the messy bother of gas chambers or firing squads.

The trains relocating officers, soldiers, and civilians who were deemed hostile to the new Soviet regime traveled on more frequent schedules than passenger transports bound for Poznan-Warsaw or Berlin-Krakow. Formerly, most trains traveled west; now, the majority of them traveled east—to Siberia.

In 1945, orders were issued for certain Polish soldiers and civilians to leave for Russia. They were not really going there;

instead, this was just another massive transport of people with questionable loyalties to the Polish town of Brezescz, which the Soviets had turned into a labor camp. Who were these latest deportees? They were physicians, lawyers, specialists, and surprisingly, many laborers who had never had anything to do with capitalistic regimes or rightist parties. Why were the Soviets arresting these people? It just didn't make sense.

As far as the intelligentsia went, the Russians could claim that they were a privileged class imbued with capitalistic ideas and would therefore never be amicable to Soviet notions. But the laborers? After all, the Communist Party stressed in all its propaganda that it was the celebrated savior of the working class, the scourge of capitalistic exploitation. I could never figure out what the Soviets had against these innocent working people.

CHAPTER 16

Colonel Zaitzev's Diary

When I worked for Colonel Zaitzev, he more or less made me a confidant; he told me about his childhood, his wife and two sons, his women—and he was determined to also make me a dedicated communist. I enjoyed listening to him talk about his personal life and his proselytizing about communism; about how communism would relieve the world of its misery. His main theme was that man has suffered too long under the oppression of tyrants; in Russia, Poland, and throughout the world. He knew that I, as a Pole who suffered under the Nazis, could sympathize with downtrodden Russian peasants. Of course, he didn't know that I had deeper reasons for feeling a kinship with the dispossessed.

Zaitzev did not talk in theoretical terms. He told stories, and the stories made his point. There was one particular incident he always came back to—an incident he had been involved in several years before; one having to do with captured Polish officers. He would refer to them as the perfect example of Poles who needed rehabilitation and retraining to fit into the new socialist post-war Poland. Whenever the colonel took me into his confidence, I asked no questions—our relationship was not that close—but I listened to him in fascination. These sessions would only occur sporadically because we were usually occupied by our official duties. I was not to fully understand the complete drama of that incident involving Polish officers until later—when I was to realize that in Zeitzev's version to me he had always left out the true and unbelievably tragic ending.

On December 15, 1945, Colonel Zaitzev summoned me into his office at our headquarters on the fourth floor of 62 Matejko

Street in Poznan. The building had been the Gestapo headquarters only the year before. I was soon to discover how cosmetic this turnover really was.

The colonel announced that he was taking three weeks leave and going home to Russia. During his absence, I would be required to perform several additional duties. I would be responsible for certain correspondences and bureau operations. I would also be entrusted with the combination to his personal safe.

The colonel pushed his chair back and stood behind his massive wooden desk. He reached down to the desk top, lifted a piece of paper and handed it to me. It was the combination to his safe.

"I want you to memorize it," he said.

The colonel took a few steps away from his desk and stood before portraits of Lenin, Stalin, and Beria that hung on the wall at one end of his office. The communist holies seemed to add authority to the colonel's words. They suggested severe retribution for disobedience involving any order issued by a superior.

"All documents in the safe are extremely sensitive and must be considered strictly confidential," the colonel said, ordering me to be scrupulous in obeying his instructions when releasing anything.

I knew the safe contained dossiers on KGB (NKVD as it was then called) agents and informers, as well as files of Poles in the Poznan area who were suspected of being unfriendly to their Soviet "liberators."

The colonel walked over to the huge black safe and, resting his left arm along its top edge, ordered that I, and only I, could remove documents from this safe during his absence. I was not to permit anyone to learn the combination, nor was I to permit anyone access to the safe.

I was not to release any document unless Major Borchook, the colonel's immediate subordinate and second in command of the Poznan KGB unit, was in my presence and signed an authorization. Each time a document was released, I was to make a record of the time and date of both the release and the return. I was to record the name of the officer and the department to which it was released and the reason for which it was being released. No document was to be out of the safe for more than twenty-four hours.

Later in the day, I returned to the colonel's office and he watched me open the safe, using the combination numbers I had memorized. We burned the paper containing the numbers in an ash tray, and then the colonel crushed the burnt paper.

Colonel Zaitzev left for Russia within the hour.

The colonel had barely disappeared down the snow-choked road toward the railroad station when First Lieutenant Michalek entered my office. He asked for the dossier on a little known Polish underground organization.

"Sorry," I said, "but you'll have to get Major Borchook to come here and sign the authorization. Colonel's orders."

The lieutenant became indignant. He insisted that I knew him perfectly well and that I knew the reason why he needed the dossier. He claimed that all this business of making the major come to sign a piece of paper was sheer nonsense. But as he raged, I could see the precise reason for his hostility. It was all an act designed to test me. Major Borchook wanted to know if I would carry out the colonel's orders to the letter. I refused all of the lieutenant's demands.

Lieutenant Michalek stormed out of my office. In a few minutes, my telephone was ringing. It was Major Borchook.

"I want you to give that dossier to Lieutenant Michalek," he ordered. "He has my full authorization."

"I'm sorry," I replied. "Colonel Zaitzev left the strictest instructions. You must come here in person and sign the authorization." I remained adamant, even when confronted with the major's growing hostility and his claims of being too busy. But he eventually relented and said he'd stop by in a few minutes to sign the authorization.

The major arrived about ten minutes later. I heard the heavy footfalls of his boots as he climbed up to our fourth-floor office. He stalked toward the safe.

I stood before him.

"Comrade Major, I don't wish to appear disrespectful, but I must be the one to remove the file from the safe," I said. "Please wait here." While the major signed the authorization, I opened the safe. Its massive steel door swung open, revealing a cavity about four feet high, three feet across and nearly three feet deep.

The files were not in any systematic order, and it took me some time to locate the file.

The major became irate at my slow progress, or perhaps he was still testing me. He started to push his way beside me so he too could search the contents of the safe. I reminded him of the colonel's strict orders and insisted that he step back.

The major stepped back in silence. I knew I had scored well on the KGB test. The major now knew that I would keep the safe secure, even in the face of threats and intimidation from a superior officer who could make life very unpleasant for me.

As I returned to my search, I found several black notebooks bound together. They obviously were not part of the standard KGB files. I set them aside and continued my search. In a few moments, I found the file they wanted and handed it to Major Borchook. I closed the safe, completed the entry in the record book and saluted the major and his lieutenant.

As I heard their footsteps descending the wooden stairs that led to the major's office, I returned to the safe and reopened it. I removed the bound notebooks and looked closely at them. The volume was about five hundred pages, written on common school notebooks that measured about eight by eleven inches. As I opened the book, I quickly realized that this was Colonel Zaitzev's private diary; the personal record of an important Soviet commander.

I flipped through the pages and recognized Polish names that the colonel had mentioned when he was talking to me as a confidant. I skimmed some pages about the execution of a priest and the shooting of prisoners; and, I became engrossed in the diary, its revelations and damning indictments.

The sound of footsteps climbing the stairs thundered into my ears like an unexpected barrage of artillery. I quickly replaced the diary in the safe and closed the steel doors. Whoever it was kept walking past the colonel's office. But fear kept me from approaching the safe for the rest of the day.

The following morning, I resolved to start reading the diary again. But this time, I had to devise a scheme that would protect me, even if I was caught with the safe door open.

Major Borchook came by that morning to return the dossier. As I was replacing the folder into the safe, I decided on my excuse for having the safe door opened. I would rearrange the confusion in the safe, placing all files in an order determined by subject matter and security classification.

I began after the major left. I partially arranged the folders in the safe and opened the door between the colonel's office and mine to allay any suspicion one might have of finding me alone in his office with the door closed.

When I started to read the diary, I was shaken by the colonel's accounts of the brutality he had used in the conduct of several interrogations. I also read about other atrocities he had a hand in as well. Each page revealed horrors beyond belief. I shuddered when I realized that if I were caught, he would be just as merciless with me. I had read enough for that day and decided to return the diary to the safe and finish arranging the files. I then closed the safe and returned to my office.

I could not sleep that night. I didn't even go home. I spent the night at our KGB headquarters, for long hours staring out into the snow and the darkness beyond. I was debating whether or not to be prudent and just leave the colonel's diary alone or to let my curiosity rule and read as much of it as possible. He had always been good to me. The war was over, and the wounds of many atrocities must be left to heal. Maybe there was no point in rattling the skeletons in millions of Russian closets. Besides, I knew the reach of Soviet might. There could be no doubt that it was entrenched for a long stay in Poland. To expose an earlier Soviet atrocity might only encourage renewed violence. And Poland was in no shape to resist.

Also, I feared for myself and the friends and relatives who might have survived the war. If I were to attempt to expose the Soviet crimes, who knows how many innocent people would pay dearly in the scourge that would be certain to follow. But still there was a nagging in my head. From what I had seen, the diary was important, and I knew that I would be just as guilty as the Russians if I left this injustice buried by ignoring it. I had to read on.

I poured a glass of vodka and drank it. And then another. I needed it to soothe my nerves. I knew I was in no shape to make any decisions. I was too jumpy, too filled with fear, too plagued with the pros and cons of stealing the diary. And the vodka only made my night more grotesque.

I paced the floor for hours, contemplating the seriousness of Colonel Zaitzev's crimes. I wondered what had passed through his mind as he had paced this same floor on those nights that he seemed burdened with problems. I wondered what thoughts had burned in the minds of the former occupants of this building, the ghosts of this very room. I wondered what secrets and screams were muffled within these walls a mere year ago, when 62 Matejko Street was Gestapo headquarters.

Gestapo, KGB, what was the difference? Surely, the pictures on the wall had changed, and the colors on the flag. But the horror was the same. And so were the tactics. Poland had merely exchanged one gang of hoodlums for another. And I was out of necessity in their employ.

My mind reeled with sorrow and anger. My predicament seemed unsolvable. I was caught in a hideous trap.

Shortly before dawn, I made a tentative decision. I would read the diary through. I would then make a final decision. If the atrocities were sufficiently documented, I would have to steal it—and somehow reveal it.

I collapsed onto my chair and slept there for two or three hours. The next morning, I transferred the diary from the safe to my own desk. I spent the entire day reading the colonel's scrawl. It was now clear to me that the Third Reich's defeat had not meant a new beginning for Europe. The Kremlin's bosses were no different from Berlin's.

Suddenly, what had been one of Colonel Zaitzev's obscure parables began to make sense to me. Yet, as I read in his own handwriting about this one particular incident, I still found it difficult to believe that he had been involved. The diary's revelations and my sleepless night guaranteed that the hours of that day would be filled with misery. Not only was I in constant fear of being caught, I was also fearful of the danger I was in should anyone suspect I had any documented knowledge of this particular Soviet atrocity. I was reading about the events that led to the Katyn Forest massacre that later was to become suspected as one of Russia's most infamous crimes of the war.

After perusing the diary for a few more hours I learned how the Russians had unsuccessfully tried to brainwash seventeen thousand Polish officers, and how, in the face of the Nazi advance, five thousand of those officers were secretly murdered in the Katyn forest by their supposed Russian allies because evacuation was logistically more complicated than mass execution. I also learned of the types of torture inflicted upon Poles and Jews in Russian labor camps deep in the Byelorussian forests. Indeed, I even learned how the colonel had, less than four years before, executed his own mistress on Beria's orders.

I finished reading the diary that evening. I knew that somehow I would have to steal it because eventually history would demand an accounting for these murderous crimes and the diary would provide powerful incriminating evidence. The truth would emerge about the Katyn Forest massacre—just as I knew that those responsible for the atrocities and suffering of the Jewish people would also be brought to justice.

I locked the diary back in the safe and waited until there were few people on the street. I feared meeting one of my fellow officers. I feared he would read the anxiety on my face. I feared he would ask, "What's wrong?" And, if he were a Pole, I feared I might tell him.

I was home in a few minutes. When Sabina saw me, she said, "Mietek, what is it? What happened? I was so worried when you didn't come home last night!" I told her about the colonel's diary. I told her about the massacre in the Katyn Forest.

"Sabina," I said, trembling while revealing the horror of Katyn, "the Russians held almost five thousand Polish officers prisoner in a camp in Smolensk Province, a camp in the Katyn Woods. And during the Nazi advance, the Russians secretly executed all of those innocent men. Colonel Zaitzev commanded that camp . . . he had a hand in it."

"I don't understand," she said. "How could this have happened?"

"This must be the way the Russians operate," I told her. "It seems there are official ways they get things done, which we know about, and there are unofficial ways. Katyn was unofficial." I was still trembling with shock and fear of my newly gained information.

Sabina sat beside me for some time, I can't remember how long. She comforted me and helped me regain some composure.

A knock at the door brought terror to both of us. It was like living in the Warsaw Ghetto again. I went to hide in the bedroom while Sabina answered the door. It was only our neighbor, but I could not let myself be seen, for I was sure that my anxiety could be read all over my face.

Later, after I had calmed down, we talked about what must be done.

My mind was made up: I somehow had to use the diary to document the atrocity at Katyn. It had to be done without the least suspicion. The greatest secrecy had to be maintained to protect myself and the people dear to me. I could not make the diary known until I had assurances that anyone in danger of reprisal was far from Soviet reach.

I tossed all night. My first impulse was to tear the Katyn pages out of the diary and make a run for it. With any luck, Sabina and I could be in Berlin within two days. If we escaped during the weekend, we might be in the American or English sector long before anyone could notice we were gone, and long before Colonel Zaitzev could learn what had happened.

But no. With a simple foul-up we'd be caught. Running was too risky and entailed obtaining forged travel papers, transportation, and even an acceptable excuse for going to Berlin. Even if we did get out, we would be endangering Sabina's mother, Lila, as well as other relatives and friends. And if our escape didn't succeed, the diary would be seized and the world might never know the truth about Katyn.

Sometime later that night I thought I might try to copy the diary. With my own copy, I could be more flexible in my planning and timing. I wouldn't be under the constant pressure and deadline of the colonel's return. But, as I soon realized, the diary was too long. I would never be able to copy it in its entirety. Instead, I decided to copy critical passages, then copy key names, dates, and places, committing the sequence of events to memory. The stories I had heard from the colonel's own lips helped round out the details in the diary, and I knew I could never forget what those pages revealed. I would do my copying in Yiddish, so even if the Russians managed to get hold of it, they wouldn't immediately realize what they had, and I might have a chance to escape.

The following day I went back to my office. When all seemed quiet, I went to Colonel Zaitzev's office, opened the safe, removed the diary, and brought it into my office. I copied four pages that day—the pages revealing the events of the Katyn massacre. That night, after returning home, I found myself pleased with my successful day's work.

But I said nothing for more than an hour.

Sabina and I ate supper and after dessert we relaxed on the couch. She was always tactful and never asked questions when she sensed my uncomfortable moods. She knew that I'd tell her what I wanted her to know in my own time.

"I have a gift for you," I said finally, as if I were a schoolboy hiding chocolates behind my back.

"You've been home for more than an hour, and now you tell me there's a gift for me?"

I reached into my pocket and handed her the pages I had copied. She stared at my Yiddish writing and asked me what it was.

"Four pages from Colonel Zaitzev's personal diary, copied in Yiddish. You hold in your hand hard evidence indicting the Russians for their duplicity in the Katyn massacre."

She stared at me. "Oh no, Mietek. They'll find out. They'll shoot you. No, Mietek, destroy them, please."

"Sabina, my dearest, don't worry. No one saw me do it; no one else knows. We have important evidence here. Now we must decide what to do next."

We could not think of a good plan that evening. That night, I did not sleep well again. I was exhausted, but my mind raced on.

Late that night Sabina came up with a solution; "I have an idea, I will go to Father Kwiatowski, maybe he'll hide those pages for us."

I thought for a moment, and then said, "But how do you know he has no contact with the KGB?"

"I'm sure he doesn't," Sabina said. "When the Gestapo shot my family, he was the one who saved my life. He hid me, at the risk of his own life. I know I can trust this man."

The next day, I went back to copying key elements from the diary. On my way home, I met Sabina on the street. She kissed me on the cheek and whispered in my ear: "Everything is okay, he'll hide the papers for us." The next day I went with Sabina to his church which was called Zmartrychstantov, located in Poznan. He was extremely interested in my documentation of these Soviet crimes against the Polish people and he asked me to bring the actual diary to him so that he could see for himself the parts dealing with the Katyn massacre. I returned the next day with the original diary and the Father spent hours reading the parts about Katyn. He advised me to continue copying the names, places, and dates. He agreed to hide the material that I copied until the time was right for its release.

I spent the next two weeks reading and re-reading the diary. By the time Colonel Zaitzev returned, I knew its contents as well as he did.

I also became a good actor. I played the role of a loyal aide even though I now had bad feelings about the colonel and all he stood for. I saw blood on his hands and blind cruelty in his face. He was a party man who was sickeningly loyal to his Communist masters. I knew that if the Kremlin ordered it, he would torture his own mother. And yet I knew he was not entirely responsible for the terrible acts I had read about. I could not shake my feeling that he was on some level still a good man. Whatever the case, I was now involved in serious intrigue, and could afford no mistakes. My greeting became warmer, my salute snappier. I even made an effort to improve my job performance, for I knew all my energetic service to the Soviets would one day explode in their faces.

The colonel was pleased with the way I had arranged the files in his safe. He was so happy with my performance that he would go out of his way to help me whenever he could. Through his personal intervention, identification papers were drafted documenting Sabina's age as eighteen. This enabled us to avoid a lot of red tape and finally get married.

The colonel gave me two weeks off for a honeymoon. During those days, Sabina and I were friends, lovers, and co-conspirators. We planned some day to escape the Soviets' control and to expose the massacre of innocent Polish officers at Katyn. But that was in the future; we had some living to do first.

CHAPTER 17

What the Diary Revealed

The Katyn story—which I have reconstructed using the colonel's words, either as I heard them or as I read them in the diary—began for Colonel Grigory Zaitzev in October 1939, when he was living in Sverdlovsk, in the Ural Mountain region, some 1100 miles east of Moscow, where he was the local KGB chief.* He divided his time between the two women in his life—his wife, Nadya, and his mistress, a young Jewish girl whose father had been placed under political arrest.

A telegram had arrived from Laurenti Beria, Chief of the KGB (then called the NKVD), summoning him to the Central Office in Moscow, at once. There he was briefed by Beria and his personal aide, Colonel Kondrashchev, in a meeting that was full of double-talk, innuendoes, and hidden meanings. "It was hard at times to catch their drift," Colonel Zaitzev wrote, "perhaps I have been away from Moscow too long; too long cloistered in the provincial air of Sverdlovsk. . . ."

Colonel Zaitzev learned from Beria of his new assignment: the command of one of three prisoner-of-war camps to be built by and for some 17,000 Polish officers from among the 250,000 Poles captured by the Soviet army when it invaded Poland in 1939. His base camp at Kosielsk was top secret and held the most important of the three groups: the highest ranking officers (including prominent physicians and other professionals), numbering nearly five thousand men. The camp was located approximately twenty-five kilometers from Smolensk, in the Byelorussian region about three hundred miles east of the Polish border. These

---

* Portions of the diary as I copied them, along with a translation, are shown in the Appendix.

prisoners were to receive intensive political indoctrination, which would "transform" them into Polish Red Army and civilian cadres useful in the future Soviet-dominated Poland. Colonel Zaitzev was to employ the method of "confusion neurosis": intimidation, interrogation, and cultural annihilation.

Zaitzev told Beria that the Poles were a tough people, ready to sacrifice their lives for the independence of their country. He reminded him that when the Red Army marched into Poland, the Poles fought back, surprising the Russians and inflicting heavy casualties. The Soviets sent in heavy armored cars against them, but the Poles threw themselves on the cars with fuel in their hands. Even after the Russians sent fifty bombers to the Polish front, it took them a whole week to prevail over the Poles.

Beria then told Zaitzev to change his tactics and said, "The Poles have never been our friends; they have always fought against us, have sabotaged work in our plants. Whenever they could they've tried to damage us. We've always known this, and, therefore, never in our history have we allowed the Poles to have an independent government. Right now, however, we must change our tactics and train these Poles to become Russian patriots. When the Germans finally liquidate England, we must have a Polish People's Army ready to free Poland from the Germans."

Beria handed Zaitzev instructions for establishing camps in the Smolensk woods, as well as the exact plans for the project, which I saw in the safe. The title page of these instruction sheets read: "The Training of Polish Officers to Become Soviet Patriots."

Beria bade Zaitzev good-bye and sent him to the personnel department. He hadn't said anything about how the barracks were to be built or where the Polish officers were to stay after they were removed from the present camps. Zaitzev did not wish to bother him with such petty details. After all, as the head of the military section of the KGB, he was supposed to know what steps to take, and so he asked no questions.

The personnel department gave Zaitzev a list of the officers who were to help him in his assignment: Major Borchook, intelligence; Lieutenant Colonel Frolov, political affairs; Major Vakchetov, interrogation. The following officers were to come to Smolensk later on: Captain Piskunov, Captain Kochetov, Major Prestupa (in charge of camps and officers for agency work), Captain Alekseyenko, Captain Ivanov, Captain Czasley, First Lieutenant Segalyevich, First Lieutenant Kolisayev, First Lieutenant Dvoraninov, First Lieutenant Gryshenko, First Lieutenant Lebiedev, and others. Zaitzev then went to Smolensk. He visited the head of the military KGB there, a major. He stayed overnight.

The next morning Zaitzev met his staff in the building of the regional KGB. They headed for the village of Kozielsk and occupied a two-story building there.

Colonel Pomarenko, who had been in charge of the Polish officers, came to confirm the arrival date of the first load of prisoners. He advised Zaitzev to watch these Poles, reminding him they were all educated religious fanatics. Wherever they are, Pomarenko declared, be it in the barracks or in the fields, they always sing with their military chaplain. Zaitzev asked him how, as a loyal communist, he could allow them to carry on like this. Pomarenko replied, "What can we do with them? We can shout and that is all." Zaitzev assured him that he would teach them to pray to a new "God," but was clearly annoyed with Pomarenko's impudence; the nerve of the man to ask about his future plans concerning the Polish prisoners! A true Bolshevik, Zaitzev proclaimed indignantly, does not ask a KGB officer questions, *any* questions.

The first four barracks and the barbed-wire fence were built by the local population. When the Polish officers began to arrive, Zaitzev was favorably impressed. They sported excellent uniforms and tall stiff boots, already stained with Byelorussian clay. Zaitzev welcomed them, asking them to sit on the ground. The officers, however, didn't want to soil their fine uniforms and continued standing. Zaitzev, pretending to be a concerned superior, addressed them: "Comrades, Brothers, Poles. We have brought you here, not far from the Polish border, so that you might survive the terrible situation which the Germans have brought on. We Russians, with the aid of the Soviet authorities, who represent the working class, are coming to help the Polish people free the territories that once belonged to them. We cannot permit the population on these lands to be taken by the Hitlerite barbarians. We will do our best to see to it that you are not harmed, politically or morally. We will help you to build yourselves a better and happier life right here in these beautiful Byelorussian woods."

The camp regimen was established and the indoctrination programs implemented: regular interrogations, propaganda lectures, films, Russian language broadcasts; a well-illuminated reading room full of Soviet propaganda literature; a punishment hut; and a "special" hidden interrogation basement. The Poles

were put to work constructing the camp buildings and later
filling lumber quotas in the surrounding woods. Conditions were
deplorable, rations meager. High-ranking officers were forced to
perform humiliating tasks. All religious practices were furiously
repressed and punished, and chaplains were ferreted out. Zaitzev's
diary noted several prominent Polish personalities: the insouciant
Captain Radomski, the "troublesome priest" Jozwiak, the clown-
ing Urbanski, the Jewish doctor Mendel, the Russian interpreter
Colonel Golominski, the detached contemplative Pawlik, the
young and desperate Captain Voyda, and two Polish generals
who were quartered separately.

Camp construction was slow as the Poles deliberately dragged
their feet. An attempt was made to arrange a network of collaborators and spies, which yielded paltry results. Suspicion
arose that resistance cells were being formed to plan acts of
violence. The priest Jozwiak incited them to resist "morally and
spiritually." Zaitzev suspected there were other chaplains secretly scattered among the prisoners, working to defeat the propaganda program. The Poles consistently failed to fill lumber
quotas set by Moscow. One of Zaitzev's aides, Frolov, was
suspected of sending private reports to Beria about the colonel's
inability to discipline the Poles. The recalcitrant Poles boycotted
the reading room, lectures, and literature. Their only interest in
Russian newspapers was for rolling cigarettes of *makhorka,* the
crude Russian tobacco.

Colonel Zaitzev complained that during his eighteen years of
work for Soviet Intelligence he had never had so much trouble as
in these camps at Katyn. In his day he had taken care of the
Petlyura gangs, participated in battles with the Bender followers
(Ukrainian nationalists), and ordered mass arrests of Trotskyites,
priests, and rabbis. But this really topped everything. Zaitzev
had serious misgivings about the conversion of these Poles. They
were educated, aware, and hostile to the idea of a Soviet-
dominated Poland. They were also dreamers, patriots, and religious zealots—formidable foes of the Soviet Union if ever
permitted to return to their homeland.

The Katyn camps were located in three areas: Kozielsk,
Ostaszkow, and Starobielsk. Each had its large contingent of
Russian guards. The Kozielsk camp had twenty-six barracks,
twenty-two used as living quarters, and four as shelters, along
with a kitchen, library, and health center. The latter contained a
hidden interrogation room. Each barrack housed approximately
two hundred and twenty-five people. Inside the barracks there

were triple bunk beds made of wooden boards two yards long,
each able to sleep five people. The mattresses and pillows were
filled with straw. The prisoners were fed three times a day: in the
morning and in the evening they would get black army coffee
and four-hundred grams of bread for the day; the midday meal
consisted of two courses. The soldiers had to wash their own
laundry. Shaving was allowed twice a year, on May 1st and
November 7th, the Soviet holidays. Wake-up time was at 5:00 in
the morning. From 5:00 to 6:00 the prisoners had to get dressed
and eat breakfast. At 6:00, the Poles would leave for their work
details in the forest. They would have their midday meal while
working in the forest, returning to their barracks at 6:00 p.m.
Each barracks had an officer of the Counterintelligence Section
in charge.

"I have been in these camps now for five months," Zaitzev
wrote, "but I cannot perceive any positive results in our work.
The KGB has not been able to convert these more and more
hostile and difficult elements to our Soviet way of thinking. I
told Borchook to appoint the Polish Lieutenant Colonel Golominski the prisoner's supervisor, with special privileges, to get
him to cooperate with us. Borchook, who misunderstood my
intention, tried to convince me that everything was all right and
assured me that the prisoners were working and would fulfill
their quotas. I saw that Borchook, in spite of his excellent
qualifications, would need a little help, and so I told him to
make out daily reports. The first report dealt with his conversation with Golominski. It quoted Borchook as saying: 'I am
turning to you, because as far as the camps are concerned you
are the most important and intelligent prisoner, and I think that
you will understand me well.'

"Golominski answered: 'Well, I don't know about that. One
of our proverbs says: Appearances are deceptive. And I'm afraid
we may not be able to help you Soviet heroes.'

"Borchook replied: 'It is not we who need the help. On the
contrary, I am concerned about your country's existence and
your own future. Tell me, how long can two neighboring nations
fight each other and squabble? From the beginning of time the
Poles have hated the Russian nation. Why? Our government is
not the government of the Tsar anymore; it represents the working class. Ethnic origin doesn't matter to us. Even if you were a
gypsy, it would not matter to us. We are interested in all workers,
and for them we are willing to do everything.'

"Golominski: 'We don't have to go back into the past. I

should like to know your regime's attitude regarding the territories you recently took away from us. Why did you have to attack us at such a critical time, making use of the trouble our Polish nation was having with the Germans? None of us asked for your help and nobody was going to attack your borders.'

"Borchook: 'God forbid! We didn't attack you. We merely wanted to protect you from the Germans. As far as I know, your troops began to shoot at us. Wouldn't it be better if your officers, your educated and experienced people, would side with us in the Red Army and fight for the happiness of both our nations?'

"Golominski: 'As a Pole I know my nation. None of us has the desire to dictate to other people, and we do not want to have other people dictate to us. We are neither a Fascist nor a Communist nation, but a devoutly Catholic one.'

"Borchook: 'Very well. But I assure you, we don't want to impose our Communist system on you. We just wish to fight the Fascist regime with you. We would like your assistance in helping us to motivate the other prisoners to be more cooperative and productive.'

"Golominski: 'Major, allow me to think it over. Give me a little time, before I give you an answer.'

"It gave me great pleasure," Zaitzev went on, "to read Borchook's report. It encouraged me to continue working.

"I thoroughly disliked Beria's aide, Colonel Kondrashchev. Whenever he visited the camps, he always made excuses and then returned to Moscow to carry on with his rascally life. In March 1940, during one of his short stays, I thought I'd go crazy. He didn't like the barbed wire fence around the camps, and the interrogation room was not conveniently located. He claimed that the KGB's activities with the prisoners weren't working out the way they should. He complained that we hadn't found out where the Poles had stashed their arms in 1939. He found fault with everything. I once said that perhaps I was not suited for such a position and that I couldn't get any better results. But that only made things worse. Now he comes more frequently.

"In the subsequent reports of Borchook I learned that Lieutenant Golominski had accepted the position of supervisor. But on the other hand, in political matters he didn't want to follow our instructions. He thought that, above all, the Poles should be permitted to return home. He didn't know that there was no power in the world to prevent us Communists from reaching our goal. And so the inevitable happened. Major Borchook and

Colonel Frolov became involved and threatened to have Golominski shot if he refused to sign an agreement in favor of a Polish-Soviet alliance. Golominski then signed the pledge and gave lectures to the prisoners which we had composed.

"Once, when Golominski began to make a speech to the prisoners, the Polish Army chaplain Jozwiak lifted up the crucifix he wore and began to chant a prayer. The prisoners followed suit. Thus, the talks only served to remind the prisoners of their Polish heritage and increase their resistance.

"Realizing what authority the priest had, we decided to try to win him over or else get rid of him. We instructed our Soviet cook to throw some poisonous powder into the priest's soup dish, so that he would develop stomach trouble. When he got sick that night, we took him to the interrogation room which could be reached through the same room that led to the sick room. Unknown to the prisoners, Major Vakchetov was in this room with all the necessary interrogation equipment. Colonel Kondrashchev was also present during the first part of the interrogation. Major Vakchetov was an expert in these matters, but in his reports this expert had to admit defeat. The use of electrical currents on Father Jozwiak's eyes and body didn't help. Nor was the Chinese method successful, where the prisoner was stripped from his waist down and forced to sit over an open cage of starving rats. We couldn't allow the priest to go back to the other prisoners in the condition he was left in, so we finished him off.

"Golominski was told to hold a funeral mass. We figured that now the prisoners would finally be scared enough to cooperate with us. After the ceremony, though, they began to rebel and sabotage our work. Our production dropped to fifty percent of its former low level, which caused Colonel Kondrashchev to show up again. Seeing him disgusted me. After we had said hello, all he did was ask questions. Why this, why that, always criticizing. He didn't accomplish anything, but succeeded in making my men dislike him. When I told him that our production decline had been caused by our killing the priest, Kondrashchev got all excited and shouted: 'I now order you to lower the food rations for those who don't fulfill their quota. Instead of four hundred grams of bread, you are to give them two hundred grams. You will also withhold their cigarettes.' Up to that time the prisoners used to get a pack of makhorka once a week, which allowed them to roll about fifteen cigarettes.

"I was forced to give these orders, which only made the

situation worse. The prisoners were not even capable of carrying the axes for felling trees. Colonel Kondrashchev didn't want to understand that a starved man wouldn't have the strength to work at all. He told us that they always treated prisoners in Lvov this way and we should never trust the Poles. He claimed to know them expertly. When I asked him what to do when they didn't work, he told me that he would come along to the forest before daybreak the next day to check their efficiency. He told me that then I would see for myself how much they could do. I'll never forget that day. It was raining hard. Kondrashchev and I went in the forest to see how the prisoners were working in the soaking rain. Colonel Kondrashchev told Piskunov to report on the production quotas. Whoever had not done enough work was to be shot then and there. Piskunov looked at me with surprise and reluctance in his eyes. But I was in no position to change Kondrashchev's order. Piskunov approached one of the prisoners and told him: 'Oh, that is not enough. It's got to be much better than this.' He spoke to about ten people like that, but didn't shoot anybody.

"Kondrashchev went over to Piskunov and yanked the production figures from his hand. The figures indicated that the men had done about forty percent of their quota. Kondrashchev began to shout at Piskunov and told him to carry out the order. Piskunov then pulled out his pistol and shot one of the prisoners. When the Poles saw this, they wanted to rush Piskunov, but our guards came running with fixed bayonets. The Poles stopped in their tracks. After a while, Piskunov responded to this mutiny by shooting another prisoner. The soldier shouted 'Long live Poland!' before he fell. The rest of the Poles then attacked our Soviet guards with their axes, managing to injure some of them. Kondrashchev ordered the soldiers to shoot. Within five minutes, 192 prisoners had been killed, and even more wounded.

"Kondrashchev seemed to take perverse pleasure in the riot he had instigated. In his usual fashion, he created a bigger problem than we had before his arrival—and then he returned to Moscow. Everything was left for me to solve. Psychologically, I was finished. I could understand fighting an enemy who threatens you. But to kill unarmed men is repugnant to anybody, I should think. Although Lieutenant Colonel Golominski was now collaborating with us, there was no change of heart among the prisoners. On the contrary, things had gotten even worse. The prisoners didn't even listen to Golominski when he addressed them. Instead, they would begin to chant their prayer, which went like this: 'We Polish soldiers and prisoners of the Soviets have been brought here to foreign lands to die. We beg of you, Mother of God, to take care of our nation, which is impatiently waiting for your favor. You alone can save and help our brothers and sisters. Save us from German and Soviet imprisonment. If necessary we are offering ourselves as the sacrifice for the independence of our fatherland and the faith of our forefathers.'

"Our task was impossible. People who have never met these Poles will not understand how difficult it was to change their attitude toward us. No beating or abuse would make them stop their singing. They are a hard and proud people. Every day they got physically weaker, but their anger and hatred increased. On top of this, Major Borchook wouldn't leave me alone. He would come to me with every little problem until my head was spinning. In spite of all our work, Major Borchook had not discovered any secret organizations or hiding places for Polish arms. I told him that as an expert he was not very skillful in getting results.

"I came up with my own plan. I instructed him to allow the prisoners to write their families. Later, the letters would be inspected, with the addresses of those under Soviet rule to be recorded. I also instructed him to have snapshots taken of prisoners with wives and children. In the pictures they were to smile and wear nice clothes. We would send these snapshots to the local KGB heads in the given provinces, for use in threatening prisoners' wives into collaborating with the intelligence agencies; otherwise some harm would come to their husbands. This new information would provide KGB units with the leads they needed to discover the hidden locations of Polish arms, the remaining secret underground organizations, and any members of prewar rightist organizations.

"Borchook liked my proposal, adding that the wives would be very valuable to us in carrying out necessary purges in the unstable Polish border areas. It would also be necessary to obtain snapshots of the wives and children of our prisoners from the head of the KGB in Lvov, Colonel Vozhnishensky. I instructed Borchook to use these pictures to induce prisoners to cooperate with us. He was to kill the families of prisoners that did not assist us. By October 1940, 780 out of 17,000 prisoners had been enlisted for collaboration. Unfortunately, their reports were not worth much.

"On the anniversary of the revolution I suffered my first serious setback, which could have led to my dismissal—or worse.

A prisoner fleeing the camp was killed. I was distressed to learn that he had managed his escape by hiding among the logs of a loaded cart leaving the forest. He was spotted by a sentry as he jumped off the cart and fled into a wooded area. My soldiers, after shooting into every bush in sight, finally hit the right one. The Pole was riddled with bullets. What surprised me most was that he had civilian clothes on. Where he had gotten them I didn't know. Borchook called Golominski and ordered him to bury the Polish officer. His body was dragged back to the camp as an example for the other prisoners of what would happen if they attempted to escape. The entire camp took part in the burial ceremony, we Russians watching the prisoners through the windows of the staff quarters.

"During the ceremony, Major Vakchetov came running to me, saying that the prisoners were demonstrating, but without violence. They were only chanting and crying. Vakchetov told me that he knew what they were singing because he had been hearing their songs from morning till late at night. I asked him what they were singing now. Vakchetov told me: 'God who has kept Poland.' I answered: 'Well, you know that better than I do, because I come to the camp at ten and leave it at six, but you are the night butcher.' Vakchetov then began to praise himself, telling me how much he was terrorizing the prisoners. I couldn't listen to this ingratiating fool anymore so I left. I was relieved that they had stopped the fugitive, because his success would have meant the end of my career. Beria had told me that under no circumstances should anybody be able to escape. If the conditions in the camps were to become known, I would be made into a scapegoat.

"There was not a day without trouble. Not only did I have to watch my prisoners, but also my aides. I was surprised when Colonel Frolov notified me about the deportation of a Soviet soldier, a camp guard, because he had a weak character and could harm us by telling outsiders about our camp. His major crime, though, was that he had secretly given bread, cigarettes, and other provisions to the prisoners. I felt sorry for him, because he had a wife and children. But what could I do?

"One day I received a letter from Colonel Vozhnishensky that cheered me up. Whenever Kondrashchev visited our camps, he never liked anything, but Vozhnishensky, who was so far away, wrote this:

" 'Thank you for your interesting communication concerning my territory. To make a long story short, the pictures and last names you gave us enabled us to uncover some secret organizations which were operating in the western Ukraine and Byelorussia. We also discovered many hiding places for arms. I hope that you will continue this kind of work. I wish you a happy New Year and every success. Your loyal comrade Colonel Vozhnishensky.'

"I told Major Borchook to pursue our scheme with a prisoner named Morawski. Borchook delegated this task to Captain Alekseyenko, whose efforts, I was distressed to learn, proved completely ineffectual. In the middle of the night Morawski was called to the interrogation room. With the best smile he was capable of, Alekseyenko greeted him and asked if he would like to go home and see his wife and children in Lvov. Then he showed the prisoner a picture of his wife and daughter. Morawski stretched out his hand to grab the snapshot to have a closer look. But Alekseyenko withdrew the photo, saying: 'Oh, no you don't. This you've got to earn. There's nothing for nothing.' Morawski almost lost his temper, and said: 'I am not interested in your blackmail plots. I should like to be permitted to leave the room.' Alekseyenko tried to persuade him that he had the right to live without wasting his youth and health working so hard out in the cold. Morawski didn't pay any attention; he got up and went to the exit. Staff Sergeant Butov wouldn't let him pass. Morawski then said he was the wrong person for this sort of thing and demanded to be allowed to go to bed.

"Alekseyenko again took out the snapshot, looked at it, and said to the prisoner: 'Well, well. The wife is not a bad looker, the daughter is even better, but they have a bad and stupid father who doesn't want to go back to them.' When Alekseyenko asked him if he didn't want his family's happiness, Morawski covered his face with his hands and whispered: 'Oh God, give me strength to endure all this and don't let me break down.' After this, Alekseyenko gave him a paper to sign and said: 'Sign this. If you don't, then I will know how best to punish you.' Morawski said: 'I can't sign if I don't know what I'm signing. I don't know how to read Russian.' Alekseyenko assured him: 'Don't worry. It only states that you will keep our conversation secret.'

"And that was typical of the reports I got. I don't know why the intelligence work in these camps is so incompetent. The Ministry intelligence department sent us their best officers and not even ten percent of our work gets done.

"On May 10, 1941, I got news from Dr. Kenski that his nurse Olga was having contact with one of our prisoners named Radomski. But what kind of contacts these were the doctor wouldn't tell me. That was for me to find out. If one of the prisoners were to find out about our secret interrogation room in the health clinic, it would prove very unpleasant. I told Major Borchook to check up on Olga.

"At 6:10 a.m. on June 22, I got a phone call from Captain Pishkunov that the Germans were attacking Russia and had crossed the border. I couldn't rest anymore; sleep was impossible. I got dressed and went to staff headquarters to phone Beria. I called all Soviet camp employees together and told them not to tell the prisoners anything about the war. We did not need a prisoner revolt. When I called Beria, instinctively I felt some unrest. I didn't know why. Unfortunately, Kondrashchev answered the phone. I curtly asked to be connected with Beria. He told me that Beria was attending a conference of the Politburo, and that he, Kondrashchev, could give him the message that I wanted to convey. I told him to ask Beria if there were any special instructions that I should follow due to the closeness of the advancing German battalions. At about noon Beria called back. Without asking me any questions, he began to shout: 'Are you afraid of war? Don't you believe in the Party?' I almost had a heart attack. It seemed as if I couldn't utter a word. But somehow, I found the nerve to interrupt him by saying: 'I have been a member of the Party since 1917, and I am not some kind of enemy, as Colonel Kondrashchev would have you believe. I'm merely calling to get some hint of what I am supposed to do now.'

"Beria changed the tone of his voice right away and gently answered: 'I'm very nervous myself. You can imagine what kind of a day it has been for me. The Germans quite unexpectedly attacked us. Comrade Zaitzev, don't be offended by me.'

"When I asked him what should be done about the camp, Beria assured me that 'within two weeks our army will reach Berlin and destroy the Krauts. If there should be any new development, I will let you know myself.' After this conversation I felt much better, knowing that our army would be in Berlin soon. But after a few days of war, I didn't see any positive results. The Germans were taking our land and every day advancing some thirty kilometers. If this kept up, I was sure they would reach Smolensk soon. What was I to do? Call Beria again? He had told me explicitly that he would call me, if need be. I decided to wait a few days more.

"Ten days later the prisoners found out about the German advance. Who told them? Nurse Olga of the health clinic? I spoke with Borchook about her. Borchook surprised me by telling me that Olga was a secret informer. She hadn't filed any reports yet, but she did know that one has to keep quiet about certain things. Borchook also told me that the prisoners were in better spirits. They were singing and the comedian, Urbanski, was starting to crack his jokes again. There were wild bursts of laughter by the prisoners.

"The situation was really getting bad—the prisoners were laughing while we felt like crying. Perhaps they were right. When the Germans, in ten days, reach our 1939 borders, our Polish enemies in these camps have good reason to laugh.

"I couldn't wait any longer so I called Beria for further instructions. But again he assured me this was only a temporary situation, that the Germans would not get any farther. He told me that the Ukrainian armies of Vlassov would strike in a matter of days.

"I found that hard to believe.

"On July 14, I called Beria again to ask him what I should do now that the Germans were only fifty kilometers away. Before I could finish my question he told me to evacuate the health clinic and put it at the disposal of the Byelorussian army. As far as the camps were concerned, Colonel Kondrashchev would come in person and bring detailed instructions. This news flabbergasted me. Was everything coming to an end? Was twenty-four years of revolutionary work in vain?

"The finishing blow came from Frolov. He told me that a division of Vlassov's was captured by the Germans with all of its equipment intact. Vlassov himself had managed to flee to Kiev.

"I couldn't eat or drink. I couldn't even read the newspapers. My head was spinning. I would have liked to believe in our imminent victory but how could I? The facts spoke for themselves. There was nothing left for me to do but to wait for Kondrashchev's instructions and the order he was bringing. Probably the camps would have to be evacuated. That would be the best solution. I had never looked forward to his visits, but this time I did.

"On July 16, Colonel Kondrashchev arrived. He was not so high and mighty toward me as he used to be. Perhaps he had noticed the new impression I had made on Beria. Kondrashchev's plan satisfied me completely. He proposed evacuating the prisoners to Arkhangelsk over the course of three days, one camp a day. Kondrashchev had finally become a decent person in my eyes. His plan encouraged me.

"On July 19, Colonel Kondrashchev called all officers together and told them about the plan to evacuate the three camps. He decided that Camp Starobielsk should go first, the next night. He put Major Borchook in charge of the operation. Thirty railroad cars were waiting at the Starobielsk station to transport the prisoners. Kondrashchev handed Borchook a short instruction sheet which he had brought along from Moscow. Major Prestupa's camp, Ostaszkow, was supposed to be moved on the twenty-first of the month and again thirty railroad cars were to be ready at the station. The last camp, at Kozielsk, was to be moved together with its staff. Kondraschev and I would be responsible for Kozielsk. As we were preparing the prisoners of Kozielsk for evacuation, Kondrashchev came running and told me that he hadn't been able to get all the railroad cars needed for the evacuation. Instead of a hundred cars, he got only sixty cars. We went right away to the military railroad management of Smolensk. But they didn't even have enough cars for the evacuation of the factories. The laborers had to destroy tools and fixtures so that they would not be left for the Germans. I began to think that my worst fears were coming true. I saw that only two camps were evacuated and one entire camp still remained. We had one military truck at our disposal and thousands of prisoners to evacuate.

"Kondrashchev was supposed to contact Beria. While Kondrashchev talked with Beria, I watched his face. Apparently he hadn't achieved anything. When he was through talking, I asked him about it. He told me angrily that Beria himself didn't know what to do. Beria was to contact me, after talking it over with Politburo members.

"On July 23, 1941, at 6:00 p.m., Kondrashchev received a phone call from Beria instructing that the camp be liquidated. He was sending a special messenger with precise instructions. At 10:00 p.m. Kondrashchev took some soldiers with him and got some German rifles and cartridges from the warehouse, where the captured war booty was kept. Before daybreak the messenger arrived. After I read the instructions, everything went black.

"The commands were brief:

"1. The population within a radius of five kilometers should be moved on account of alleged maneuvers.

"2. In the vicinity of Kozhy Gorky, five kilometers from the camp, deep ditches should be dug by the Soviet engineers (Brigade No. 162) who are stationed in Smolensk.

"3. Delouse the prisoners with chemicals so we

have good reason for making them change clothes. Give them their own winter clothes. The light clothes are to be burned then and there. (The chemicals will be brought by our messenger.)

"4. Lead the prisoners to the liquidation site in groups of one hundred.

"5. At Kozhy Gorky the Soviet soldiers should be masked, so that the prisoners won't see their faces.

"6. When the truck returns for the next group, nobody should betray himself to the waiting prisoners. None of the waiting prisoners should know what is going on.

"7. After the task has been carried out, all barracks are to be burned to the ground and ploughed with tractors so that nobody will be able to tell that camps ever stood there.

"8. After completing the entire assignment, do not leave the area but relay me a report.

Signed, Beria.

"After reading the instructions I asked Kondrashchev if he thought we would have to stand trial some day if the world should find out about this massacre!

"Kondrashchev laughed: 'What? This is your first big liquidation, but for me it is not the first. Don't be afraid. It will be done in such a way that nobody will be able to tell that we have done it. Everybody will suspect the Germans. Everybody knows that they shoot our prisoners on the spot. And about a few thousand Poles nobody will talk.'

"I couldn't listen; I got dizzy. I could still see the prisoners falling to the ground. I hate the Poles. I know that they are not our friends, but why did fate want me to liquidate them? These thoughts kept me awake all night.

"At 4:00 a.m. on the morning of July 26, we began the process: I had to make sure that the prisoners were loaded on the truck; Kondrashchev looked after the liquidation itself. I was glad Kondrashchev didn't insist on my being a witness to the killings.

"It was hard to watch people waiting to be executed. Every hour on the hour the prisoners would get on the truck in groups of one hundred people. If a load was delayed for ten minutes, right away Kondrashchev would call me and accuse me of sabotaging the whole action. Every once in a while Lieutenant

Colonel Golominski would ask me where they were going. I had to play the part of the friendly Russian. I had to explain that they were going to the railroad station in small groups because we had only one truck at our disposal.

"Upon completing the liquidation, Kondrashchev reported to Beria that the assignment had been carried out according to instructions. For that he got a gracious *spaseebo* (thanks).

"The night after the massacre, Kondrashchev waited coolly propped against his car, while I climbed the stairs to my mistress Ludmilla's room under orders to execute her. No amount of protest could convince Kondrashchev that she was ignorant of the Katyn affair. Ludmilla sensed that my anguished look and strained lovemaking concealed a deadly finality. Amid my words and caresses her eyes strayed to my holster.

"My hand shook violently as I repeatedly fired my pistol into the girl's body. Below, Kondrashchev greeted me with a broad smile, then bounded up the stairs to check for himself. In the truck en route to the railroad car, Kondrashchev was in high spirits, talkative, relaxed. 'Only trusted KGB men emerged from the Katyn Forest yesterday,' he remarked."

During the first few weeks after his return, I was strongly tempted to confide in the colonel. I had developed a high regard for the man and, despite the revelations of the diary, I still believed there was a basic goodness to him. Indeed, at Katyn he was assigned to a task that he hadn't asked for, and had it not been for the Kremlin, I believed he would have run the camps with a substantial amount of justice and consideration. And I believed that if Beria had not sent the execution orders, Zaitzev would have tried to march the Polish prisoners away from Nazi lines by himself.

But I never mentioned anything to him. I continued working for him with mixed emotions. He still showed an almost paternal care for me, and he was an exemplary leader. Colonel Zaitzev had worked hard to defeat the Nazis, and after the war he worked with relentless spirit to destroy all vestiges of Fascism. He deeply believed in Communism and its inevitable victory. He believed that this victory was in the ultimate interest of mankind.

I was to remain within the sphere of Soviet control for another eight years, and during that time the pages I had copied from the colonel's diary remained safely with the Catholic priest. When we finally did make our escape, we took the papers with us. I still have them in my possession—Yiddish characters penciled on brown Russian graph paper.

   Since then, the world has generally agreed upon Soviet responsibility for the Katyn massacres. Many authorities, including the U.S. Congress, have studied and reported on the incident. No one, save the Soviets, disputes their culpability. The Soviets continue to blame Nazi Germany and have even gone so far as to inscribe a misleading and ambiguous commemoration on a recently built Polish government memorial. It states: "To the Polish soldiers—victims of the Hitlerite Fascism that arose on the soil of Katyn." It is most significant to recognize the following fact when judging the Soviet guilt for this heinous massacre: if the Russians were innocent of planning, executing, and later covering up this murder of innocent officers, why have they never included the Katyn massacre in their lists and accusations of German war crimes that took place on Soviet land? Why would any innocent party not mention such a substantial crime against humanity in their condemnations of a ruthless former enemy? The answer must be because the Soviets know that such claims are insupportable and can only stand up in their own closed society, where no one is ever allowed to prove them wrong. If they were innocent, they surely would have made some reference to the tragedy and would have blamed someone for it over the last forty years. Instead whenever the Soviets are accused of committing this massacre, they conveniently deflect blame by invoking the guilt of the Germans.

   Today we have plenty of evidence concerning Soviet complicity in many atrocities. Records of the Stalinist purges fill many shelves. Contemporary writers shock the world with their stories of the Gulag Archipelago. There are living witnesses who can bitterly recall the Soviet invasion of Hungary, its treatment of the Ukraine, and countless other abuses of power. The most recent Soviet crimes include their takeover of Afghanistan and the frequent massacres of innocent civilians committed by Soviet troops.

   The martyred Poles of Katyn still lie in mass graves. And justice has not been done. Indeed, it is difficult to say which was the more repulsive government—that of the Nazis or that of the Soviets.

CHAPTER 18

Fascists and Comrades

On February 26, 1946, Colonel Zaitzev called me into his office and told me that we were to search out two active anti-Soviet Polish partisan groups in the Krotoszyn region. The groups—both Fascist—were called "Bor" and "Cien," and their leader was named Lopazko.

The colonel filled me in on the details. The Sixth Group of Light Artillery was stationed in Krotoszyn under the jurisdiction of the Fourth Infantry Division and was headed by Major Piskunov, a name I recognized from the colonel's diary.

The Intelligence Officer of the Krotoszyn regiment was a Major Dvoraninov, who was unable to uncover the location of these two partisan groups. Colonel Zaitzev, a soldier with far more experience in these matters than the major, divulged his plan to me for capturing these hostile groups. I was dispatched to Krotoszyn to serve as Major Dvoraninov's aide.

The major and I did our best to carry out the colonel's maneuvers, but the partisans were elusive. We were constantly criticized by Major Piskunov, who complained that two intelligence officers were accomplishing less than one.

We attempted to track down the wanted men by establishing the whereabouts of all former members of rightist parties, as well as all prewar officers. A prewar lieutenant named Swiderski, who lived in Krotoszyn, and an undercover agent whose code name was "Zajac" were able to compile a detailed list of these men.

Zajac owned a restaurant and a retail bakery opposite the railway station. His daughter, who acted as a double agent for us by collaborating with the partisans, had an assignment from the leader of the Bor group to discover the names of officers and soldiers stationed in the local regiment who were against the Communist regime.

The regiment barracks were located near the bakery. Since the military men often went there for pastries, the baker's daughter proved to be an excellent decoy.

Our plan got underway with a ruse. Lieutenant Swiderski, whose code name was "Cukier," was purposely discharged and publicly branded as an enemy of the working class. By posing as an ousted officer, the lieutenant was able to get close to the guerrillas with the proper introduction from the baker's daughter.

Within two months, thanks to the undercover work of agents Zajac and Cukier, the two guerrilla groups were captured and arrested, and all documents pertaining to their activities were sent to Polish KGB Headquarters at 7 Chelbinski Street in Warsaw.

The partisans were turned over to Major Piskunov, Intelligence Chief of the Division. When I reported to his office one day to turn in my monthly report, I saw the major and Captain Ivanov beating the prisoners and holding live electric wires against their shins. Their only crime was the understandable desire to free their homeland from the hated Russian regime.

Among these pitiful men was a young lad of twenty named Zakarzewski. He was handsome, intelligent, and obviously courageous. When the crude major asked him in Russian why he was fighting against the Polish Army, the boy answered in Polish, "First of all, I don't speak Russian, and secondly, I'm apparently held by Russians not by Poles."

The major spat in his face. "So much for your insolence. I'll see to it that you die like a dog."

The boy wiped his face with his sleeve. "Better to die like a dog than live in a Poland dominated by Russian savages."

Piskunov jumped up, the veins in his neck throbbing. He looked as if he would like to strangle the boy, but he didn't dare do it in front of me. He sat down and fumed in silence. I dreaded what would happen to the boy after I left.

I felt very sorry for young Zakarzewski. What he had said was true—better to die like a dog than live in a Russian Poland. We had just conquered one beast; now we were in the hands of merciless rapists, masking their crimes against the Polish people with their convenient Communist ideology.

But were we, the Polish officers, to blame? We had joined the Polish Army of our own free will to fight for an independent Poland, for the freedom of its people, and for the liberation of its territories seized by Hitler.

It had never occurred to us that the Polish Army, fighting side by side with the Soviet Army to drive the Nazis out of Polish territories, was also helping to establish a Communist slave regime in our own country.

What could we do? We received diverse military and political orders, which we were forced to carry out or face sure and swift execution. Should we have deserted? There were some who did, but to this day, as far as I know, they have never been heard from. As for young Zakarzewski—none of us ever saw him again. He was not at the trial of the other partisans, nor at any prisoner interrogations. Yet not one of the Polish officers dared inquire about him.

The war was over in Europe, and there was confidence that it would soon be over in the Pacific. It was a time of rehabilitation and readjustment, especially for the handful of European Jews who had managed to survive. I too should have been happy about my survival, but I was gnawed by confusion and uncertainty. It was not easy to continue masquerading as a Pole. While I had achieved recognition as a war hero and enjoyed a comfortable way of life, I feared that someone would eventually unmask me. One of my recurring nightmares was that someone from my past life—the face was always blurred—would point me out on a crowded street and shout "This man is not a Pole—he's a Jew!"

My main frustration at this time, however, was my lack of confidence in either the Soviets or the Poles to rehabilitate the strong anti-Semitic bias that pervaded our country. On the one hand we had the Russians who had executed five thousand soldiers at Katyn, including many who were Jewish. On the other hand, I constantly read in the papers about the Polish Fascist underground killing of Jews who had survived the Nazi bloodbath.

A tragic event ocurred in 1946 showing that the Poles still bore their deep hatred of Jews. The government discovered that it was the Polish underground who had entered a synagogue in Kielce, where worshippers were at prayer, and killed forty-one of them for no reason. It was an international scandal and clearly showed that certain Poles still wanted their nation rid of all Jews. I found myself just as fearful of the Poles as I was of the Soviets.

In the middle of this personal dilemma, I learned that my superior, Colonel Zaitzev, was being recalled to Moscow. I was surprised at how sorry I was to see him go. Despite what I knew of his past, I had enjoyed working for him. He was an interesting man, and he trusted me. Even though I could never accept the atrocious things he had done, to some extent I could understand them—even the cold-blooded shooting of his mistress. The Kremlin had demanded it. It was a dog-eat-dog system, and if he hadn't killed her, they would surely have killed him.

In May of 1946, while serving under Major Dvoraninov, I became disgusted with his boorish behavior toward Polish women. I knew that he had once raped a fifteen-year-old girl in front of his orderlies. He drank vodka that he stole from Polish merchants by threatening to blackmail them falsely for their political beliefs. He urged me to imitate his debaucheries. He was well aware that I was happily married, and I believe this bothered him and made him feel guilty about his behavior. He grew furious that he couldn't corrupt me. I knew that I had to get away from this sickening pervert. If I stayed much longer, I was afraid that I would lose control and say what I thought of him.

I filed my application for a transfer, and two weeks later I was questioned in Russian by Major Grachook of the personnel section. I answered his questions in Polish, which infuriated him.

"You hate us, don't you?" he barked. "That's why you're answering in Polish."

"I speak Polish much better than I do Russian; why shouldn't I speak it when it's my native tongue?"

"This hostility of yours is unhealthy."

"If you're going to take that attitude," I said, "I'll simply ask for a discharge instead of a transfer."

When the major realized that I meant what I said, he played it safe and had me transferred to the staff of Colonel Voznishensky, the KGB's military intelligence chief in Koszalin. His position was parallel to that of Colonel Zaitzev.

Before assuming my new post, I was granted a leave of absence, which gave me a little time with my neglected wife. She and her mother, Lila, greeted me with tears in their eyes. We all hoped for a time when we could be together without these extended absences on my part.

Colonel Voznishensky assigned me to Major Banski, chief of the border army, as head of his intelligence section in Sopot, on the Gulf of Danzig. This was a promotion for me.

Major Banski was an undercover agent who was unfavorably disposed toward prewar officers, although he had been an officer himself in the prewar reserve. He was responsible for ferreting out spies on vessels calling at the nearby ports of Gdynia and Gdansk. His reports were sent directly to Major Alekseyenko, a notorious Russian assassin, who, according to Colonel Zaitzev's diary, was responsible for the mass murders at Katyn.

Major Alekseyenko proved, if possible, to be a bigger pig than Major Dvoraninov. When he arrived in Sopot for inspection, his first questions were, "Where are the whores? Where are the hot spots? Where can I get American cigarettes?"

I told him that cigarettes were available in most stores.

"Why should I spend my money? A man of my rank shouldn't have to pay for anything."

He soon proved his point. The major became notorious for helping himself to whatever he wanted, be it women, cigarettes, liquor, chocolate, or "souvenirs." Taking advantage of his rank, he conducted night-time raids on such Polish vessels as the *Batory, Sobieski, Slask,* and others. After the major would arrive, the sailors were fleeced of practically everything except their underwear. The victims were warned not to press charges against the officer, or their families would suffer.

These raids were jointly conducted by Major Alekseyenko and Major Banski. They would arrive with a truck, and when they were through with their so-called inspection, these two would load it full of cigarettes, cocoa, coffee, and sugar from the United States. The stolen items would be taken to the town of Slupsk, about sixty miles west.

The two majors were certain to stage their raids when there were no Polish officers on board the ships. They feared, and rightly so, that their scandalous behavior might be reported to the head of Poland's KGB, Colonel Kuhl, who was Polish.

Major Alekseyenko liked to boast that Colonel Voznishensky was his best friend. After a few drinks, he would start enumerating how much of his stolen booty he had given the colonel.

When I visited these ports, soldiers who were stationed there told me how indignant everyone was over the looting by these corrupt officers. They were certainly not doing much for Soviet public relations. Whenever a Russian officer came on board, blackmail and barbarity followed.

Alekseyenko soon became a hated figure in Slupsk. There wasn't a resident in the town who didn't know and fear him. He seemed worse than Major Dvoraninov in his despicable excesses—if that were possible.

The major had a knack for organizing harems. He had four or five young women who were kept in a dark cellar, fed dry bread and army soup, and summoned for sex whenever the major was in the mood, which was frequently.

Fortunately, he went too far and was eventually discovered. In the fall of 1946, he attended a ball at the Astronom Ballroom with Helena Kozlowska, his tall, blonde, nineteen-year-old secretary. During the evening he got roaring drunk, took off his pants, and started to strike the girl until she passed out. After she fell to the floor, he raped her in front of the assemblage. There was a horrified silence. Civilians who were present didn't dare protest his behavior for fear of reprisals.

But some of the Polish officers who witnessed the act were nauseated enough to report him to his superiors. The KGB transferred the major immediately, and the populace of Slupsk was assured that he had been sentenced to ten years of hard labor in Siberia. I later discovered that in reality the major had been transferred to East Berlin and promoted to a higher post. So it went in the kingdom of the Soviets.

Toward the end of 1946, the Ministry of National Defense issued an order about the reorganization of the 12th Section of the Polish Border Patrol in Sopot. The KGB appointed Major Czarley, the man who had helped me in the eviction of Captain Olshewski from my wife's apartment, to head this section.

Sabina and her mother were permitted to join me at this time, and we found a lovely house. We hired a young German girl, whom we had grown very fond of, to be our housekeeper. She had lost her entire family in the war. And, much as I despised the Germans for liquidating my family, I took pity on this sad girl who had no one left in the world.

Unfortunately, Major Czarley came to stay in our house for a few days and perpetrated an ugly scene. One morning, just as Sabina and I were getting up, our bedroom door opened, and the German girl rushed in, crying. During the night, the major had gone to her room, beat her, then raped her repeatedly. She begged us to find her some other place to stay.

We were both shocked. The major had seemed such a mild-mannered person. My wife comforted the girl, and I placed her in a friend's home where she would be safe. Sabina and I promised to take her back as soon as Major Czarley left.

I could understand the Russians' hatred of the Germans, but why take it out on this unfortunate girl who had nothing to do with Hitler or the war? I was sure that the major had to have been drunk to do such a thing.

He immediately noted the girl's departure and our displeasure. "Why are you so upset about this Kraut?" he said. "Look at what her people did to the Jews. And you're worried about the loss of her virginity. You're both hypocrites."

Sabina gasped. "Better to be a hypocrite than a pig," she said and left the room.

"Major," I said, trying to control my temper. "This is our home and we have been honored to have you as a guest. However, we have certain standards that we observe, and mistreatment of human beings—whatever their nationality—will not be tolerated under our roof."

The major packed his things and moved to a hotel. We promptly brought back our grateful German housekeeper.

Soon after this, during the Polish plebiscite in 1947, I received another lesson in Soviet morality. Intelligence appointed Major Czarley to supervise the plebiscite in the province of Gdansk. Czarley was on the board of a secret provincial commission composed of a dozen men in responsible positions. It was their duty to make certain that the Communists won the election.

One day, after Major Czarley emerged from a session of this board, he summoned all intelligence officers to his office. The gist of his message was that, for the moment, we were not to oppose certain elements propagating hostile publicity against the Soviet-controlled People's Party of Poland.

The reason he was being so impartial was that he knew the Communists were going to win. He knew this because with typical Soviet duplicity, two sets of ballot boxes had been readied: empty ones for the voters to use, and others filled with affirmative votes to be used by the Russians to "fix" the election. The empty ballot boxes were conspicuously placed in the election hall and guarded by security agents to show that all was fair. After the election was over and the polling center had closed, the ballot boxes were stored on trucks and brought to the central hall for counting.

When these trucks arrived, the Russians delayed their unloading by inviting the delegates of the various parties and factions to a dinner. Since these people hadn't eaten all day, they readily accepted the invitation. While the dinner was in progress, the fraudulent ballot boxes were substituted for the true ones, and the Communists won the election by a landslide.

If the true boxes had been opened, the communists would have suffered a humiliating defeat. At a meeting several days later, the major informed us that only seventeen percent of the Gdansk Province had voted for the Soviet-controlled regime; the rest of the votes had been for Mikolaiczyk, the Prime Minister of Poland, who was living in London.

"Things are not good for us here," the major said dourly. "These votes show what a small percentage of the populace thinks that our regime has done a good job."

In the province of Poznan, the major revealed, there was another deplorable situation. Only sixteen percent of the populace had come to the polls. Had the correct ballot boxes been opened, the results would have been a ninety-eight percent vote for Mikolaiczyk and only two percent for the Soviets. "It's obvious," the major said, "that our party members in that province are two-faced. They joined us for materialistic reasons, but not all of them voted for us or even showed up at the polls."

As a result of the fraudulent elections, Major Czarley received the Silver Order of Merit from the Polish Government.

Some months after this, the major summoned all intelligence officers in his section to another meeting. He read us Bulletin No. 16, issued by the KGB. It divulged that Russia was constructing a large underground city containing an enormous atomic power plant. The finest Russian scientists would be involved in this project, along with five thousand German scientists captured during the war.

"The Soviet Union," said Major Czarley, "will leap ahead of all nations in atomic power. This will be our greatest hidden weapon in the liquidation of all capitalistic countries."

Then, as an example of the Soviet Union's largess toward her loyal intelligence officers, the major opened a safe and took out some fancily wrapped gifts for us. All we found inside, however, was some pieces of leather! All that could be done with it, we supposed, was to use it for new soles on our shoes.

Meanwhile, the major was getting rich from the stolen loot. At his instigation, First Lieutenant Karol, an intelligence officer stationed in Leborsk, together with two orderlies in his section, had rounded up a group of thieves to do the major's bidding. Their plundering was done in the vicinity of Lebork, where ninety percent of the population was German. During the night, the gang would break into homes and barracks, and steal watches, jewelry, linens, valuables, food, cigarettes—anything that caught their fancy—at gunpoint. The stolen merchandise was piled on a truck and brought directly to the major. He kept most of the loot for himself. Whatever he didn't want he gave to intelligence officers under his command.

The plundering continued for a long time, despite the outcry from the populace. The major's gang became boldly ruthless. They even went so far as killing a mother of six children just to remove a gold wedding ring from her finger.

After that murder, the major grew apprehensive that there would be an investigation. He wrote to KGB headquarters and requested that Lieutenant Karol be transferred to another post. In just a few days, the officer was transferred to an equivalent post in the city of Eiblag. No further mention was ever made of the murder.

Before Lieutenant Karol left for his new post, I asked him how he had the conscience to sleep at night after killing a mother of six children.

"I'm a soldier, and I do what I'm told," he said.

A short time later, the two orderlies who were his accomplices in these raids were imprisoned. They had continued their operations after the lieutenant's transfer, and without his political protection they quickly landed in jail.

Those days were filled with almost as much brutality and tragedy as our days in the Warsaw Ghetto had been.

In 1947, while I was serving with Intelligence in Slupsk, I roomed briefly with a very affable officer, Lieutenant Zielinski, who was Colonel Voznishensky's aide.

The lieutenant was about to leave on a special assignment: to be the bodyguard for General Swierczewski, who was scheduled to inspect a unit stationed near Sanok in the province of Krakow.

Polish guerrillas were very active there. They had many followers and were well equipped with modern weapons. There was also a pro-Soviet partisan group located in that area. Poland's KGB had many agents operating in this organization. In fact, the group consisted of prewar officers who were either well paid to be members or were forced to join with threats to their families if they did not. Their orders were to spy on the guerrillas, and to cause provocations involving persons who were enemies of the Soviets.

First Lieutenant Paczko, an intelligence officer with the KGB unit stationed in Sanok, was told to have a secret meeting with the partisan leader and to inform him that General Swierczewski would be arriving in Sanok in a few days with a cadre of fifty soldiers. The partisan leader had already been briefed on what was to happen to the general during his inspection tour.

One night, just before his departure, Lieutenant Zielinski got drunk and began complaining to me how much he hated the army and how sick he was of military life.

"You never used to feel that way," I said to him in our quarters, "and you never drank before, either."

"You would drink, too, if you had my assignment."

"What's so terrible about being the general's bodyguard—unless somebody takes a potshot at him?"

He took a few more swallows of his drink, then said, "Yes, and I'm the one who has to take the potshot."

"I don't follow you."

"When I go on that inspection tour with the general as his bodyguard, I have orders to shoot him."

"This can't be true!" I said.

"Yes, it is. I swear to you on my mother's life that it is." He burst into tears.

I couldn't fathom this. The general had been a staunch Communist since he was a child. He had fought against Franco in Spain's Civil War and had been in charge of the Dabrowski Brigade there. After the Communists had been defeated in Spain, the general had served in the Red Army. He had always been connected with the Communist cause.

But it didn't take me long to find out why the Soviets wanted to be rid of him. At meetings of the party's Central Committee, he had vehemently opposed the Soviet plan for collective farming in Poland. The general was well acquainted with the political feelings of peasants and laborers. Since the end of the war, he had been an adherent of land reform. He supported the theories of Gomulka, First Secretary of the Communist Party in Poland.

The general made the mistake of voicing his opinion at an officers' ball. "We didn't give these poor farmers land in 1945 so that we could take it away from them now." He also explained that there was almost no farm machinery in Poland, not even horses.

The officers cheered. "Long live General Swierczewski!" they shouted, singing and applauding. They were a hundred percent behind him.

But Poland's secret KGB operatives lost no time in reporting his views to headquarters. The general was politely informed that he had better alter his ideas on collective farming in accordance with the Kremlin's plan for Poland, but the old man ignored the warning. He became the scourge of the Communists so much so that the KGB resolved to do away with him. Poland's Soviet-dominated KGB wasn't afraid of Gomulka, who also opposed collective farming, because he did not control the army.

Unfortunately, Lieutenant Zielinski did not know the entire

plot. Although it was later agreed by both Ukrainian and Polish military sources that the general was killed by a band of Ukrainian partisans, I discovered what really occurred: When the general's train arrived, a mob of partisans (Ukrainians who had joined with Poles) fired at it. In the confusion, by arrangement, Lieutenant Zeilinski shot and killed the general; but he himself was immediately shot by one of the so-called partisans. Zeilinski was really killed by a KGB operative to cover up any trace of the conspiracy.

Later secret investigations revealed that the general was killed by a Soviet-made bullet that was in use by both the Ukrainian and Russian units; however, Zeilinski was killed by a Czech bullet, which was used only by the Russian forces. If this true story had been revealed earlier, the Soviet leadership could have been entangled—most damningly—in the killing of a Polish Nationalist general who resisted the Soviet system of collective farming that was forcibly instituted in Poland.

After the assassinations, there was an investigation by the general's many supporters which revealed that the partisans had been tipped off by First Lieutenant Paczko about the general's arrival. He was looked upon with great disfavor by the old man's friends and followers. These citizens were angered by the killing of their hero and protector, and the Soviets had to think of something that would quiet them.

With their usual hypocrisy, the Russians tried the lieutenant publicly and sentenced him to ten years in prison. I later found out that the officer was sent to Moscow right after the court-martial, where, instead of being imprisoned, he continued to flourish as an intelligence agent for the KGB.

At Lieutenant Zielinski's funeral, I had a chance to talk to his deeply bitter mother. She said she had found out from her son's friends that he had been shot by a Czech bullet. All of her attempts at investigating the tragedy had been blocked by her son's superiors. "There is something very devious about this entire situation," she said.

I did not wish to risk my life by telling the distressed woman what her son had confessed to me in our quarters.

My world was so full of intrigue, plots, sub-plots, counterplots, and double agents that I was not surprised to discover soon after this incident that another rub-out was being planned—that of Field Marshal Zymierski. Major Czarley let us in on the big secret. I was in a conference room with another intelligence operative, Lieutenant Kasprzak, when Czarley entered and motioned for us to be quiet. He told us that he was taking us into his strictest confidence and then revealed that Marshal Zymierski was to be killed. The reason: Zymierski had gathered about him a group of government dignitaries who, like himself, opposed the Soviet regime and wished to restore the old capitalistic rule in Poland.

The field marshal owned a summer residence in Sopot where he loved to fish. Early in the morning, Lieutenant Lichtenko was to accompany him on his daily fishing trip, while Lieutenant Kasprzak and I patrolled the border waters in a Coast Guard cutter, which wouldn't arouse suspicion.

Lieutenant Lichtenko could not speak Polish well, and Major Czarley was afraid that the real Polish Coast Guard might pick him up and charge him with the field marshal's murder. Despite the fact that the lieutenant was wearing a Polish uniform, he was Russian and the Soviets did not wish him to be accused of the crime. It would be bad publicity for their glorious party. Consequently, Lieutenant Kasprzak and I were instructed to pick him up after the murder and hide him on our boat.

All of this was to happen on the morning of October 10, 1947, but the night before, after I had gone to bed, I received an urgent call notifying me that the plan was off. I was to forget about it. They had simply changed their minds.

Shortly after this, the field marshal was replaced by Marshal Konstantin Rokosovski, a Russian with a Polish name.

One day a proposed assassination, the next a picnic for the workers. I never knew when I got up in the morning if it was going to be blood or beer that afternoon.

The things I was observing were making me increasingly uncomfortable, but it was only with my next assignment that I began seriously to question my position. The assignment centered on the small island of Bazak, a former Nazi concentration camp near the provinces of Gdansk and Stuthot.

Stationed on this island was an army platoon, headed by First Lieutenant Wicherkievich, who also acted as a contact for the Polish KGB. The lieutenant had discovered that a local man by the name of Karol Niemiets was engaged in undercover activities. He lived in a house surrounded by water that could only be reached by boat.

The officer had observed that numerous people made visits to this isolated house, including the prewar head of a regiment in Modlin and a Mrs. Stulinska, the daughter of a prewar colonel who had been an aide of General Anders, the pro-Fascist Pole who had fled to England. An investigation showed that Mrs. Stulinska lived in Gdynia and had an unsavory reputation. Among numerous other charges, she was supposed to have had affairs with German officers during the war.

Captain Uryga of Intelligence passed on this information to headquarters, confronted the woman, and succeeded in coercing her into working as one of our agents. She was assigned the code name "Hania."

As a result of Hania's snooping, a Captain Lopatynski, was arrested for aiding Polish citizens escaping to Sweden aboard the Swedish liner *Victoria,* which made the trip twice a week. His arrest led to the capture of eighty-five additional persons, who were also helping people in their escape from Poland.

It was then that I developed even stronger misgivings about my participation in Poland's military establishment. The great liberating sword which helped drive the Nazis to their destruction was now being turned against the Polish people. The nationalists who wanted only good for their people, land for the peasants, and independence from Soviet domination were either liquidated or driven away. Those who wanted to escape faced the same difficulties I had encountered as a youth on the Zionist march out of Poland. The Nazis had been driven from the land, but the repression of people continued. I decided that I would have to resign from the KGB. I would have to seek my own escape from this worsening tyranny.

CHAPTER 19

Haganah

My spirit was nearly broken as I traced the tragic web in which I was caught. There were no grand dreams of freedom and fulfillment. There was no hope, not even the slender hope that had burned in the Warsaw Ghetto. Poland was sinking into medieval autocracy, and I had become an instrument of injustice.

Just as one intrigue would end, another would commence. Toward the end of 1947, I became involved in an explosive situation involving a Major Stern, who was a doctor in our health department.

It all began when one of our Intelligence officers, Captain August, who was Jewish, sent me a confidential note mentioning that Major Stern was recruiting Jewish soldiers and officers for the Haganah Army in Israel.

I was astounded that a Jew would spy on another in this manner. I decided not to relay the information to our headquarters in Warsaw until I had an idea how to handle it.

That night, I consulted with Sabina, who always seemed to know the right thing to do. She suggested something that had already occurred to me. Could this note from Captain August be a ploy to test my loyalty to the State? It had all the earmarks of that type of trap. This might be a trumped-up charge against the doctor to ascertain whether I would report the information to headquarters.

Sabina mapped out a plan, and I agreed to it. The following day she visited Dr. Stern in his office, ostensibly for a medical check-up. When the nurse left the room, Sabina whispered to the physician that her husband, an intelligence officer, wished to see him that evening.

"I do not have meetings with strangers," the doctor snapped. "If your husband, whoever he may be, wishes to see me, tell him to come here during visiting hours."

Sabina lost her temper. "Don't be an idiot. My husband has been informed of your activities. He's Jewish too, and wants to help you before the Soviets hear about your actions. This is a very serious matter. It may cost you your life."

When the doctor heard this, he changed his tone. "Yes, I understand. Please give me your name and address and tell him to expect me at eight."

Sabina gave him the information and shook his hand. She felt pity for the man. His hand was trembling. She came right home and gave me the news. To assure complete privacy when the doctor arrived that evening, I gave my orderly and my cook the night off.

Precisely at eight, Doctor Stern arrived. He shook my hand nervously and looked about the apartment as if he expected to see agents secreted behind the drapes.

"Could you tell me what this is all about?" he asked in a tremulous voice.

"Sit down and relax," I said in Polish. "Sabina will make us some coffee and we can talk."

"Are you really Jewish?" he asked.

I replied in Yiddish, and he smiled in relief. "Now I know you're one of us."

"You've made a big mistake," I said.

"You mean that you're not Jewish?"

"I most certainly am. The mistake you made, however, was in trusting other Jews like Captain August. These men are our enemies. They're working against the cause of the Jewish people and only for their own gain."

Dr. Stern was too stunned to speak. Afer a moment, he said, "I should have known. He's always asking me questions about the *Yishuv*, the Jewish community in Palestine, and what's going on there."

After that, the ice was broken. The doctor trusted us, and I promised to deliver to him the names of reliable men who would be perfect candidates for the future Israeli Army.

"We have to operate very carefully," I said, "or we both could be executed. Leave the details to me. I've had years of experience in the KGB and I know just how it operates."

Dr. Stern was so happy that he had found an ally he could trust that he seemed years younger than the man who had knocked on my door an hour before. I told him my entire story—my escape from the Ghetto and from the Gestapo train—and how I had used a fraudulent I.D. card all these years. He was fascinated by my account. It was almost midnight when he bade us farewell. I told him he would hear from me in a few days.

The next day I decided to deal with the traitorous Captain August in an appropriate manner. I contacted a Polish informer whom I knew and told him to get the goods on Captain August. I explained that I suspected the captain of working in secret to mobilize the new Jewish Army in Palestine.

My informer friend came up with some damaging information that could be turned against the captain. I entered these facts in my monthly report, charging that the captain was a double agent, working for the Poles on one hand and for the Jews on the other. I recommended that he be dropped from the intelligence service.

Two weeks later, the captain was transferred to another post, and that was the last I ever heard of him.

In the weeks that followed, Dr. Stern was able, with the aid of my list, to round up eighty-five military men—officers, non-commissioned officers, and privates—for the Israeli Army. Our problem now was how to get them across the border.

We formulated a plan. The doctor succeeded in recruiting a Swedish yacht for the transport of the men. It was docked at Port Gdynia, near Gdansk, and we were able to have the men meet there singly and in twos so as not to arouse suspicion.

We had been able to raise a great deal of money for our cause by confiscating American goods which had been smuggled by the Polish marines. We sold these for cash and raised over a million dollars for the Jewish soldiers who wanted to defect to Palestine. Armed with guns and ammumition, they boarded the boat in excellent spirits. Dr. Stern, together with the Israeli Ambassador Barzilay, his assistant, Moshe Dagan, and my wife, supervised the shipment.

The yacht sailed for Sweden, and all went according to plan. From there, the soldiers were transported directly to Israel.

We were very proud of ourselves. To cover our tracks, I made out a report listing the missing soldiers as "deserters." I did not mention that they were all Jewish.

About two weeks later, the phone rang in my office. It was Sabina asking me to come home early that afternoon.

"Why?"

"It's a surprise."

"I don't like surprises."

"Please—believe me—it's important."

When I got home, she told me that we were invited to Dr. Stern's house that evening to meet someone of importance.

"I'm not going," I said.

"Why not?" she asked in surprise.

"Because if someone of importance is going to be there, it's probably the Israeli ambassador, and if it's the ambassador, it would be dangerous for us to be seen with him. These dignitaries are closely watched by the Soviets. They might even take a photograph of us with him. It's much too dangerous, and I'm not going to risk it."

Sabina agreed. I called Dr. Stern in his office and said that I was not feeling well. Could he possibly come over and examine me? He said he would come immediately.

When the doctor arrived, I explained why I couldn't meet with him at his house, especially if the ambassador was going to be there.

"Yes, but how did you know it was he who wished to meet you?"

"I'm in intelligence; I surmised it. I'm eager to meet him, but he must come to my secret meeting room in Sopot, where I meet with my agents. There are two entrances; he must come in one, I in the other."

I drew a diagram for the doctor to give to the ambassador. Dr. Stern thought this an excellent plan. We made arrangements for the ambassador to meet me there at 9:00 p.m.

All went well. The ambassador arrived punctually via the special entrance. He greeted me warmly and thanked me for my help, then came right to the point.

"We are desperately in need of weapons," he said, "and I know that you can be of help. At this moment, there are fourteen railway cars here loaded with German ammunition."

"How do you know that?" I asked. "It's supposed to be a closely guarded secret."

"I happen to know that because Captain Berman, who was in charge of those cars, was one of the men we helped send to Israel. He urged me to talk to you about securing those arms for Israel. Can we depend on your help?"

"This is difficult," I said honestly, "without risking my life. Give me a few days to mull over a plan. If there's any chance of my doing it, you have my promise that it will be done."

"We shall forever be in your debt," the ambassador said,

shaking my hand. He took one door, I left through the other. I was certain no one had detected us, but I was troubled by the ambassador's request. There was nothing more that I wished than to help my struggling people in Israel but it would take a very clever maneuver to swing this hazardous mission.

For the next few days, I did little but map out plans for turning the ammunition over to the ambassador without facing a firing squad, but nothing I thought of seemed right.

Then, suddenly, in the middle of the night, an idea came to me and I jumped out of bed.

"What's the matter, darling?" Sabina said.

"Sssh—go back to sleep. I'm okay."

She turned on the night light and peered at me with half-open eyes.

"There's only one way to do what the ambassador wants—and I just thought of it," I told her.

We sat up half the night discussing my idea. Sabina agreed that it sounded workable.

The next morning I called Dr. Stern and asked if he could drop by my house for tea later in the day. He said he would be there by 5:00 p.m. We never discussed private matters over the phone; it was too risky.

When the doctor showed up, I requested that he arrange a meeting for me with the ambassador's assistant, Moshe Dagan. I specified that he was to meet me in Sopot at 9:00 p.m. as the ambassador had, and once again I drew the diagram of the two doors.

The following evening, Moshe Dagan entered my secret headquarters. After a brief greeting, he asked why I had summoned him.

I repeated the ambassador's request for the ammunition, then outlined my plan for letting him remove it. "I will turn over to you fourteen cars full of ammunition on one condition: you must sign this document."

"What document?" he asked.

I handed it to him and he read it. "You want me to sign this paper stating that I'm acting as an undercover agent for you in the Israeli Embassy!" he exclaimed.

"Correct. It's the only way this can be done. Don't you see? If my superior officers in the KGB call me on the carpet and demand to know why in heaven's name I would turn over all this ammunition to a Jew, my only recourse would be to say that the

Jew is an undercover agent for us. I know their mentality. This is the only answer they would accept. And it must be in writing.''

''Yes,'' Moshe said, ''I see your point. It's a clever idea.''

He signed the document and acknowledged receipt of the fourteen cars in writing. We parted friends and on the next day the ammunition was in the ambassador's hands.

I wrote a detailed report to my superiors in Warsaw, stating that we now had an excellent undercover man working for us in the Israeli Embassy under the code name of ''Gibon.'' I noted that, in exchange for his services, I had made the transaction involving the ammunition.

Colonel Krezeman, National Chief of the 2nd Intelligence Department, was elated over the deal. ''What a fortunate and ingenious move—having an agent in the Israeli Embassy.''

During all this time, I constantly wondered whether I would ever have news of any members of my family. Then, in March of 1948, a lawyer named Dr. Zaremski paid me a visit with a surprise letter. It was from my brother, Nathan. He was living in New York, where he was rabbi of the Warsaw Synagogue at 60 Rivington Street. It was typical of Nathan not to write a warm letter rejoicing in my survival as well as his. Instead, he chronicled how he had made his way from Poland to Japan to Shanghai, where he had been welcome all during the war. When the war ended, General Eisenhower had assisted him and many other rabbis who had found asylum in China in their efforts to relocate to the United States.

Nathan expressed his sorrow that he had not been able to find any traces of the rest of the family, but on the whole his letter had the tone of a business message rather than a reunion with a long-lost brother.

Still, it was wonderful to hear that at least one other Shainberg had survived. I decided to write to him as soon as I had some spare time.

The lawyer who brought me my brother's note was a close friend of mine. I had helped him some time ago when he had gotten into trouble for hoarding American money. I happened to be in Captain Lewandowski's office the day he was questioning this lawyer, Dr. Zaremski, about the money. He threatened to put him in jail for three years. I noted that the lawyer appeared frightened, and I knew why. Instinctively I realized that he was a Jew masquerading as a Pole, and I decided I would help him.

I asked the captain to come to my office when he was through questioning the lawyer. He came to see me a half hour later, and I said, "Instead of putting this man in jail, why don't you put him to work on the liquidation of German goods? We need an informer there. We have no inkling of what's going on in that department."

"I don't think that would be advisable," the captain said.

"Why not?"

"Because I suspect that he's a Jew, and nobody would work with him. They wouldn't trust him."

I was appalled to hear this. The Polish KGB was supposed to be rid of anti-Semitism, yet here again was one of our officers sounding like a Nazi storm trooper. I wanted to reprimand him, but thought better of it.

"Maybe you're right," I said. "Let me handle this case. There must be something other than putting this man in jail."

The captain shrugged and left.

I was able to save the lawyer from going to jail, and he was eternally grateful to me. With his American contacts, he was able to do me a favor and track down my brother. But all his investigation concerning the rest of my family came to a dead end. There was no record of what had happened to any of them.

In May, 1949, we received a bulletin translated from Russian to Polish for KGB counterintelligence officers. It was the text of an appeal to Stalin made by a man named Slanski, head of the Communist Party in Czechoslovakia.

Slanski and a group of activists in the Czechoslovakian Politburo had traveled to Moscow to seek Stalin's help in backing the new Jewish fighting nation. These were Slanski's remarks to Stalin as I remember reading them:

You are now the father image and leader of most nations in the world. Millions of people look to you. Your past shows that you have always fought for equality for all.

Now, we students and followers of your ideology come to you for help. We have been successful in every direction—we have freedom, we have a plan to follow which has proven infallible, we have improved education, and we have better industrial conditions. What we now request from you is help to build a stronger Jewish nation. For over two thousand years our people have experienced nothing but discrimination

and bitterness and have suffered massive pogroms or-
ganized by our enemies.
PLEASE HELP US. DONT LET OUR
NATION DOWN.

Stalin's written reply was:

> Yes, I will help you build your new nation. Russia
> will be the first to recognize Israel as the new Jewish
> State. In exchange, please remember that we are inter-
> ested in building up a big arsenal in the Middle East
> and in dividing the capitalistic countries. The Mediter-
> ranean must be ours. Israel can have the Suez Canal
> and they can use it; that will be preferable. But we will
> control it.

Slanski's reply was: "We shall do everything in our power to
make this come true." When I read this bulletin, I felt a greater
hope for the emerging nation of Israel.

CHAPTER 20

Moscow

My enthusiasm for working with the Zionists, and joy over the May 14, 1948 proclamation of the State of Israel, was dampened by a confidential note I received one morning. It contained orders that would cause a major change in my life and entangle me more deeply than ever in the dangerous Soviet web.

The note came from Colonel Kohl, Chief of Polish counterintelligence, who informed me that because of my brilliant military career and unblemished work in Intelligence, I had been chosen to attend a special five-year program in the Military Academy of Moscow.

The news was received with less than enthusiasm at home. Sabina was raising our year-old daughter Dina and didn't like the idea of my being gone for five years while she stayed in Poland. But appointments of this nature were not easily rejected. Indeed, to turn down such an honor would have invited substantial displeasure and suspicion by the authorities. And in many ways, I was enthusiastic about the appointment. It was a chance to learn the true workings of the Soviet system, a chance to learn if the Soviets really meant their oft-proclaimed intentions of building a better world, a chance to learn if they practiced the tolerance of varied ethnic groups they were so fond of preaching, a chance to learn if a Jew truly had a chance in the Soviet world.

I called our headquarters in Warsaw, and my fears about long periods away from my family were calmed. "You will be permitted to go home for three days every month," an officer assured me. "Tell your wife not to worry. We're not sending you to Siberia. She will see you once a month."

I called Sabina and gave her the good news. She was overjoyed and said that now she could care for the baby in peace. I was relieved that her mother was still living with us. Without her, life would have been very lonely for Sabina.

The night before my departure, Sabina, Lila, and I had a farewell dinner in a local restaurant. We were all somewhat sad. Once again we were being separated, and at a time when my wife needed me.

I had heard both pleasant and forbidding things about Moscow, and I almost felt as if I were being sent to another planet to study the manners and mores of a mysterious people. I would have to leave my fears in Poland and go east with confidence and faith.

The following day, after much embracing and crying, I left Sabina and Lila on the railway platform and joined twenty-four men on a train headed for Moscow. One of my traveling companions was General Dushinski, but I wasn't on friendly terms with him. There were two men from Czechoslovakia, however, who were amiable. We all spoke Russian and greatly enjoyed one another's company on the trip. That seemed to be the language of the day, and we rarely reverted to Polish.

Moscow turned out to be as extravagantly bizarre as I had anticipated. It was a predominantly gloomy city with a grim-looking populace; yet, set in the middle of all this depression was the magnificent Red Square and the resplendent buildings in the Kremlin.

During our first few days in the city, we were taken on tours of landmarks, always escorted by a guide who lost no opportunity to inject political jibes against capitalistic nations in her commentary.

We visited Lenin's tomb and the museums in the Kremlin, many of which were former cathedrals that still stunned the senses with their ornamentation and rich furnishings. But all the golden domes and minarets didn't excite me as much as the wild exoticism of St. Basil's Cathedral right outside the Kremlin walls. Here, in one edifice, was embodied the alternately comical and tempestuous nature of the Russian people. I could have contemplated its passionate allure for hours, but our guide rushed us on to still another landmark glorifying the great revolution.

Despite the endless propaganda we were fed about the triumph of Communism in Russia, the average Russian I observed in the street looked ill-clothed and ill-fed. Later, I discovered that he was also ill-housed.

Our courses at the Military Academy began almost immediately, and it was somewhat like being back in Yeshiva. We attended classes ten hours a day and had exams every Friday. It was an entirely new life for me with an expanding horizon about the world we were living in.

We studied the development of the Communist Party and the history, geography, economy, and politics of all the world's nations. Most fascinating to me was our study of intelligence systems and how they operated.

Our professors demonstrated the vast infiltration of communist agents all over the globe. The communist plan, based on Lenin's teachings, was to take over the world without physical struggle. Our instructors all drummed this point into our heads.

But the major thrust was always how to take over the United States. The inner workings of the U.S. intelligence system were studied in great detail. America was regarded as the king in a chess game. One of my instructors, Professor Yarmuloff, was a great chess player and frequently used the terms of the game in his classes. Pawns could be expended and pawns could be destroyed, but the object of the game was not to wage genocidal attack on pawns. They were merely tools for getting at the real objective, the checkmate of the enemy king. And our enemy's king was Washington.

Indeed, the game of chess, which is much loved by Soviet leaders, was a strong influence on Soviet planning. The bishops, knights, and castles of the chess board represented various defenses of the enemy society, namely, military force, intelligence systems, and industrial capacity. The true chess master is not interested in destroying these pieces, but only in getting past them. And in the end, the object is not to destroy the enemy king, but to checkmate him. The Soviets were deeply committed to an international communism that precluded the shedding of blood. Instead of tanks, we were taught to use intrigue. Instead of artillery, we were taught to use propaganda. Instead of bombs, we were taught to use intelligence.

The Soviet Union was thoroughly unwilling to wage an armed confrontation against American economic and technical strength, and Professor Yarmuloff constantly lectured us on the need to outflank the United States without a military struggle. Instead we would use superior Soviet strategy.

Professor Yarmuloff's classes also focused on the ethnic groups of the world, primarily Blacks, Hispanics, and Arabs, and their potential roles in a communist takeover. Yarmuloff saw Blacks as pawns in the international struggle, currently under the direction of the capitalists; but with proper strategies, he believed they could become willing pawns of the communists.

Professor Yarmuloff claimed that the race's tradition of being exploited meant that Blacks were culturally and intellectually incapable of self-determination; in other words, we shouldn't expect to see any substantial communist revolution springing spontaneously from within a Black community. Blacks would forever be dominated, he told us, and the dominating power would simply be whatever outside power held the most influence within their society.

Yarmuloff lectured: "In the United States, Blacks are dominated by the capitalistic system that forces them either to work as second class citizens or starve. Blacks resent this as a mule resents the farmer's whip, but like mules they are also stupid and powerful. Given the right circumstances, Blacks can be used as our pawns to threaten the U.S. government."

A communist America would treat Blacks better, Yarmuloff taught, but there is the key: Blacks would be treated better by a dominant power, but they would never assume leadership. His bigoted remarks demoralized me.

Yarmuloff also had his theories about Hispanics. There were then about 300 million Spanish-speaking people spread through a dozen countries, and each of these societies tended to be intensely religious. Hispanics, Yarmuloff told us, "will be very difficult to convert to communism because they are too severely addicted to the opiate of religion." Although there might be a few minor successes, there was no reason to believe a mass of Hispanics would disown their religious culture and rise against their Catholic states, no matter how repressive those states were. At best, Hispanic people could only be manipulated to revolt, assisted by our agents, gradually being absorbed into international Communism.

The Arabs posed a more serious problem for Communist planners. They supplied and controlled much of the oil that fueled a large sector of Western industrial and military might. It would be extremely difficult to bring this vital community within the Communist sphere. There were several elements in Arab society that worked against us. Even worse than the Hispanics, Arabs were intensely religious, and they would spill blood across their deserts before they would forsake their Koran for an atheistic Communist ideology. Surely Arabs could be made radical, and perhaps driven to build something like a socialist state. But in the end, Arab devotion to the Koran would mean that they

would never truly accept an essential ingredient of Communism—
the recognition of man's supremacy in the universe, and the need
for man to determine his own destiny. Also, Arab culture was
decidedly reactionary, feudal in character, and a long way from
the capitalistic, free-market decadence and greed needed to in-
spire the masses to take the ultimate step to Communism. Finally, Arabs were unusually egocentric and were convinced that
their society was far superior to anything in the infidel world.
The lowliest Arab camel trader, in his own mind, felt superior to
the highest executive officer of any infidel state, and it would be
easier to convince his camels otherwise.

Another of my courses at the Academy focused on the blue-
print for international Communism. General Zacharin lectured us
on the tactics necessary for the overthrow of capitalistic society,
how to find the proper seeds in the capitalistic farm and enrich
them with Communistic fertilizer. Most of his lectures were
aimed at methods of sowing discontent within capitalistic society—
the divide-and-conquer theory. Internal dissent, he taught crip-
ples a society and thwarts the efforts of its leadership. When a
population is reluctant to follow its leadership, it is as weak as
Czar Nicholas II was in 1917. When capitalistic rulers are incapable of imposing their wills upon the workers, these leaders
become emasculated, defenseless, and ripe for overthrow.

"The best way to realize our goal is by dividing a country and
turning it against itself. This is achieved by sowing mistrust and
suspicion among the populace so that they do not present a
unified front against us. If we cannot attain this dissension, we
shall not realize our aims in the twentieth century."

Professor Bashkatov's lectures explored further methods for the
defeat of capitalistic countries. "The Soviet revolution erupted
because of the deplorable conditions of the Russian worker and
peasant, and we succeeded because our cause was just and
imperative. Capitalist countries subsist on a class system whereby
one class exploits another."

In his classes Bashkatov outlined the Comintern's plan to take
over the world. It was a complex scenario that would take
twenty-five years to succeed. Bashkatov's lectures on world conquest included the following major points:

> The Communist Party is based on the ideology of
> Marx and Lenin. We are the representatives of the
> proletariat of the world. The Party has a responsibility

to the working class. The 1917 November Revolution
was just the beginning of our struggle against capitalism.

The Communist Party cannot hold world leadership
until it takes over the world through revolution, evolu-
tion, or counterrevolution. Even when the world is
ruled by one regime, we will still have to fight for
leadership according to the teachings of Marx and
Lenin; the Russian Communist Party has to lead the
International Politburo.

It is impossible for the Russian Communist Party to
fully succeed in establishing Communism in other countries because of the following conditions:

1. Communism cannot control nor fully survive as
long as there are competing systems of government in
the world.

2. At the present time we work according to the
needs and live according to the opportunity. When we
have one regime in the world, the agenda will be
reversed. We will work according to the opportunity
and live according to the needs.

3. Our system is struggling with internal problems
that take time to correct:

    a) we still use money in our transactions;
    b) we still have to maintain an army;
    c) we still have to maintain a police force;
    d) our economy is labor-intensive with a severe
       shortage of capital investment;
    e) sixty percent of the Russian population lack
       technical know-how and a basic education.

Without reforming the above conditions, we cannot
think of having secured Communism as the dominant—if
not only—system in the world. This is how we propose
to accomplish our aim of world domination:

First, we must take over the leading capitalist an-
tagonist—the U.S. The United States is the most dangerous enemy of Communism for several reasons:

    a) They have the highest and most advanced
       technology in the world today.
    b) When we were fighting the war, Ameri-
       can businesses grew rich selling military sup-
       plies to both sides, without regard for the
       human cost.
    c) They are very knowledgeable in propa-

gandizing and playing the "double game."
They play both sides, yet they come out as
the good guys.

d) The United States has the same large population that we have.

We Russians will never attack another country to start
a war. Lenin taught us to fight with white gloves. This
means that when we do take over a country, there are
no reasons for creating conditions of war. We must
employ subversive strategies and turn the country against
itself by encouraging discontent from within. We will
not take over a country just for pleasure, but for good,
solid reasons such as the following:

a) If it offers a strategic location for another,
future takeover.

b) If it will provide training bases preparing
us for assaults on the "religious" countries.
We can learn their customs and conform to
their lifestyle.

c) If it is suitable for setting up military
bases near the United States.

We have spent several years cultivating "friend-
ships" with Western nations. Now we must begin
organizing a tremendous underground network to assist
in our takeover of the West. We must begin planting
Soviet agents or underground "moles" in Western
society to further our intelligence-gathering activities.

How can we take over the United States without a
war?

We have to maintain friendly relations with them.
Our methods must demonstrate that we want to work
together in all fields, such as economy, arts, technol-
ogy, etc. Let the U.S. think of us as their friends, and,
in the meantime, let us continue with our plan behind
their backs. Then, we propose to do the following:

a. Organize five military bases around the
United States.

b. Organize a back-up security system for
the bases.

c. Develop a powerful conspiracy in the United
States.

The scenario to achieve these goals will develop as
follows: The KGB will train and educate members of

the Black, Hispanic, and other minorities. We will also engage in a program of smuggling young Americans, with the consent of their parents, for placement in our specialized training schools. These young people will be prepared in Rayzan, two hundred miles from Moscow. There they will be carefully indoctrinated and eventually returned years later to the U.S. They will be resettled with new identities into American society and await our signal to assist in the takeover of the country. These trained young products will be placed in jobs and schools and will appear on the surface to be ordinary U.S. citizens. They will support their local politicians, attempting to become close to and gain influence with them. They will give financial and political support as the Soviet Embassy directs them. From 1950—our present time—give us approximately one-quarter of a century and we will have implemented a major portion of this resettlement program. They will be called upon from time to time for assistance in the KGB's underground U.S. activities. As we continue these training and resettlement programs each year, we will develop an army of U.S.-based KGB agents that will facilitate our impending U.S. takeover.

The Rayzan Military Training Academy was founded by the Soviet Union in 1943 to train officers from Poland. By 1945, when the war had ended, the school was enrolling officers from all of the Soviet satellite nations. The program was expanded in 1947, with the school transformed into a political training center that would indoctrinate candidates—young and old alike—from the various Soviet satellites. The smuggling of young people—primarily children of Communist Party members in the Western nations—didn't surprise me, but I was later to learn that under Khrushchev the school's recruiting tactics were changed in a most shocking manner. When I visited the school in 1953 along with a group of fellow officers, I was to see thousands of adolescent children from around the world—all races and nationalities—who had been kidnapped for the purpose of indoctrination and the eventual resettlement in and infiltration of their native countries. Khrushchev, we were to learn, viewed this as one of many ways to influence the masses in hostile nations around the world, especially the United States. As far as I know, these kidnappings are still going on today.

Bashkatov also lectured us on the internal problems that were impeding a Communist takeover of the U.S.:

> Before the U.S. takeover can be implemented there are substantial adjustments that we must make in our own ranks, especially the cleaning up of Trotskyism within our Communist membership. The job begun by Felix Dzherzhinsky* is not over yet. We still have many Trotskyite leaders around the world; we must undermine and destroy them, whether they are in Spain, Greece, Hungary, Rumania, Bulgaria, or France.
>
> We have not succeeded in our opposition to Tito of Yugoslavia or in the elimination of many other leaders in countries outside the Communist Bloc. But we are getting stronger. Our KGB is eager to dispose of these leaders, and eventually it will. We have only one way to achieve total Communism—and that is *Stalin's* way.
>
> We have many difficult problems to overcome. During the Communist Revolution, we lost over a million of our fighting members. We are the first people in history fighting to unite the entire world's working class. We must effect the transition from socialism to communism. But if we rely on elections only, we, the Russians, can lose the leadership because of our small population.
>
> We must unite the proletariat as well as other ethnic groups. We must train them properly so they do not pose a threat to Russian leadership. Then we will not have to resort to liquidating more than three billion of these people to preserve our Communist leadership, and we shall be able to attain a secure and pure political system according to Marxism and Leninism.
>
> In many countries, especially the United States, there are shameful unions which pose as the protectors of the working class, but they are really tools of the capitalist owners. In most cases, the union management is operated by major American criminals.
>
> This evil union system works well for Communism;

---

* Dzherzhinsky was responsible for the formation of Russia's notorious CHEKA, which was the original predecessor to the KGB. He also instituted the "Red Terror"—the arrest and instant execution of anyone deemed to be a potential enemy of the state.

it plays right into our hands. It demonstrates that the
capitalist system is wrong and that we are right. It can
be exploited to open the eyes of the working class and
open the door for our entrance.

In order to establish ourselves in every country—
especially in America—we require an initial penetration. Once this is done, we can send in our agents to
coordinate our serious activities. We are not alone in
this infiltration. There are twelve other socialist countries in league with us to liquidate capitalists. Every
one of these allies has a specific task to perform in the
takeover.

One of Bashkatov's favorite topics was the need to break the
U.S. labor unions. In the long run, he taught, the hypocrisy of
these unions would help a Communist revolution because workers would one day comprehend that their unions were not organized for their benefit, but instead were working against them.
Until this awakening came, however, U.S. laborers would be
duped into blindly following the charade. In the immediate
future, he taught, American workers would be hostile to Communism because of the influence exercised over them by the
capitalist-dominated unions.

Bashkatov said that American unions had become the clergy of
American workers, a clergy that was just as powerful and persuasive as the Russian Orthodox clergy during the days of the czars.
They preached from the pulpit of the union hall and guided the
workers to believe in the distorted American concepts of freedom, justice, and the eight-hour day—and all the while they
fleeced their congregations. American labor leaders drove around
in Cadillacs and collected large unearned salaries, while the
workers sweated on assembly lines.

According to Bashkatov, there was occasional unrest within
U.S. unions, but the unrest was superficial. They would strike,
protest, and conduct various other actions for a few dollars more,
or a few hours less. But they never had the nerve to challenge
the system itself. This is what we were to lead them to do.

Bashkatov claimed that an elite of about a hundred people,
America's untitled nobility, essentially ruled the nation's political, economic, and social life. These people dominated a country
of almost two hundred million people which in turn dominated a
world of three billion people. This elite hundred was made up of
White, Anglo-Saxon Protestants, and would never tolerate a

serious challenge. They would occasionally throw a few "liberal" bones to the people, as goodies from a benevolent state. But they would never compromise their own power.

Bashkatov impressed upon us the great power of this elite and taught that it might take as long as half a century to destroy it. But eventually Communist ideological currents running through the American working class would become too powerful for the elite to resist, and they would be swept up in a general revolution.

> Russia lost twenty million people in World War II because of international capitalistic concerns which brought Hitler to power in Germany so that he could destroy the Communist majority and their leaders. The Americans thought that they could destroy the fruits of the Russian Revolution. But we took them by surprise. They now want to be prepared for us in the future.

He would tell us about conditions in Russia before Communism prevailed. The lecture went something like this:

> Our people had no food, no clothes, no decent houses. We had no freedom or human rights. However, the priests told us we had one thing we could be thankful for: God. Unfortunately the priests never explained the reality which was that God has created two types of people: those who work and those who enjoy the fruits of that work.
>
> This injustice gives us the opportunity to create a strong base because justice is on our side. We realize that the capitalists are strong. We cannot possibly destroy them in one generation. But we will accomplish our goal before the twentieth century is over. We will be busy with our development programs. We are rebuilding our towns and our industries destroyed by the Germans, thereby developing our nation and its vast natural resources so that we may eventually forcefully challenge the capitalists. At the same time, we have to rebuild the twelve socialist countries which became our allies after World War II. With a strong foothold in capitalistic countries, we can act freely and wisely according to our Comintern—especially in the United States.

Another professor, General Nechlis, instructed us on large-scale economic sabotage of the free world:

> The first step is to strip England and France of their colonies, to reduce their economic viability. Then, we must reduce U.S. influence in the smaller countries—the American equivalent of colonial holdings. Consider the shocking fact that forty million French dominate three hundred million subjects and that forty-five million British dominate five hundred million subjects. Despite the scores of countries in the economic and political grip of America, England, and France, these nations call themselves and their systems democratic!
>
> After our underground penetration is completed in these capitalist nations, our intelligence network will be worldwide. It will receive its orders directly from the Soviet Comintern. Our goal is to make each political party in these countries hate the others in order to dull their awareness of our underground work and activities. We must prepare bases for taking over key industrial units in every state of the United States.
>
> We know that U.S. intelligence is weak. It does not have the experience and cunning of the German or British systems. Their agents are too open in their actions, too revealing. And Americans are preoccupied with three things: money, women, and alcohol.
>
> There are various methods for bringing these countries to our side. First of all, we must establish a spy network to penetrate every branch of industry, to organize—or buy off if necessary—agents who will maintain contacts for underground activities. At times, we will have to use sabotage to accomplish our aims. Besides physical sabotage, we may have to use black-mail, taking advantage of compromising situations. Any method is condoned, as long as it secures our goals. The end will justify our means.
>
> Subtlety is the keynote of our penetration. We need active underground groups that will not be identified as Communist proxies. They can call themselves ''New Democrats'' or something similar, but they must not reveal their true purpose. They must be double agents, assuming legitimate positions in government or industry but working for us undercover. These people must

be well-trained agents who can monitor mail and memoranda without being caught. They should be well educated and placed in every state. As these agents operate without being detected, our cause will be furthered toward its inevitable success. We can quietly establish the foundations of Communism without intervention from capitalists who are busy with their own problems: racism, strikes, unemployment, and political corruption. By the same token, we must not allow our adversaries to strengthen their political platforms.

It would be useful to induce the United Nations to have two hundred nations represented, not just seventy-five. We could then more easily sway these countries to our side—a useful tool in the struggle to liquidate capitalism.

Lenin taught us to fight capitalists with white gloves. We have to infiltrate their lives and minds with smiles on our faces, with no let-up in our resolve. One step back, two steps forward—such is the choreography in our march to establish world Communism.

I found little amusement in any of our courses at the Academy, but one day I almost burst out laughing in class. As was inevitable, one of our lecturers spoke to us on the subject of Jews. I had already noted the bigoted comments about Blacks. If anyone had thought that the Russians in Poland were free of racial prejudice, he needed only to observe the school I was attending to learn the true picture. Professio Nechlis went on to lecture:

It's very easy to spot a Jew. Don't think that just because a man has a long, sharp nose or a heavy accent, he's a Jew. He may well be or he may not. There are other, more tell-tale clues to pounce on. Jews are very emotional. They must dominate the conversation. It is almost impossible to get a word in edgewise with them. Also, they pay lip service to Christians, fawning over them, bowing and scraping before them, agreeing with everything they say in order to ingratiate themselves. There is nothing the Jewish male covets more than a Gentile bride. That is his ultimate conquest. Also, Jews eat extremely quickly. Whenever you see a man eating quickly, you can be

sure he's Jewish. Finally, they are very pushy people,
whether they're waiting in line or in any social or
business situation. They will do *anything* to get ahead
and make money, because they think that money will
buy them the social acceptance they lack. So, just bear
these traits in mind, and you will have no difficulty
spotting a Jew.

I had a strong urge to leap up and laugh in the man's face.
Here I had been fighting, working, and living alongside Russians
all this time, and not one of them had ever suspected that I was a
Jew. If this was the sort of provincial mentality our professors
had, I began seriously to doubt the efficacy of the Moscow
Academy.

At the time, anti-Semitism was not as big a problem in the
Soviet Union as it was in Poland, but it did exist. Usually, Jews
were simply regarded as another minority ethnic group with
strengths and weaknesses. After the war, the Soviets maintained
a relatively benevolent attitude toward Jews and were inclined to
support Zionist aspirations in the Middle East. This was, however, a self-serving benevolence. For centuries, Russia had tried
to gain access to the Mediterranean, so Odessa could become a
truly international port. Traditionally, Istanbul had blocked passage of Russian fleets, keeping them bottled up in the Black Sea.
The Communist successors to the Russian Czars were faced with
the same problem. The Soviets sought to outflank the Turks and
force guaranteed passage through the straits at the Dardanelles.
Alliances with Arab states bordering Turkey to the south and east
were out of the question. The Soviets regarded the Arabs as vile,
unpredictable, and potentially dangerous. So the next best place
for them to gain influence in the area was within the new Jewish
State. Israel was already organizing a socialist government, and
some Jews had expressed strong interest in Communism.

Thus, the Communists in Moscow saw the Jews as a vehicle
of international Communism, another pawn that could be used
now and abused later.

During this period, I was still plagued by indecision concerning the value of Communism and I had doubts about my
own future. I felt as if I were in the cave of the Russian bear and
in the lion's den at the same time. Nevertheless, I took up a
part-time journalistic career at the suggestion of my superiors,
and sent articles to Warsaw newspapers and magazines in which
I promulgated the Party's doctrines.

I became increasingly engrossed in the Biblical Book of Daniel and found great inspiration in it. Surely, my case paralleled Daniel's in many ways. I, too, had been carried off to a Babylon, to a burgeoning empire in the East. And as Daniel had changed his name to Belteshazzar, mine was now Pruzanski. And as Daniel, I gained access to the court of my bestial Nebuchadnezzar, reading and interpreting his awesome global dreams.

Like Daniel, I was miraculously passed over by hungry lions. And like Daniel, I started to have visions, acquiring an insight into the ways of the world. I pondered the moral and political issues confronting my destiny. I began to see how things worked, but I couldn't yet understand why.

> And I heard, but I understood not: then said I, O my Lord, what shall be the end of these things?
>
> *(Daniel 12:8)*

CHAPTER 21

The Russians

There is an important distinction between the Soviet Union and the Russians. The Soviet Union is a political entity, an amazing and extroverted accomplishment of the human mind with grandiose visions of internationalism. The Russians are a people in themselves, curled in the comfortable ball of introverted nationalism.

I initially fell in love with the Russians during my years at the Moscow Military Academy. Behind the bleak and silent masks I first met in Moscow there were some people capable of great warmth and humanity.

During my years there, I became friendly with Colonel Karlov of Leningrad. He was my age, and we shared many interests. He enjoyed dancing and the theater, opera and ballet. He also enjoyed my company, and took me along when he visited his relatives.

Although I went to Poznan often to visit my family during my five-year training period I took several opportunities to travel with Karlov to the Caucasus, Odessa, Sverdlovsk, and other regions. I enjoyed these trips immensely and met a wide range of Russians: the peasants, the workers, the city dwellers, and the intelligentsia.

Once, we went to visit the Colonel's cousin who lived on a collective farm, "Krasny Borets" (Red Fighter) in the province of Saratov. I was very impressed with the set-up. There were over one hundred families on that farm. They had a beautiful club with a library. Three miles away was a school that the children had to walk to in all kinds of weather. The parents felt the young ones had to harden themselves to become strong Russians, and this daily walk helped build their bodies and their resistance to the elements. This particular village was fortunate because it had electricity, while twelve other villages in the vicinity were still using kerosene lamps.

Each family had its own house with a straw-covered roof. Their huge mud and cement ovens served as stoves and radiators and, at night, served still another purpose: the family slept on it.

Most of the houses had only one large room which functioned as kitchen, living room, and bedroom. The bathroom was outside and no matter how cold it was, that's where you had to go.

Each family was allotted one cow, two pigs, and up to thirty-six chickens. In return, each family had to pay the state a tax in the form of four hundred gallons of milk, thirty-six dozen eggs, and 150 kilos of meat per year.

The principle of Soviet collective farming was that each worker was credited with a "work-day" for toiling in the field. The tractor operator was credited with five work-days for one day's work, because his task was so arduous.

There were no clocks on collective farms. The workers toiled from sunrise to sunset, fewer hours in winter, more in summer.

The aim was for each family to amass as many work-days as possible. At the end of the year, at harvest time, the administration divided the harvest in the following manner: eighty-five percent to the government and an undisclosed amount to the secret police and local dignitaries. Whatever was left was then divided by the number of work-days to the farmer's credit. For example, that year, a work-day equalled three kilos of wheat, one pound of potatoes, and up to two pounds of vegetables.

In other words, these poor people worked the entire year for the same amount of goods that a Western worker received for a few days' or weeks' work. And this wretched system was installed by the Soviets who supposedly fought against the exploitation of man!

But in the final analysis, things were infinitely better than in Czarist days when nobody could determine exactly how much the landlords would take, and often farmers who had produced an abundance of food would starve. Furthermore, the farm workers seemed to accept the burden. Life was hard, and physical rewards were few, but they found some satisfaction in the joy of life, and in the peace that sweetly blessed them after their terrible war.

One morning during my stay, Karlov and I noticed that there was no breakfast on the table. His cousin, Clara, who usually prepared our meals, was nowhere to be seen. Feeling distraught, my friend went in search of her. When he returned, he said to me, "Can you believe this? I found her waiting on a long line at the store. And do you know what the store is 'giving' today? They're giving ladies' panties for eight rubles. I could have bought Clara panties in Moscow for four rubles without standing in line. They are really taking advantage of these country folk." (In Russia, Karlov explained to me, you never ask a clerk what he's selling today; you ask what he's giving.)

That same day, Karlov and I went to visit a tractor brigade. These men and women didn't go home at night, but slept in covered wagons. I looked forward to meeting these hardy farmers.

We had to walk twelve miles to get to them. The foreman was very cordial and invited us to have lunch. We sat at a big table with a dozen people in an open field. A cook served two bowls of soup with chunks of meat floating in them, and everyone dipped bread into these communal bowls in an uncivilized manner. When I saw these smoke-blackened tractor operators dipping their bread and filthy oily fingers into the soup, I couldn't bring myself to eat.

My friend noticed this and diplomatically asked the cook to give me a small separate bowl, since I didn't like fat in the soup. I must confess that despite the unsanitary conditions, the soup was delicious.

Walking around a collective farm was not easy when you were the only ones in the area with shoes on, so we took them off. For these farmers a pair of shoes was an unattainable dream.

When we were through with lunch, I noticed a girl of about twenty get up from the table and walk toward some bushes. The sun was strong, and it made her body visible under her dress. She was powerfully built and carried a large piece of newspaper. Without any shame, she squatted down in the bushes and relieved herself. When she returned to us, she clasped the bottom of her stomach and said, "Now I feel good."

The language of these simple people was earthy, filled with sexual terms and blasphemy.

That night I couldn't sleep because of the strange conditions I was confronted with. These people all slept close together in a wagon, packed like sardines. They obviously had never heard of soap and water. The stench in that wagon was unbearable! I left and was content to sleep outside and breathe the clean, warm country air. It was so lovely and tranquil under the clear, starry sky that I couldn't imagine why these workers didn't sleep out here in comfort instead of in that abominable wagon. I soon had my answer.

I heard a commotion by the wagon and went over to investigate. I looked inside the wagon and could hardly believe my eyes. The workers were engaged in sex, noisily, freely, with men going from one woman to another. The women who hadn't been serviced yet lay there with their legs open, waiting their turn. It was a revolting sight, for, as I have said, these people were quite dirty. The men didn't even bother to take off their filthy underclothes. They performed their acrobatics in a tangle of pulled-down shorts.

I walked away from the offensive, malodorous orgy and paced the fields, savoring the wonderful night air. One of the tractor operators jumped out of the wagon for a drink and asked me why I wasn't sleeping.

I couldn't tell him the truth, so I said, "It's this invigorating air you have here. I'm enjoying it while I can. We have nothing like this in Moscow, you know."

He laughed heartily and invited me for a night ride on a tractor. I hopped on with him, and we drove around the field. I noticed that he was plowing at a setting of seventeen centimeters down instead of the mandatory twenty-two. I asked him about this, and he said, "My quota is five acres per shift, and if I don't reach that goal, they'll put me in jail for sabotage. It is much easier to plow with less resistance from a shallower soil setting than it is in twenty-two-centimeter-deep soil. They're not looking for quality here—just quantity."

"Doesn't anyone check over your work?" I asked.

"No. Immediately after plowing, I rake the soil, and nobody knows the difference."

Back at the wagon, the sexual smorgasbord was still in progress. These farmers were jumping on each other like grasshoppers in heat. It occurred to me that this was an economical no-nonsense solution to the sex drive. There was no need for an expensive date with flowers, a costly dinner, and a show, with the hope of some lovemaking at the end of the evening. Here one took what one wanted as often as he or she felt the need, and that was that.

The colonel and I returned to Moscow the next day, and the ritual of classes and long study hours resumed.

CHAPTER 22

Policy Shift

Life was good to me. By the spring of 1950, I was well into my course at the Moscow Military Academy, learning much and believing only some. My family was doing well in Poland, living comfortably on my salary and getting together once a month on my leaves.

I remember one spring day when I thought the world was particularly good. It was the first warm day of the new season, when clear skies and balmy breezes swept the last remnants of the winter snows from Moscow—one of those incomparable days that bring joy into men's hearts. I looked forward to the morning's classes, little realizing that a storm was approaching.

We had no sooner than assumed our seats in Professor Bashkatov's class when he announced that the Politburo of the U.S.S.R. had declared that Israel had become an "enemy of Communism." I was shocked.

Soviet Intelligence agents he said, had discovered that Swiss and Israeli agents were collaborating with the United States in an effort to establish a mutual intelligence network to counter Soviet Communist agents around the world. Bashkatov then attacked Israel, recalling the aid that only Communist countries had offered when the helpless Jews were struggling for independence. He reminded us that the United States and Britain had both collaborated on an arms embargo to the threatened Jews of Palestine during the critical months in 1948. He reminded us how the capitalists had maintained a hard line against Jewish immigration to Palestine at a time when every able-bodied man and woman was needed to defend their settlements against Arab attack.

Had the ungrateful Jews of Israel sided with the Soviet Union, he said, they would have expanded their territory to include everything that had been ruled by King Solomon three thousand years before—plus a bit more. Israel would have become secure, he said, and its people could have lived in peace.

Bashkatov's lecture went something like this:

> To think that this nation, which we helped set up to guarantee freedom for millions of Jews, to build her economy and technology, prestige and morale—to think that this ungrateful nation would stab us in the back.
>
> Under our protection, Israel would have become the only major power in the Middle East, with the Suez Canal in its hands. But no—they have forgotten their lamentable history, the Spanish liquidation of three and a half million Jews, the Russian Czarist and Ukrainian pogroms against Jews, Hitler's gas chambers and ovens, and the world-wide anti-Semitism that has held them back for centuries.
>
> The leaders of the international proletariat wanted to extend their helping hands to this small nation, but they have chosen to join with the greedy capitalists. These ingrates want to oppose us who fought and defeated Hitler's forces for the world's survival. They haven't analyzed their history; they have learned nothing from it. They don't realize that the capitalists will bring only death and disintegration to the Jewish nation.
>
> We cannot tolerate such treachery. We are now going to seek a relationship with the Arab nations. We are sending a group of political scientists to Egypt to see what can be done. The Middle East is an important strategic location for the expansion of Communism.
>
> The Suez Canal is a major communication link between East and West. We can't afford to give it up. It is essential to our aims.
>
> We made a big mistake thinking that the untrustworthy Jews would be our allies. We will destroy Israel; that will be our answer to their betrayal. They are now our major obstacle to the planting of Communism in the Middle East.

I was extremely disturbed by Bashkatov's harsh words. I wasn't sure how truthfully he was telling the story. Perhaps the Communists had been unsuccessful in gaining substantial influence with Israel and were covering up their failure by accusing the Jews of anti-Soviet activity. Perhaps they thought they could gain more influence among the Arabs, and had to have some excuse for disowning Israel. Whatever the reason, I vowed to myself that I would not be part of any activity that would make Jews suffer again.

Bashkatov went on to condemn my other country of allegiance—Poland. He told us that the new Polish communists were mostly Trotskyites, and we should therefore be wary of them. He said that in 1939, Russia had found it necessary to kill certain members of the Communist Party—Alfred Lampe, Marian Buczek, and Leon Lenski, secretary of the Communist Party in Poland before the war—who came to Moscow on a visit.

"Building Communism," he said, "is not like building a house. Lives must be sacrificed—even that of your own brother, if need be—to achieve your goal."

Now I was more confused and depressed than ever. "Is this the kind of system I want to live by?" I asked myself. I had grown up believing in God and the teachings of the Bible. "Thou shalt slay thy brother" was not one of the commandments.

I was distressed by Bashkatov's veiled threat to Poland. Again, I couldn't determine the truth of his statements, but I could see that it might be used as an excuse for a major purge in Poland and the initiation of a greater Soviet presence. I knew that I didn't want any part of that bloodshed.

On my next leave home, I discussed the problem with Sabina. After a long conversation, we came to the conclusion that as long as I remained a student at the Moscow Military Academy, I would not have to participate in Soviet schemes that were against my conscience. But unless there was a new policy shift in the Politburo, I would have to resign and somehow escape the country before graduation. I would not be able to work within an intelligence system that sought to destroy both Israel and Poland.

Back at the Academy, I continued my classes and worked particularly hard to learn the machinations of the Soviet intelligence system. I secretly knew that someday I would go to Israel, and all the information I was accumulating would be useful in helping the Israelis resist Soviet pressures and clandestine activity. I became proficient at both the theory and practice of Soviet intelligence and, by the spring of 1953, I knew the system down to its finest details.

During my years at the Academy, I observed the shift in Soviet policy from the euphoria of the postwar years to a nightmare of intrigue, suspicion, and murder as the Communist bloc solidified. Serious conflicts erupted as the Soviets enforced Stalinism throughout Eastern Europe. As these conflicts were crushed, the state became ever more repressive.

Even in Moscow there was an atmosphere of tension, as the son of a Georgian shoemaker named Dzhugashvili withdrew to the inner chambers of the Kremlin. This man, known to the world as Joseph Vissarionovich Stalin, degenerated into macabre paranoia. There were accusations, and there were executions. The "man of steel"—which is what "Stalin" means—discovered that he had feet of clay. The defiant dictator, who had snubbed Hitler's entire army and spat at it in contempt, was now afraid of shadows behind the Kremlin walls.

The entire Soviet political system had descended into Byzantine decadence by the spring of 1953. It could not maintain and follow through on a single policy. Simple procedures became suspect.

Shortly before I was to finish my course at the Academy, Joseph Stalin's death was announced on March 5, 1953, leaving the Soviet political system in unworkable chaos. His death brought an immediate power struggle, and there was much talk of coups. Bulganin, Malenkoff, Beria, Khrushchev, and a half-dozen others scrambled for the seat of the dead war lord. Within a month, we in the Academy understood that no matter who took over, more executions would follow. There was much talk of collective leadership, but we all knew better. The possible ascendancy of Beria was the most feared, for, if anything, the Chief of Soviet Secret Police would be more repressive than Stalin during his worst days. He would not strive to make the Soviet Union a viable, twentieth-century industrial state, as Stalin had.

The situation looked grave, and my prospects for assignment after graduation looked even worse. No matter where I was placed, I would be working in a system that was by then strenuously plotting the destruction of Israel. In addition, I would be new to any unit where I was assigned, and therefore suspect.

With the prospects as bleak as these, I had no alternative. On May 4, 1953, I did the unthinkable: after more than a decade of posing as Mieczyslaw Pruzanski, I drafted a memo to the headquarters of the Polish Army in Warsaw, tendering my resignation and revealing that I was Jewish and hoped to emigrate to Israel.

CHAPTER 23

Imprisonment

My letter proved a bombshell, but I must say that my arrest wasn't very theatrical. Within a week's time, I received a telephone call from the Special Department of Central Military Intelligence. I was commanded to report to that department in Warsaw on May 14, 1953.

We were then living in Sopot and Sabina, pregnant with our second child, became terrified at the prospect of losing me. I was also concerned, because after spending five years in the Moscow Military Academy, I knew how devious the Russians could be—but I tried not to show it, for Sabina's sake.

As for the Poles, having experienced their anti-Semitism from the day I was born, I expected little help from them. So many military officers had been liquidated since the war's end that one more would not rest on anyone's conscience. Another possibility was that I could be shipped off to Siberia and never heard from again, as was the fate of so many officers and civilians who had opposed the Russian takeover.

Before I left our apartment on the day of my appointment, Sabina cried, fearing she would never see me again.

"Don't be ridiculous," I said. "I haven't done anything. All I'm asking for is an army discharge. I have that right. They can't keep me in the service if I don't want to stay."

"I know that," she replied, "but you shouldn't have told them that you wanted to move to Israel. If the Russians are so anti-Israel, they will regard your resignation as an insult and a rejection of their regime."

"That's the risk I must take."

She held onto me for a long time. Our little girl, Dina, had never seen her mother cry before and couldn't understand what was happening. I tried to laugh and make jokes to appease the two of them, but the atmosphere in our small apartment remained grim.

"I have many friends in high places—you know that," I said. "I'm sure they won't let me down."

That seemed to cheer her a bit. "I'll expect you for supper," she said. I kissed Dina tenderly, then she and Sabina followed me downstairs to the street. My wife was so big with the baby that when we attempted to embrace, her huge stomach got in the way. I was certain that our neighbors laughed behind their curtains at this tenderly comic farewell scene. None of them knew my true predicament.

When I arrived at Special Headquarters, I instantly saw that Sabina and I had every right to be frightened. I knew it the moment I ran into one of my fellow officers who had always been friendly with me. Instead of his usual cheery "Good morning, Colonel," he passed in cold silence.

My orders were to report to Captain Kotlas. I knocked on his door, was instructed to enter, and was greeted by chilly stares. Seated next to the captain was his assistant, Lieutenant Sternman, who was obviously serving as a witness to my statements. I was not asked to sit down.

Captain Kotlas had pad and pencil ready and came right to the point. "Why do you wish to resign and take up residence in Israel?"

My intelligence background had prepared me for this question and I had formulated a reply days before. "In Poland, every stone is stained with Jewish blood. I can't rid myself of that nightmare. I can't sleep at night. I can't continue to masquerade as a Pole. I want to move to Israel with my family to help build that nation—and to ease my conscience."

In truth, after five years in Moscow, I had realized that I wanted no part of the Soviet system. My only hope was to break my ties by leaving the Army and going to live among my own people in Israel.

Lieutenant Sternman jumped up, strode over to me, and despite my higher rank, snatched the gun from my belt and bellowed, "Colonel, you are under arrest."

That was it. No hearing, no trial, no further questions. It was the typical Soviet solution to any problem. Lieutenant Sternman further humiliated me by searching me in front of the other officers, taking all my personal belongings, and refusing to answer any of my questions. "Silence!" he barked and escorted me to a small cell crowded with twenty other jailed intelligence officers.

"If I have to stay here very long," I thought, "I'll lose my mind." The cell was dark, with only one small bulb in the ceiling for illumination, and no windows. The small beds were in tiers, and each had to accommodate two officers.

"What are you doing here, Colonel?" one of the men asked in surprise. I recognized Lieutenant Gerski, an officer who had fought for the liberation of Poland with me. I shook his hand and told him only that I wished to resign from the Army.

"They won't stand for that," he said, shaking his head. "After all, they sent you to the Military Academy of Moscow. You know too much."

I asked the officer why he had been arrested. "For the same reason most of us are in here—because of some innocent remark that has been misconstrued as criticism of the Soviets."

I discovered that most of these men had been confined to this cell for months, cut off entirely from the outside world. No newspapers or visitors were permitted, no radio, no mail, no communication with loved ones.

I sat on one of the bunks and buried my face in my hands. I had lost my entire family in the war—my parents and four sisters—with the only survivor being my brother Nathan. I had handled this tragedy with stoic control, believing that once the Germans had been crushed, our problems would be over.

Now, trapped in this nightmarish cell with these doomed men, I reached the point of despair. One holocaust had simply been replaced by another.

My first thought was of Sabina, waiting for me at home, preparing a supper that would never be consumed. I sobbed quietly. My friend put his hand on my shoulder and begged me to stay calm: "The only way you'll survive this dungeon is by keeping control of yourself."

A guard unlocked the cell door and began distributing bowls of murky soup and some bread. My stomach was so upset that I declined the bowl, but my friend took it for me. "I'll see that he eats," he said to the guard.

He attempted to give me the bowl, but I pushed it away. "You eat it," I said, "I couldn't keep it down."

The other prisoners drank their soup greedily. "You'd better have a little," I was advised. "They only serve us twice a day." I shrugged and refused the soup.

Word soon got around the cell that I was a war hero because some of the officers had earlier heard of me. They were a friendly lot and offered their condolences, but their pessimistic outlook on our chances only made me more depressed.

Lieutenant Gerski showed me an empty bunk and advised me to try to get some sleep.

How could I sleep when faced with the uncertainty of ever seeing my family again and with the possibility of Siberia or death?

I lay on my bunk and turned from side to side. All my life, I had been a forceful, decisive person. There was one human condition I could not tolerate: uncertainty. I wanted to know immediately why I was being detained, how long the authorities planned to keep me here, and what would happen to my family if they had no further news of me. My impatient nature demanded that someone answer these questions immediately, yet I knew that was impossible.

The thought that these other men had been caged here for months, with no hope of escape or pardon, caused me to tremble. I remembered Lieutenant Gerski's caution to control myself and heeded his words.

But anger inflamed my brain and made sleep impossible. My nerves got the best of me, causing a cramp in my foot which made me jump off the bunk. Two of the men came over and asked if I was all right. "Yes," I said feebly, "just a little cramp, that's all."

"That's the least of your troubles," one of them replied.

Although I had never understood the motives that drove people to suicide, if it weren't for my wife and children, I might have contemplated calling it a day. Prolonged life in this cell seemed far worse than death.

I lay down again and tried to relax. The men around me were so defeated and so forlorn and hopeless that they spoke in low, weary tones. Their conversations sounded like the buzzings of insects. "Wait . . . wait . . . that's all we do . . . ," I heard one of them complain.

"The Jew has taught me how to wait . . . ," I suddenly remembered. It was a line from an Ibsen play that had always fascinated me. I couldn't remember the exact quotation, but it had something to do with learning something from each nationality—manners from the French, industry from the British, good fortune from the Americans, *dolce far neinte* from Italians. And from the Jew—how to wait.

For centuries the Jew had been waiting for the Messiah, for deliverance from bondage, for the promised land, for freedom from persecution, for the death of tyrants like Hitler. Although I was a Jew, I had never mastered the virtue of patience. My father had preached patience all his life, but I could never exercise it. The tranquillity of resignation was not for me.

But now, I had no choice. My only hope lay in help from the outside—from some of my influential friends—but that would take time. I regretted not having given Sabina more specific instructions as to what to do if I didn't return that day. My fear of upsetting her had made me play down the danger of my situation. There were many people she could turn to for help, and I should have discussed this in detail with her. It was too late now. If no visitors or letters were permitted, it might take months before she could persuade one of my military friends to intercede on my behalf.

I found myself dozing off, but only for short spells. Images of the past flashed through my mind, of faces long dead and forgotten, of happy childhood days when I could sneak out and play soccer, and of less happy occasions when I was forced to attend the Yeshiva.

But every time I dozed off, I was sharply awakened by the guard calling out a name. Each time, it was a different name. Whoever was called left the cell under escort and seemed to stay away for hours. It was probably some all-night work detail, like cleaning the latrine or some other menial task.

Once when I awoke, my eye caught sight of a black shape moving about on the floor below my bunk. It was a huge rat surveying the cell for food or human flesh. I made a noise, and it scurried away.

In the morning, when the guard brought our 7:00 a.m. soup, I still couldn't drink it. I gave it to Lieutenant Gerski, who would have preferred me to have it.

"Did you sleep, Colonel?" he asked.

"A little. That guard kept waking me up. Why was he calling out names in the middle of the night?"

"You'll get used to that. They'll be calling your name out soon enough."

"What for?"

"Interrogation." He lowered his voice. "You know the Soviet system."

Of course, it should have dawned on me. It was an old

psychological trick of the Russians to interrogate a man when he's groggy, to further break down his morale and resistance.

"My wife is pregnant," I confided to Lieutenant Gerski. "I don't suppose they'll give me any news of her?"

He shook his head. "And don't ask the guards for information. It's only a waste of time."

I felt myself shaking again, but put a stop to it immediately. There was nothing to do but wait.

As the days went by, I gradually grew accustomed to the monotony of life in that cell. We were fed only twice a day, allowed only one shower per week, and confined to the cell at all times, except when being interrogated at night. We were not permitted to sleep during the day and it was impossible to have a full night's rest with the incessant noise of the guard calling out prisoners.

Days slipped by and since there was nothing else to do, I began to fill them with memories of the past—daydreams about old Warsaw, the war, and my postwar life. This was what was expected of me anyway, for the Soviet penal system is based, in part, on the prisoners own review of his life and the faults that have brought him to ill fortune.

A few weeks after I was imprisoned, I awoke from my sleep in the middle of the night and, from the corner of my eye, saw an unfamiliar shape at the far end of the cell. My eye was riveted to a shadow. When you're trapped in a small room for any length of time, you grow accustomed to the unchanging sights, sounds, and smells of your entombment. This shadow was new and frightening. I tried to focus my gaze. The shadow swinging to and fro and appeared to be cast from the end of the cell where the bathroom was.

I sat up in my bunk and realized what I was looking at. It was a human form suspended from the ceiling of the bathroom.

I cried out and ran toward the light. Some of the prisoners woke up and cursed me for the commotion I was causing. Soon everyone sat up and followed me into the bathroom.

There, hanging from the ceiling, his trousers serving as his noose, was young Carl Zbigniew, a 23-year-old Pole. Although I never had a lengthy conversation with him, I knew from what I heard around me that Carl had been a brilliant student in the intelligence school in Warsaw. Six months after his graduation, he was imprisoned by the Soviets because he refused to arrest a Catholic priest.

"I'm a Socialist, but I'm also a Roman Catholic, and I would never arrest a man who is God's representative on this earth,'' he reportedly told the authorities who interrogated him.

We cut his noose and lifted him onto a table, but it was too late. He had forfeited his own representation on this earth. My cellmates said he had been talking about suicide lately, but no one took him seriously because suicide threats were a dime a dozen in that cell.

"He felt guilty about having attended a Soviet intelligence school,'' Lieutenant Gerski told me. "As it often happens with the young, he didn't know what he was getting into. Then, when they ordered him to arrest a Catholic priest, it violated his basic religious beliefs. He realized that in order to be a true Communist, he must renounce his religion, and that proved too much for him. He went into a state of shock, and committed an act that, according to his religion, will condemn him to hell.''

The young man's suicide shocked me, but I was even more disturbed by its aftermath. Shortly after we cut down the body the guards appeared, then a battery of Soviet officers. As usual, they were well prepared with printed forms that swiftly disposed of this unpleasantness. We were asked to sign these forms, which served as a promise that we would never reveal what we had witnessed in that bathroom. The Soviets could not bear to acknowledge that anyone would be unhappy in their paradise, even if the person was in a jail.

We all returned to our bunks, but sleep was impossible. I had seen countless deaths during the war, had even killed numerous Germans without feeling any pangs of conscience, but this boy's suicide depressed me beyond consolation. Although I didn't know him well, he seemed to be a fine young man, brilliant, well-mannered and soft-spoken. Any other nation would have found him a sterling asset.

A month passed, and still I was lingering in uncertainty. There had been no interrogation, not a word of what was to happen to me. Nor did I have any information about my family. Sabina must have had our baby by now.

My pain was eased only because I knew precisely what my jailers were doing to me. They knew that my wife was expecting a child; they knew I would be desperately searching for the slightest clue as to the fate of my family. As time passed, they knew I would worry about my family's financial stability and future. Time was on their side. The longer they waited, the more I would worry, and worry would wear me down. That was why they never interrogated me or even recognized my existence except with my daily bowls of soup. They would continue this psychological torture until they thought I was ripe.

I waited too, and reviewed everything I had learned at the Moscow Military Academy. I became involved in a mental chess game where I sat across the board from my captors.

I was dubbed "The Silent Man" by my cellmates, for I rarely engaged in conversation with them. I took no one into my confidence and told no one that I was a Jew. There were surely informers slipped in among the prisoners, agents who would carefully observe each of the cellmates. I offered these informers precisely what the jailers were looking for, a silent man plagued by worry.

But I knew what I was doing. I could worry, but I would keep my wits. When the interrogation did come, if it were to come at all, I would be as formidable as possible.

By mid-June, I was still enveloped in silence. I had lost about twenty-five pounds and played my role as best I could. I had also become one of the senior prisoners in the cell, for most of the inmates who were there on my arrival, including Lieutenant Gerski, had disappeared into the midnight interrogation and never returned. I never did learn of Gerski's fate.

New prisoners replaced old ones, and, frequently, they plied me with questions. But most often I told them I simply didn't know. Nor did I bother to ask them questions about the outside world.

For a while, I tried to play a mental diversion game of trying to identify which of my cellmates was most likely to be an informer. I had a few suspects, but no means of confirming my suspicions, so I gave up the game before I was frustrated.

The beginning of August marked the tenth week of my imprisonment, and still I had not left the cell. There had been no interrogation since Captain Kotlas's single question so long ago. I was weary. I avoided looking at my face in the bathroom mirror. I was becoming so haggard that I didn't want to see myself. My jailers were pushing me to the limit.

Then it came. The guards marched to the cell door in the middle of the night, summoning me for interrogation.

Nothing jars me more than being awakened from a deep sleep late at night. It upsets my stomach and makes me irritable, which is exactly what the Russians wanted. It is much simpler to successfully interrogate a man whose nerves are on edge.

I was escorted out of the cell by silent guards. We walked down a long, dank corridor and entered a small, harshly lit room. I could barely keep my eyes open. After my vision adjusted to the glare, I noted that Colonel Kohl, Chief of Polish Intelligence, was seated at a desk, flanked by two Jewish assistants, Colonel Kozemien and Colonel Feigen, a well-known lawyer and defender of Polish Communists before the war.

Standing before these men in that unnerving room made me feel like the accused victim in a Kafka novel.

I was not greeted or asked to sit down. I had known these men during my years in intelligence. Now, they regarded me with frigid stares.

"Are you a nationalist?" Colonel Kohl asked for starters.

"No, Sir."

"Then why do you wish to go to Israel when we have spent a fortune training you for Soviet intelligence?"

"I feel that what I would be doing here, I could do just as well in Israel."

The response took him a little off guard, but he was still suspicious. "Then why didn't you request a transfer before tendering your resignation?"

"I agree. That's what I should have done."

Colonel Feigen then put a very delicate question to me. "If we refuse to allow you to go to Israel, would you comply with our decision?"

I took a moment before answering. I realized that I was not dealing with human beings, but with ruthless totalitarian puppets. I decided to take the advice of their master, Lenin: "Fight your enemies with white gloves."

"Surely, I wouldn't attempt to contradict the Party's wishes. But I would like to say what I feel."

"And what exactly is it that you feel?"

"I feel that my place is in Israel. I do not feel at home in Poland, where my people's blood has stained the landscape. I am depressed and unable to function efficiently in this atmosphere."

"When you applied for intelligence work, you did not state on the questionnaire that you were Jewish," Colonel Kohl snapped. "That lie alone could land you in jail for five years."

"I didn't lie," I said. "I answered every question truthfully. My nationality is Polish. There was no question about my religion on that form."

The interrogation continued for several hours, and I did my best to stick by all the Leninist philosophy and tactics that had been pumped into my head throughout the past decade. I kept my "white gloves" on and went as far as I could to avoid offending anyone. "One step back, two steps forward." Somehow, I felt all the training I had gone through had taken control of me. My responses were nearly automatic, quick enough to convince the questioners that my words were spontaneous and I was a true Party man.

"Do you have any questions before you return to your cell?" Colonel Feigen asked.

"Yes," I said. "My wife, she was about to give birth when I was arrested. Did she have the baby? Does she have enough to live on?"

"She had a baby girl," Colonel Kohl replied. "And they are being provided with ample funds."

I returned to my cell feeling somewhat optimistic. I felt that I had handled myself well through the interrogation. I had also learned about my family. I looked forward to new developments and to the day I would finally leave my prison cell behind. It was my first moment of relief since I had entered this sadistic, wretched place.

Weeks later, I had a dramatic and tearful reunion with my wife whom my tormentors finally allowed to visit me. We sat in a small visitors' cell while a stony-faced guard at the door looked on grimly. They let her bring some provisions, kielbassa, and some cheese, but confiscated the sweets. She brought no bread in the mistaken belief that this was all I was fed. When she heard I rarely received bread she wanted to go out to get some, but of course, neither the guards nor the prison officials would consider this. They told her all she had was a half-hour with me. I was so happy to see her that nothing else mattered. Before she left, I whispered to her that she should discreetly try to get help from the Israeli Embassy.

After Sabina's departure, the dreary routine continued for days and weeks with no end in sight. I was turning into the most senior prisoner in the cell. Then, one morning, when I was in the depths of depression, a guard entered the cell and called out, "Pruzanski! Step forward!"

There wasn't the usual complement of guards, so it was obvious I wasn't being taken anywhere.

"Here," he said, offering me a razor, "Use this."

I took the blade and looked at it. "Do you want me to cut my throat," I asked, "or my wrists?"

"Shave," he ordered. "And be fast about it! After you've shaved and had breakfast, you're free to go."

I couldn't believe what he said.

"Is this some kind of joke?" I asked.

"No joke," he replied glumly. "They're letting you out. You better not ask any questions, or they may change their minds."

"Get out while the getting's good," one of my cell-mates shouted. "I wouldn't even bother to shave or have breakfast."

"He must shave," the guard warned. "He can't leave here in this condition."

"Don't worry," I said, "I'll do what you want."

I rushed to the bathroom and shaved in record time, cutting myself but impervious to the blood. Some of the prisoners watched me. I felt great pity for them. They all craved their freedom as desperately as I did, but at the moment they had little hope. Several of them asked me to give messages to their wives, families, and girlfriends. I swore to each of them I would deliver their messages, remembering my own earlier suffering, when I had no idea how my wife and my chlld were surviving without me. A few of them cried when I shook their hands and said my farewells.

The guard brought me the clothes I had been arrested in, including my heavy winter overcoat. I dressed quickly and decided to skip breakfast, even though I was hungry. At any moment, I expected an officer to enter and announce that my pardon had been rescinded. The faster I got out of there, the better.

On the other hand, at the last moment, before shaking all my cellmates' hands, I had another dark notion. Knowing the Soviets as well as I did, could it be possible that once I stepped out of that building, I would be an easy target for an assassination? I would have to keep a sharp lookout for cars following me or agents tailing me.

As much as I loathed that cell, I felt distressed at leaving behind so many unhappy men. I wished I could take them all home with me, but that was a fantasy. I told them all not to worry. After all, I had been in that prison longer than any of them. I told them to be patient, and they, too, would be liberated.

The guard escorted me to Special Headquarters. Lieutenant Sternman wasn't there, and that gave me some hope. Colonel Kohl was talking to some friends. He turned to me, rather stiffly and said, "You are free, but before you go there are papers you must sign. You will swear that you will not attempt to leave this country and that you will follow the Politburo's instructions. After all, they have spent a fortune educating you in Moscow to be an intelligence officer."

I found myself signing about twenty different documents without bothering to read them. The colonel made certain that I had properly signed all the papers, then handed me the few personal belongings I had when I'd arrived at the prison. He did not shake my hand or wish me luck; he merely resumed a conversation with his friends, who were eyeing me curiously.

If you have never been in prison, you can't imagine the exaltation of walking out of one into the balm of freedom. I felt like dancing in the street.

I had no money, I was starved, but I was deliriously happy. I stopped at the street corner, wondering which way to turn. Here I was in the city of my birth, broke, with no job, and a wife at home in Sopot with two small daughters. There were no members of my family left in this wasteland to help me. My only hope was help from old friends. But I didn't even have a few coins for the carfare to get to their houses.

My immediate concern was to notify Sabina about my liberation. I stopped at the post office and made a collect call to her. When she heard that I was free and was calling from the post office, she let out a cry of joy. "Don't worry, it's true. I'll be home with you tonight," I assured her.

My next stop was to obtain some money so I could get home. I could go to some of my Jewish friends who lived within walking distance and tell them, at last, that I was a Jew. It suddenly occurred to me that my new-found freedom also gave me the liberty of saying, after all these years of suppression, "Yes—I'm a Jew."

There was one drawback, however, to unmasking myself. If I suddenly revealed that I was Jewish, they could conceivably turn against me, for Jews who had become Communists tended to be more dedicated to the cause than the Pope to Catholicism. They might now perceive me to be an enemy of the state because I had been jailed for so long. It was difficult to speculate how former "friends" might react to the prison cloud that was hanging over my head. These self-righteous Communists might wonder if I could be trusted as a loyal party member or if I was now too dangerous to be a "friend."

Finally, I decided to contact Stefan Matuszewski, a friend and a Socialist ex-priest who was now director of the Party's Revision Committee. I walked to the Central Committee building and told a receptionist that I was an old comrade wanting to see Mr. Matuszewski. The woman looked at me somewhat suspiciously, but relayed my request to her boss. I suppose I must have appeared shaky to her because I had lost so much weight in prison that my clothes didn't fit properly—not to mention my sloppy shaving job. When he heard that I was waiting, he came down himself to greet me.

Stefan was thoroughly shocked at my appearance. He asked me to come upstairs to his office, and before we talked, he ordered some breakfast for me.

"I don't want you to say a word until you've eaten," he said. "I'm afraid I might lose you unless I get some food in you first."

The breakfast tasted like the finest meal I ever had. After the slop we were served in prison, this restored my spirit and my energy.

Slowly, I recounted to Stefan everything that had happened to me after I had sent in my letter of resignation. He listened quietly, never interrupting, and I could see that he was moved by my plight.

When I finished my tale of woe, Stefan put his hand on my shoulder and said, "Don't worry—I'll help you. Before you leave this room, I'll not only give you money, but I'll manage to find a decent job for you. With your education, background, and experience, you belong in the academic world."

"I would like that very much," I said.

Stefan told me to relax while he made some phone calls. I sat down on a comfortable couch and started reading a newspaper. Even that small act seemed a luxury after months of deprivation. Soon I was fast asleep. The excitement of getting out of jail and suddenly finding myself in warm surroundings with a kind friend was overwhelming for me in my present weakened state.

I felt a hand gently shaking my shoulder and, for a split second, I thought it was a guard waking me in my cell. Fortunately, it was Stefan, and for a change there was some good news.

First of all, he had been able to secure a brand-new, two-bedroom apartment for me in a recently constructed building with modern conveniences. Secondly, he had been able to place me in a professorial position at Poznan University to teach the history and principles of Marxism and Leninism. As a final gesture of generosity, he gave me three thousand zlotys, which would support my family for more than a month.

I was pleased at the prospect of returning to my wife's hometown. What's more, Stefan told me that my old friend and benefactor, Conrad Janasek, was there, although things hadn't gone well for him. He had opposed the coalition of the Polish

Socialist Party and the Polish Labor Party. As a result, he was ousted from his party and now held an insignificant post.

There was no end to Stefan's aid at this time. He used his influence to ensure that my membership in the Writers' Union would not be canceled, despite my jail experience, so that I could continue with the journalistic work I had begun in Moscow.

When he had finally finished the phone calls that reorganized my life and it was time for me to leave, I embraced him and thanked him for his kindness. "I shall never forget how you helped me at the lowest ebb of my life. I only hope that someday I can repay you for your generosity."

"Please don't embarrass me," he said. "After all you've been through, it's the least I could do."

I promised to keep him informed of my activities and also promised to pay him back.

"Don't worry about it," he said. "Just be very careful of your movements from now on. I'm sure you're being watched."

Stefan was more than right. I took a cab to the railway station and after a few moments, the driver said to me, "I think we're being followed by two men. Look in my rearview mirror. Do you recognize them?"

I looked in his mirror and saw a car following us. As far as I could tell, I had never seen these men before. My mind started conjuring up fantasies. Were the Soviets going to fake an accident in order to get rid of me? Thank God I hadn't gone to the Israeli Embassy; they surely would have assassinated me.

"I can lose them—if you wish," my driver said.

"Good—do that. I don't know them, but they have no business following me."

The driver knew all the city's twists and turns and quickly lost them on the way to the railway station. I gave him an ample tip and he happily drove off.

Luckily, my train was there when I arrived and I was able to board it without being detected. I watched the station platform through my compartment's window, but did not see the men who had earlier been following me. By the time the train departed, I was fast asleep.

Once again, a hand was shaking my shoulder. This time it was the train conductor. I thanked him for awakening me at my stop.

By the time I arrived at our apartment, it was 2:00 a.m. Sabina was waiting for me, and when I knocked on the door, she opened it so quickly that I almost fell into the room. She held me close for several moments, then said, "Now come and see the baby."

She brought me into the bedroom and there in a crib lay the loveliest surprise I have ever seen. "Her name is Elizabeth," Sabina said. I wanted to pick up this baby and hold her in my arms, but she was sleeping so peacefully that I didn't dare wake her. Then I felt a tugging at my leg. It was Dina demanding her share of attention. I scooped her up into my arms and danced around the room with her. I was so exhilarated at being home that I talked for hours.

"I have so much to tell you," I said to Sabina, "that I'm afraid I'll have to put it all in a book. It would be easier. But I can give you some good news now."

I told her the wonderful things that Stefan had done for us and showed her the two documents he had given me: one for the apartment, the other for my new position at the university. Then I took the money he had loaned me out of my pocket.

Instead of seeming happy, Sabina looked pensive. She got up and walked to the window with a frown on her face.

"What's wrong, darling? I thought you'd be grateful for Stefan's help."

"Of course I am. He's a saint, as far as I'm concerned. But I had my heart set on leaving this country and settling in Israel. Instead, you've found another apartment in Poland, which means moving again, and a job in Poznan, which means staying in this country. Here we are, stuck in this miserable nation where I'll live in fear that someday you'll be arrested again."

"I know. I understand your feelings. But I've had a lot of time in prison to think about our situation and I decided one thing. I know too much about the Soviet intelligence system to be let out of this country. They'll kill me if I try to leave."

I decided not to tell her about the two men who had tailed me after I left Stefan.

You're right," she said, "but with your background in intelligence and your knowledge of loopholes, surely we can find a way to get out. We did the impossible before, and we can do it again. We'll bide our time and won't tell anyone about our plans—and someday we'll find a way to get out forever."

We went to bed and I held Sabina tightly for hours, trying to make up for all of the months I was in prison alone. It was so good to be back home with my wife and precious daughters. I suddenly felt a surge of optimism and a new-found strength to overcome my uncertain future. I must now be very careful not to talk about my imprisonment or to make any political comments whatsoever. There was no doubt that I would be watched carefully. And with all of the secret listening devices being used by the government, we would even have to censor what we said at home.

We moved to Poznan at the end of September. Our new apartment, overlooking the old city hall tower with a whimsical clock, was very pleasant. Shortly after we moved in, Sabina made a confession to me.

"I knew that you would be freed from that prison," she said.

"How did you know that?"

"Remember that brief visit I had with you?"

I nodded.

"I took your advice. You told me to go to the Israeli Embassy. I went there and was able to see Moshe Dagan. When I told him your story, he called Ben Gurion, who instructed him to get in touch with a Mr. Wolski at the Ministry of the Interior. He was a friend of Ben Gurion's, and he said that he would take care of the matter. Moshe called the man, and Wolski said that he could be of help. It might take a little time, but he would do his best to get you out. And he did."

"Why didn't you tell me this before? I would have written him and all the others a letter of gratitude."

"No, they didn't want you to do that. They wanted to keep the whole thing as quiet as possible and asked me not to tell you for a few weeks."

I kissed her tenderly. "Thank God that I married an intelligent woman. You're the best agent I ever met."

CHAPTER 24

Academy

The academic world suited me. It was pleasant to be away from the military's intermittent intrigue and boredom. I was teaching political science—the doctrines of Marx and Lenin. My students were affable, eager to learn, and overly impressed with my war record and subsequent studies at the Moscow Military Academy. I enjoyed my classes with them immensely.

Most important of all, however, this new life afforded me enough leisure time to continue writing. In 1953, I pubished a book that I was instructed to write, called *Two Worlds*, which dealt with the inevitable defeat of capitalism by communism. This work became popular throughout Eastern Europe and was an even greater success, naturally in Russia. It is still widely read in Soviet satellite nations, although I never agreed with most of what I wrote. Its success brought me added luster on campus and the usual petty jealousies among my colleagues at the university.

Just as the satisfactions of college life were beginning to restore me to sanity, I received a jaring phone call. A male voice with a military tone said that I would have to report to Intelligence Headquarters in Warsaw once a month to sign my name.

"Who is this?" I asked with annoyance.

"Colonel Feigen of Intelligence," he replied coldly.

"Why can't I do that in the intelligence office in Poznan?"

"You will do as we command. We wish to see you, in person, once a month in Warsaw." He told me which day to report, then hung up.

I told Sabina what had happened and she said, "How did they ever get our telephone number?"

"Intelligence is their business," I reminded her. "You can't escape from the grasp of their tentacles."

So, once a month I traveled to Warsaw, signed my name in a record book, then returned to Poznan on the next train.

At the university, I became friendly with the school's president, Professor Szurkiewicz. Both of us were invited to a dinner in Warsaw in honor of the Jewish writer Ilya Ehrenburg, who had miraculously escaped Stalin's purges. I still found it necessary to hide my true identity, but I was interested to meet this man, whom I considered an authority on Jewish current affairs.

The dinner was delightful: good food, excellent wines, and stimulating conversations. I felt flattered when the guest of honor told us that he had read *Two Worlds* and other works of mine.

When I found myself alone with Ilya Ehrenburg for a moment, I summoned the courage to speak frankly with him.

"I would like to ask you a rather delicate question."

He regarded me with sorrowful eyes and replied, "Why not? Speak to me as you would to your father. If I can answer your question, it will make me very happy."

"I have heard something, and I wish you could verify it. Is it true that Marshal Voroshiloff shot Stalin because the Marshal's wife is Jewish and Stalin had issued orders to remove all Jews from Moscow?"

The writer thought for a moment, then answered, "It's not important who shot whom. What's important is that Stalin made a mistake in thinking that every Jew is a nationalist."

I had another question—one that was closer to my heart. "What will happen now between Russia and Israel? Their relationship seems to be deteriorating by the day."

"You seem to be preoccupied by Jewish affairs," he said. "Do you have a Jewish background?"

"Yes, I am Jewish, but in order to survive Hitler I had to pose as a Pole. I still haven't revealed my identity here in Poznan."

He made no comment. But in answer to my question, he said, "You see, Israel chose the wrong way to survive as a nation. No capitalist country will guarantee Israel's security; only the Soviet Union can do that. Only our communist nation could make the necessary investment to ensure the development and spiritual rebirth of Israel. History shows that no capitalist system survives in the long run. Look at the Roman Empire and all the empires after it. They all fell."

His words disturbed me. When I went home that night, I repeated this conversation to Sabina, who said, "Then if he's right, Israel will be destroyed again? We struggled for this country for two thousand years—and now what?"

We can do nothing but follow the course of history," I said, "and whatever happens to other nations can happen to us."

"What if he is right? I thought I wanted to go to Israel," she said, "but now I'm not sure. I'm almost afraid to leave here."

"Sabina, it's so difficult to make the proper choice in this demented world," I said. "I too wonder if you can rely on capitalist countries. Will time prove Ehrenburg to be correct?"

I gave these matters much thought, and despite my loss of faith in the Soviet system, I had to admit that there were some advantages to it. One could not deny the accomplishments of the Russians in Eastern European countries. They had rebuilt devastated towns, restored destroyed factories, put up new housing, and organized a school system that welcomed every social class in the nation. They took care of four million orphans and eight million old people who had no means of support after the war.

For centuries, Poland had been a war corridor through which marauding armies had marched, devastating everything in their path. The Russians had organized new agricultural reforms through which every peasant was allotted land. These farmers and their ancestors had been exploited through history by feudal and capitalistic systems. The Russians mobilized Poland's human resources on a massive scale and restored the industrial base of the economy transforming the Polish nation into a productive satellite state.

Poland was divided into seventeen districts. Thanks to the Soviets, some of these districts had more students in school than the whole country had before the war. Disabled veterans and senior citizens were well cared for. Those who were able to work in light industry were employed by the state and became self-supporting, instead of being humiliated by having to beg, borrow, or live on welfare. The Russians exercised their control to restore dignity and purpose to millions of broken lives in Poland.

On the other hand, if the Russians had effected so many desirable changes, why was such a high percentage of the population anxious to get out of Poland? While they'd gained economically and educationally, relatively speaking, under Soviet domination, they were still lacking the most precious gift of all: freedom. You could have all the comforts of the world in your home, but if you had to stay cooped up inside like a recluse, all those luxuries would seem meaningless.

I had been denied my freedom for six months, and could now

appreciate limited liberty. But the average person in postwar Poland felt restricted under the Soviet system. Enough people who complained had disappeared, proving that communist repression was more than wild imagination. All of the Soviet satellites were exploited in ways familiar to the Czars of old. Before the war, there had been two classes of citizens: capitalists and the working class. Now, ironically we still had two classes of citizens: the Party members, who enjoyed privileges and luxuries available only to them, and the subservient non-Party members, who scarcely received life's necessities.

The nations under Soviet rule all played significant roles in serving Russian militaristic and expansionist aims. They helped build up a mighty arsenal while working for wages that barely covered living expenses. Party members were entitled to buy much merchandise at fifty percent off, in secret discount stores, which made them feel vastly superior to non-Party members. Brains were not an asset for a Party member. All that was required was a pair of strong hands. Anyone with intelligence and independence was mistrusted, blacklisted, and suppressed.

The goods manufactured in Communist countries were sold to the Soviet Union at cost, yielding no profit at the price levels established by the Soviets. This exploitation occurred not only in Poland, but in all other sixteen Soviet Republics. The average worker could only afford a new pair of shoes and a new suit every five years. And there was no complaining. If you voiced a protest, you quickly vanished.

In 1954, the Polish Politburo organized a seminar in Sopot-Gdansk to be attended by leading writers from Communist countries. I was honored to be one of the few authors asked to sit at the presidium with Wladyslaw Gomulka's wife Sylvia as a representative of Polish journalists. Among the many distinguished guests were Madam Curie's daughter from Paris and Boris Pasternak.

Many of my colleagues at the university were jealous of the honor accorded me, but it was not of my doing. My book, *Two Worlds*, was my passport to this seminar.

The major theme of the conference was the eventual revolution against capitalist regimes and the triumphant takeover of Communism. Representatives from each Communist nation reported on the progress the Party was making in that country and the methods employed to win over the populace.

Madam Curie's daughter, Eve, made a ringing speech denouncing Trotskyism, especially as practiced in some nations. Her

plea was for unadulterated Russian Communism. She denounced
General Marcus, commander of the Greek Communist partisans,
as a deviant, to be ousted because of his Trotskyite leanings. If it
hadn't been for his obdurate stand, she claimed, Greece would
now be a hundred percent Communist and would serve Russia as
an essential military base against capitalist countries in the
Mediterranean.

The next speaker was Boris Pasternak, who gave the impression of being a cold, selfish man. He talked interminably and
never made his points clear. He seemed more interested in the
sound of his flowery prose than in the meaning of his words. The
gist of his monologue seemed to be that capitalism and communism could never merge successfully, a message that was hardly
worth the oratory expended.

One spring morning in May, 1956, on my way to the university,
I ran into a huge demonstration of working people protesting
their deplorable working conditions and the outlawing of bonuses
by local Party leaders. The protesters carried large banners
proclaiming:

WE WANT OUR 40% BONUSES BACK
WE WANT TO FEED OUR CHILDREN
WE WANT AFFORDABLE FOOD PRICES
OUR WAGES CANNOT PAY FOR OUR
    LIVING EXPENSES
WE DESERVE BETTER CONDITIONS THAN THE
    GESTAPO LEFT US

The strikers meant business. They locked the regional First
Secretary, Stasiak, in his office and demanded these changes.
Then they marched to the Polish Security Office, where about
38,000 political prisoners were being held.

The police and the Polish Army units stationed in Poznan
refused to shoot into the crowds. Surprisingly, they gave up their
weapons to the demonstrators without a fight. The rioters attempted to enter the police building to take it over, but were held
back by gunfire from the windows. They kept the station surrounded all night, and there were heavy civilian casualties. Once
again, the duplicity of the Soviets was established. During the
night, Russian Army units stationed at Poznan put on Polish
uniforms and shot indiscriminately into the crowds, killing men,
women, and children. The bodies were left in the streets for
several days, so that activists could see what happened to those

who opposed the regime. I had unpleasant flashbacks of similar atrocities committed by the Nazis, when I was an underground fighter in Warsaw.

But the demonstration had a measure of success. In a few weeks, Gomulka was restored to power as First Secretary of the Communist Party. In order to check the revolution, the Party made some concessions.

Still, about fifty thousand people were arrested as "political activists." The Poznan jail could not hold that many prisoners, so they were sent to nearby towns. The hospitals were jammed with the wounded, and when the final tally was taken, a shocking three thousand persons had been killed in the riot. That was Russia's gift to the Polish people.

The following day, the newspapers published the names of those who had led the uprising. To my surprise, I found the name of my old friend Conrad Janasek, whom Sabrina and I saw often now that we were in Poznan. I called Sabina to tell her about him, and we decided that we must try to get him pardoned.

Colonel Karol, who was chief of Military Intelligence in Poznan, and his wife were good friends of ours dating back to my days in the KGB. I called the colonel and asked if he could help Conrad. I also inquired if Sabina could bring Conrad a package of food and cigarettes.

"Yes, that's no problem. But I'll have to call you back regarding your other request."

We didn't hear from him for several hours. When he called, his tone was more official than friendly. "I'm sorry, but nothing can be done for your friend until the committee has decided how these activists are to be punished."

"Which committee?" I asked.

"Colonel Paszko and a special committee are coming here from Warsaw to investigate the uprising."

I found that of interest. The colonel was one of my former Intelligence colleagues.

The following day, Sabina prepared a package for Conrad with food, cigarettes, and newspapers. She brought it to the jail and was treated very coldly when she asked to see Conrad. However, when she mentioned that Colonel Karol had approved her visit, she was told to wait.

It was two hours before Conrad was permitted to see her, and when he finally came out, Sabina suffered a shock. His face was badly swollen and there was a nasty gash on his forehead.

"My God!" Sabina cried out, "what have they done to you?"

"Sabina," he said in a low tone, "don't say a word. They listen to everything we say. You're young, and you must not get involved with my activities."

Conrad asked about me and was relieved to hear that I, at least, was free. But before anything more could be said, a guard interrupted them and said their time was up. She handed him the package, though she doubted that Conrad would ever get to enjoy the contents.

When I got home that night, I found Sabina sitting with Colonel Karol's wife and crying. She told me how they had beaten Conrad and how swollen and bruised he had looked.

I called Colonel Karol and asked him if anything could be done to stop the police from beating Conrad.

"How do you know they're beating him?" he said.

"Sabina saw him today."

"Oh," he said very cautiously. "Well, that's the last time she'll be able to see him." Obviously he was afraid of the political overtones in the case and would have nothing more to do with it.

The colonel asked his wife to wait there for him. In about an hour, he arrived to pick her up and warned both Sabina and me not to attempt to help Conrad. "It's very risky for you to get involved—especially you, who have been in jail. They might throw you right back in using your friendship with Conrad as an excuse to brand you as a collaborator."

"He's right, darling," Sabina said. "We can't let that happen."

Still, I couldn't sit back and allow my friend to be tortured by these goons. That night after dinner, Sabina and I went to the hotel where young Colonel Paszko was staying. We called his room, and he told us to come right up.

When we arrived at his suite, he greeted us warmly and served us coffee. I told him why I had come to see him. "After all, Conrad is sixty-two years old. He should not be beaten up in this manner."

"Colonel," the officer said, "Conrad Janasek is politically dangerous. He was one of the leaders of this uprising, and he opposes our political system. It would be most advisable for you to stay out of the case."

"Can't you at least stop the beatings?"

"I'll see what I can do, Colonel." (He still called me by my official rank, remembering that I had been his boss in 1947.)

After a moment's silence, the colonel added, "You must know from your years in intelligence that sometimes beatings are necessary if the prisoner refuses to give vital information. If that's the case, there's absolutely nothing that can be done about it.''

The colonel dropped the subject entirely and asked me how my classes were going at the university. After ten minutes of irritating chit-chat, we bade the officer farewell.

A week later, Sabina returned to the jail with another package for Conrad. This time she was treated very rudely ''You can't see that prisoner,'' an officer barked at her. He snatched the package and threw it in a wastepaper basket. Sabina left without another word. She had no choice but to stay away from there as advised.

There was only one other possibility. I went to see my friend Stefan Matuszewski, who had helped me when I got out of jail. He, too, implored me to stay out of the matter. ''This case is a time bomb, and you'll be put in jail again if you try to help Conrad. Even I wouldn't try to assist him now.''

The weeks went by with no further news of my friend. Then, in true Soviet fashion, the newspapers announced that Conrad Janasek had suffered a ''heart attack'' in jail. That was the Russian expedient for anyone who opposed their strong-arm tactics. Conrad wasn't the only heart attack victim. There were many more sudden deaths among the prisoners, indicating that an epidemic of heart attacks was in order that year.

CHAPTER 25

Escape to Freedom

And so the brave partisan died behind bars like a criminal. The government could never have brought him to trial, because he was a man of too much honor. He had led one of the most vital partisan units that worked behind Nazi lines during the war. He had fought untiringly for his country. He had helped destroy the German oppression, and fought to establish some social justice in postwar Poland. To put such a man on trial would have aroused the latent nationalism that refused to be deprogrammed from the Polish consciousness. Such a trial could only have proven extremely inconvenient for the Soviet authorities.

Conrad's battered body was laid to rest and with it was buried my final hope for Poland. If there ever had been a Pole who deserved the title ''comrade,'' it was Conrad Janasek. His dignity had been sacrificed to growing autocracy. His honor had been sacrificed to political expediency. I could bear it no more.

At the university, I led a comfortable life. I was well paid, had a comfortable apartment and a chauffeured car. My books were selling well, six plays I had written were enjoying productions, and my royalties permitted Sabina and me to live in style— Polish style, that is.

Since I was a wartime hero, both in Poland and in Russia, I enjoyed special privileges. My family and I were entitled to free admission at all cultural activities—opera, ballet, theater, concerts, art galleries, movies, and lectures. My portrait hung in Warsaw's World War II Military Museum among those of the other war heroes.

Yet, in spite of all these advantages, I was unhappy. In fact, I was thoroughly miserable. We were choking in the sinister atmosphere blowing in from Moscow. If I was delayed on campus and came home just a few minutes late for dinner, my wife was already convinced that I was in jail again. She was certain that our phone was tapped; she jumped nervously every time it rang.

Moreover, after the 1956 war in the Middle East, the Soviets and their allies had stepped up their anti-Israel propaganda. Now they had a perfect excuse. Israel, they claimed, was ganging up with the old imperialist powers, England and France, to invade the Sinai Peninsula. Even some Americans lent the Soviets support, like Secretary of State John Foster Dulles. Of course, it was all politics, along with the old rivalries between the United States and some European powers. Israel, along with France and England, was forced to abandon the Sinai.

Meanwhile, some of my students were having a field day with Moshe Dayan's eye patch, which suddenly became a popular item, worn as some kind of badge, not so much of honor as of protest. This silent protest against the authorities gladdened my heart—a silent gesture of support for Israel.

But I could no longer stand the suffocating atmosphere of the country. I knew, I felt in my bones, that more oppressive measures against Jews were on the way, and that my present position and relative prosperity could vanish any day, any time some higher-up in the KGB decided that I didn't deserve a better fate than General Swierczewski or Conrad Janasek.

Accordingly, on March 12, 1957, I made a definitive move. I went to a photographer I could trust and had passport pictures taken of me and my family. Then I called on Gomulka at his home. His wife Sylvia, whom I had met a few years earlier at a Communist writers' seminar, entertained me until her husband arrived. She asked me what brought me to Warsaw, and I replied that I needed her husband's advice. I did not confide in her, because I mistrusted her. I knew that although she was Jewish, she was still violently anti-Semitic. I sat there and made small talk.

When her husband Wladyslaw arrived, he invited me to step into his den. Once we were comfortably seated, I got right to the point. "I have a secret to tell you, and I would like your assurance that it will remain between us. I would prefer that you do not even mention it to your wife."

"You have my assurance."

"Thank you. To be brief—I'm not Polish, but Jewish. By posing as a Pole, with forged identification papers, I was able to survive the Nazi liquidations. I have come to you because I find life here intolerable, and I wish to move to Israel."

Wladyslaw was so astounded by my words that his face turned red. For a moment, I thought he would suffer a stroke. When he had regained his composure, he said, "But you don't look Jewish!"

"Why—because I don't eat quickly and monopolize the conversation?"

He looked at me as if I had lost my senses. I explained to him about our lecture on how to tell a Jew at the Moscow Military Academy.

"No, I mean you do not have Jewish features," he said.

"Well, I can't help that. If I did look Jewish, I would have been dead long ago."

"What would you like me to do for you?"

"I need passports for myself and my family to get to Israel."

"I may be able to help you there," he said kindly. He picked up the phone and made a call.

I was terrified. "Wait a minute!" I begged. "Whom are you calling? I don't want to be arrested again."

"Don't worry," he said calmly. "The head of the passport office is a close friend. There will be no problems and no arrests."

He got through to his friend immediately and presented the facts. He gave my name and the names of my family members, urging his friend to keep this matter a secret.

After Wladyslaw hung up, he told me that his friend had assured me I need not worry. He then looked at me, lowered his voice, and said, "Yes, it would be preferable if my wife didn't know about this. I'll tell her that you came to see me on another matter—something to do with your university career."

I nodded. He, too, knew what a rabid, self-hating anti-Semite his wife was. We shook hands, and I thanked him.

I went directly to the passport office and was delighted to find my documents waiting for me. But Gomulka's friend froze my blood when he asked, "What party assignment do you have in Israel?"

I was so flustered by this question that, instead of answering, I put my finger to my lips. He immediately presumed that I was not at liberty to divulge that information. He discreetly nodded in secret agreement.

The whole procedure was so swift and simple that I felt suspicious. All this time I had been unhappy in a country that I hated, when I could have been in Israel just by asking a favor from a friend. I realized that I was gambling with my family's safety by this move, but I felt that it was worth the chance.

I called Sabina and asked her to start packing. Then I went to see Moshe Dagan at the Israeli Embassy and showed him our passports.

"How did you ever manage that?" he said with surprise.

"I can't tell you. Let's just say that it pays to have friends. Now, I have a favor to ask of you. Can you put us on the first available transport to Israel? You know that in my case haste is needed."

"There's a group of two thousand Jews leaving on a train tomorrow for Venice. From there, they'll board a ship for Haifa. The quota is already filled, but I'll put you and your family on as extras. You must be at the main railway station in Warsaw tomorrow morning at 6:30. It will cost you twenty-four hundred zlotys for each member of your family for transportation."

"That's no problem."

He introduced me to the man in charge of the shipment and told him to take good care of me and my family.

I called Sabina again and told her the additional good news. She could hardly believe it. "We can only take forty kilos each on the trip, and we must be ready to leave tonight on the midnight express to Warsaw."

"Oh, my God! How will I ever manage that?"

"You'll manage," I said. "And don't forget. Not a word to *anyone*. Don't even answer the door if someone knocks."

"Yes, yes, dear. Now please let me pack." I had never heard her so excited over anything.

At 2:00 p.m., I went to see Mr. Dabrowski, Minister of Finance, a personal friend of mine. He could be trusted. I showed him our passports and asked for his help in having my furniture moved from Poznan to Israel. He called the government export office and gave instructions to transfer my furniture to Haifa, at no cost to me. He also gave me a letter of recommendation to the proper authorities, stating that, as a hero of the Polish Army, I was entitled to have my belongings shipped from Poland to Israel free of charge.

I got on the 4:00 p.m. train to Poznan, saying a silent farewell to Warsaw, and praying that nothing would prevent me from leaving this bloodied land, my family's graveyard.

When I got home, the apartment was in chaos. Sabina was having a dreadful time trying to adhere to the forty kilo limit.

"Oh, Maurice!" she said. "There's so much to leave behind. It's heartbreaking."

Our daughters were in a state of shock. Sabina didn't tell them where we were going and why we were leaving in such haste.

"Is Papa in trouble again?" Dina asked.

"Hush, darling," Sabina said. "We'll explain everything to you on the trip."

"Can I call my schoolfriends and say goodbye?"

"No!" Sabina said. *"No one* is to know. Do you want us all to be killed?"

The girls looked at her in silence.

Sabina was having the same mixed emotions. She desperately wanted to leave Poland, but it also meant leaving our homeland, our first decent living arrangement, and her mother's final resting place. Lila had died of a stroke in 1953 and Sabina made weekly visits to her grave. If we escaped from Poland without incident, she knew that we would probably never be back, and this bothered her.

I reminded her that I had no idea where most of my family was buried, which was even more painful.

I remembered long ago hearing the great Zionist Ze'ev Jabotinsky's warning speeches on how the Jews must all leave Poland. I knew that he was right. It meant starting all over again in a new country, but at least we wouldn't have to jump at every door knock or telephone ring.

I didn't notify the university or the magazines I wrote for that I was leaving. I was thankful that a group of Jewish émigrés was being assembled and we would not have to wait for weeks which would have increased the risk of our plans being discovered.

I decided to have a close friend and his wife over for dinner, as a farewell gesture. He was one of the top military men in Poznan, but I knew I could trust him. We could not just disappear without saying some selective goodbyes. At dinner, which was to be our last in Poznan, I disclosed our secret to our guests. They were astounded, but happy for us. My daughters were still confused about what was happening. To spare them from suffering and fear, we had never told them we were Jews.

I gave my military friend the letter authorizing the special transport of our furniture. I asked him to wait for about three days before pursuing the matter. I wanted to be out of the country before anyone discovered our absence.

At 11:00 p.m., we quietly took our luggage out of the apartment. Our friends drove us to the railway station. When the train arrived, we all had tears in our eyes. It was difficult to say goodbye. The children made matters worse by asking incessant questions. We finally told them to just keep quiet. We would explain everything later.

In Warsaw early the next morning, we boarded our train. We joined two thousand others, all strangers and all intent on leaving Poland. We were a grim lot. The anxiety that filled all of us—the fear that at any time someone would prevent us from leaving and put us in prison—made the journey rather cheerless. No one spoke. Fear and mistrust filled the train with tension.

Our first nerve-wracking incident came at the border crossing between Czechoslovakia and Austria. It was reminiscent of the old Gestapo days. The train was detained there for six hours with no food or drink available to the passengers. But the most frightening thing was that the train was surrounded by Soviet military units of the border patrols. We were informed that a search was to be conducted.

It was torture sitting there. We were warned by the Soviet soldiers not to leave our seats. Sabina and I were trembling with fear. It was impossible to sit there for all that time and not go to the bathroom. Finally, we took a chance and escorted the girls to the toilet on the train. There was a long line, but we finally made it.

As the hours passed, our children became more and more irritable. I kept telling them that we were going to a wonderful place far away, where they would make marvelous new friends.

I had a letter from the government minister granting me permission to take out more than the usual belongings. I noticed that lots of personal items were being confiscated by the inspectors. For example, mothers were permitted only three diapers per child. One woman had five, and they took two away from her. Even the Gestapo had not been as thorough in their searches as these corrupt border patrols were.

When the guards approached us, I confidently handed him my letter. He pushed me aside without even looking at my documents and tried to open my suitcase. "Don't touch it!" I commanded in my best colonel's tone.

My order startled the soldier. "Very well," he said, "I'll call my superior."

"Please do," I said.

In a few moments, a stern-looking major approached us. I was petrified.

"What's the problem here?"

The major stopped, looked at me in disbelief, then saluted. I was astounded. He was Major Kolodriejski, a former intelligence colleague of mine. When the guards saw him salute, they sheepishly changed their attitude.

"What are you doing on this train, Colonel?" the major inquired.

I had a brainstorm. "Please," I said in a low voice, "don't ask any questions. I'm not at liberty to discuss my assignment. And please don't address me by name."

"Of course, Colonel," he said. Then turning to Sabina he smiled and kissed her hand. He glared at the guard who had summoned him. "This family is permitted to pass to the next car without being searched," he loudly ordered.

The guards quickly moved our bags to the "cleared" car ahead and found a comfortable compartment for us.

"Good luck," the major said as he left.

From our compartment, we could hear the outraged cries of passengers whose belongings were being confiscated. These were not luxury items—furs, jewels, or art objects—but inexpensive, essential possessions. From our window we could see carts loaded with coats, suits, socks, gloves, and other items.

Finally, after hours of anxiety and depression, we felt the train move. The air suddenly grew lighter. The guards may have taken some personal things from the passengers, but there was one item that they couldn't take: the intoxicating sense of freedom we all felt on having crossed the border.

When the train pulled into the station at Vienna and we saw the beautiful blue uniforms of the Austrian police, we experienced a true feeling of exaltation.

I looked at Sabina, and we both started laughing.

"We're free!" I cried, embracing her and our girls. "We're free!"

Now, at last, the other passengers loosened up and started walking about the train, shaking hands with everyone. There was such overwhelming joy, such unparalleled relief at having left Poland, that these blue police uniforms were viewed as the robes of our liberators and temporary protectors.

Our fellow passengers started singing. I had never seen a group of people restored to life so quickly in all my days. Sabina and I joined in on some of the Hebrew songs, many of which we had not sung since we were children.

Our joy increased when we arrived in Venice. This most haunting of cities mesmerized us with its ancient beauty. Our daughters became animated at the sight of gondolas and singing gondoliers, and they were thrilled when we took them for a ride in one.

It was one of those unforgettable days, with a golden sun illuminating St. Mark's Square like a gigantic set for an opera. My daughters ran around feeding the pigeons, and we had our photo taken with pigeons on our heads and in our hands. We had a fantastic meal in a restaurant recommended to us by the gondolier. Sabina was even pinched near the Bridge of Sighs, but she calmly accepted it as a respected Italian custom. It was our happiest day since the end of the war: we were all together, we were free, and we were going to Israel.

Our ship, appropriately called "Peace," was waiting for us that evening. To us, it seemed like our ark of salvation.

We sailed at midnight, and our view of the Italian coastline was an incandescent sight. The multi-colored palazzi and striped hitching posts for gondolas basked proudly in the moonlight, and the vaporetti carrying passengers to the Lido and back skirted our ship as we sailed slowly into the Adriatic.

In our cabin, we sat down with our girls and attempted to explain what this major change in our life was all about. I told them that we were really Jews posing as Poles and that for two thousand years our people had been persecuted. We had to leave Poland because our people were still being persecuted there, and we hoped to find freedom from bigotry in the exciting new nation of Israel. During the war, I had had to masquerade as a Pole in order to survive. From now on, we were Jews again, and we should be proud of our heritage.

The girls did not fully comprehend what I was saying. But being on a huge boat that was going to take them to an exotic-sounding land excited them sufficiently to allay their confusion.

The seven-day-journey to Haifa was like a luxury cruise for us. Everyone on board was in a vacation mood, full of the kind of optimism and happiness that I had only imagined possible for Christians.

During the voyage, I got to know our fellow passengers, and, as to be expected, they were a mixed lot: some good, some bad. I discovered that some of them were Jews who had embraced Communism in exchange for better living conditions. They had sold themselves to the Party and willingly cooperated with the Soviets in abandoning the history and traditions of their people.

In Poland many had spoken out against Jewish organizations in the press, on the radio, and at public gatherings. They had denounced those who wished to emigrate to Israel. But when it became uncomfortably clear that the Communists wanted to destroy Jews as much as Hitler had, whether or not the Jews were good Communists, they left Poland at the first opportunity.

These people were not headed for Israel because they loved their Jewish origins or their native land. They were leaving Poland to survive. Many still had their Communist ideologies intact. Fortunately these characters were not in the majority; most of the escaping passengers were decent people and good, proud Jews.

There were about twenty Israelis on board. They represented various political parties in Israel and their mission was to enlist as many new members as possible for their particular parties. I thought that the new nation must be rich to afford such a welcoming committee for new immigrants.

Each party representative had a table on deck, like a market-place stall, with leaflets and information promising all kinds of jobs and favors if you signed up with that party. All parties operating in Israel were represented except Betar.

I observed that the Mapai party was extremely popular with the passengers, especially those who had sold their souls to the Communists. Now they wished to secure their future by joining Ben Gurion's party.

The political agents pursued me endlessly but I notified all of them that I wanted a long vacation from political activities.

There were three representatives on board from the Sochnut, known as the Jewish Agency. These men interviewed passengers to become acquainted with their professions and to attempt to place them in jobs upon arrival in Israel. Only ten couples on board were assigned to Jerusalem and Tel-Aviv. The rest were settled in rural areas. I was fortunate to be located in Bat-Yam, about fifteen minutes from Tel-Aviv.

When we got to Israel, my family and I were assigned to a *maabara,* a temporary settlement in Bat-Yam, composed of ten huts. We were in hut 115, with the sea facing us on one side and sand dunes on the other. It was desolate, but comfortable and peaceful.

Our hut consisted of one large room and a small kitchen, with a shower outside. We had four new beds, a table and chairs, and a kerosene lamp. As a welcoming gift, we were allotted fifteen pounds of potatoes, flour, and other provisions to keep us going for a few days. Best of all, our daughters could play outside without having to worry about traffic.

On my second day in Israel, I visited some old friends: Lichtenstein, the lawyer, whom we knew from Poznan; and Dr. Stern, director of the Tel-Aviv hospital, whom I had helped to recruit soldiers for the Haganah.

I also took a quick tour of Tel-Aviv, which impressed me with its busy streets, businesslike air, and contented-looking people. There was an air of freedom about the city that exhilarated me. It reminded me of prewar Warsaw, without the hated police.

One thing about Israel, though, bothered me from the very beginning: the intense heat. Here it was March, and the temperature was torrid. People I spoke to assured me that this was not usual weather for March. We were having a heat storm—a *hamsin*—one of those freaks of nature that sometimes occurs out of season.

During my trip into town, Sabina took our girls to the beach. When I returned to our hut, I found two visitors waiting for me. They were from the Mapai political party. One of them, the chairman, offered to send me to a Hebrew language school for three months, after which I would be given a government post. They indicated that they knew "all" about me.

I was a little put off by these political approaches. I had just arrived, and I didn't care to rush into anything—especially of a political nature. "I need a little more time to get acclimated," I said. "Let me get acquainted with the situation here; then I'll give you an answer."

Later in the evening, I had another caller, Simon Baker, chairman of the Mapam party, a more left-leaning organization. We had a long talk. I liked him, because he wasn't rushing me. He seemed genuinely interested in my family's well-being and asked me to let him know if there was anything he could do for us.

Next day, I went to see his brother Aaron, a big-shot in the labor movement, who offered me a job in a corrugated carton factory in B'nai Brak, about fifteen minutes from Tel-Aviv. That offer interested me because it was the same kind of business I had helped my father run in Warsaw. Also, there were no strings attached to the offer.

Aaron was delighted that I had experience running a corrugated carton plant. He set up an interview for me at a large factory called Cargal. I was not only hired the same day, but was offered a fine salary. I stayed with this company for as long as I remained in Israel.

The education system in Bat-Yam was rife with conflict.

There were two schools in the town. One was a religious school which emphasized the teachings of the Bible and the history of our country; the other was a state-supported school, left-oriented, with red flags flying in front. To me, the red represented blood and misery, of which I had had enough. I preferred the colors of peace: white and blue. Consequently, I decided to send my girls to the religious school.

The area in which we lived was growing fast. In about six months, five hundred immigrant families had settled around us. These included Jews of many nations: Rumania, Hungary, Egypt, Syria, and others. Each had a rich cultural heritage, and each had struggled to survive terror, hate, and discrimination. Some of these people brought their customs and prejudices with them to Israel, causing a good deal of dissension.

I couldn't understand this. After thousands of years of serfdom and slavery, these people had come here to be free. Instead, they were planting seeds of prejudice in their own country. That was not my way, and I don't think it was the way of Abraham, Isaac, and Jacob.

When my neighbors noted that I was sending my children to the religious school, they started doing the same. This angered the Mapai representatives, who came to complain to me about it.

"Why are you sending your daughters to a religious school?" they asked. "Now, everyone is following your example, which spoils our efforts to fill the state-supported school."

"Your school has red flags in front of it," I said, "and I don't trust what they stand for."

"But we're not Soviet-styled Communists."

"I still don't like red flags, and I will not send my girls to any schools bearing those symbolic banners."

I made many enemies, but I stood firm. Only Simon Baker seemed to understand my attitude and stood by me. Our friendship grew stronger because of this.

My friends from Poland did not approve of my girls' playing with children of Egyptian and Iraqi Jews. I replied to these people that my girls did not know the meaning of discrimination. They had been reared to respect and love all people.

One evening in November 1957, three members of the Israeli Communist Party presented themselves at our hut. They did not request my cooperation with their party—they demanded it.

"At the moment," I replied sternly, "I do not wish to be affiliated with any party. My main concern at this time is to get settled here. If I change my mind, I'll be happy to let you know.''

One of the men said, "We know you attended Moscow Military Academy. We know *everything* about you. Why are you sending your children to a religious school?''

"Because I want them to have a Jewish education, to know something about our country as it is taught in a religious school. Later, they can make up their own minds as to which way they want to go.''

"The trouble is,'' their spokesman said, "that you've obviously changed your political thinking.''

"Maybe I have,'' I said. "One is apt to, as one gets older and wiser.''

They left, dissatisfied with my answers and my attitude. My wife and I were disappointed by this confrontation. We had just escaped one political nightmare and now found ourselves swirling in what appeared to be the beginning of another.

Once again, Sabina became disquieted. She was worried about our girls. "I'm afraid to let them go out. These political fanatics may try to harm them.''

I told her to stop worrying. "They wouldn't dare. They are simply using pressure tactics.''

About a week after this incident, the Communists decided to hold a meeting almost directly behind our hut. Delegates knocked on all doors, inviting families to attend.

When they banged on my door, I gave them short shrift. "Please leave me alone,'' I said. "I don't wish to attend any meetings; I don't want to engage in any political activity.''

Their constant badgering was beginning to wear on my nerves. I had come here to live in peace, and, once again, was finding too much political dissension.

I decided that I should try to prepare an "out" for myself just in case things got too unbearable. I wrote a long letter to my brother in New York and explained the situation to him. I requested that he begin the procedure to apply for our relocation in the United States. He accommodated me and the papers arrived in about a month. Now I had to make up my mind.

CHAPTER 26

America

On the same day that our visas arrived, we had an unexpected visit from Meir Wilner, the first secretary of the Communist Party in Israel. He left a companion in a car outside and came alone to our hut.

"How are you, Mr. Pruzanski?" he boomed.

"Shainberg is the name."

"Ah, yes, but you are remembered for your achievements during the war as Pruzanski."

"That is correct, but now I prefer my true Jewish name, which is Shainberg."

"Admirable, admirable. And how is your family and your job?"

"Both are fine."

"Excellent. I won't take up any more of your time. I merely dropped in to greet you. Please visit us soon. We would be honored."

"Thank you very much," I said indifferently. I shook his hand. He gave me his card and left. I crumpled it up and threw it away. I had no intention of ever visiting him.

The Communists continued having meetings within earshot of our apartment—orchestrated to try to win us over.

Even though we had escaped racial prejudice in coming to Israel, I did not feel comfortable and free in my new land. I knew that the Communists were watching my every step, and that I would have to be careful. I wanted to warn my people of the dangers that Communists posed to their personal happiness and freedom, but I couldn't effectively do this without endangering my family.

Once again, Sabina and I had to do serious soul searching and admit to ourselves that Israel was still not the ideal place for us to settle. Was there any place, I wondered, where I could live in complete freedom to do, speak, and write whatever I pleased? After what we had been through, I was looking for a land where we would not have to deal with the Communist threat and Communist propaganda on a daily basis. The only logical place left seemed America.

I wrote my brother Nathan a lengthy letter explaining my unhappy predicament and I asked if he would assist my family and me to resettle in the United States. He responded with a letter stating that if I was unhappy in Israel, he would begin making the necessary arrangements for us to visit him. The letter insisted that only I would be able to remain in America and my family would have to eventually return to Israel because of the complicated U.S. immigration laws. Once I was established, the letter went on, my family would be able to relocate to America. I wondered what Nathan meant by my being "established" in America before my family could join me?

On the day before Yom Kippur, in 1958, we were notified by the United States Embassy in Tel-Aviv that our visas for America were ready and that we should come over and pick them up.

We went to the United States Embassy where a red-haired, freckled-faced girl told us we would be taken care of in about an hour. Our optimism diminished considerably when one hour turned to four. Finally, I lost all patience. I demanded to know why we were being detained there so long. The information clerk checked on the matter and asked us to step into the adjoining room where someone was waiting to speak to us.

A young Israeli girl was seated at a desk and seemed a bit flustered at seeing us. "I'm afraid I have bad news for you," she announced.

"We are used to bad news," I said simply. "What is it this time?"

"It seems that your brother in New York has decided against sponsoring you, and so we cannot issue your visas."

For the first time in my life, I didn't go to synagogue on Yom Kippur. It was my form of protest against my brother, the rabbi, who could be so heartless. I couldn't imagine what had motivated him. It couldn't have anything to do with his past grievances, or he wouldn't have approved the visas in the first place. It must have something to do with my present situation.

I spent hours and hours going over my life and wondering

what could have changed his mind. Was it the fact that I had been a KGB officer living in Moscow for five years—in a godless country? Did he imagine I was a hard-core Communist who wished to come to the United States as a spy? Didn't he realize that I still loved him despite the many abuses I suffered as a child because of him?

After many sleepless nights, I sat down and wrote Nathan another long letter, in which I detailed the anguish he had caused me and my family and demanded an explanation for his behavior.

In my bitterness, I remembered the old superstition about babies who were born "with a hat on," as I had been. They were supposed to be blessed with good fortune all their lives. "So where's my good fortune?" I acidly asked Sabina one night when I couldn't sleep. "I've had nothing but trouble all my life. First of all, I'm born a Jew and have to suffer a lifetime of prejudice. Then, I'm reared in a family whose only love is religion. Next I have to hide my identity for years in order to survive. And now, I must wander from country to country trying to find a peaceful haven. So where's my luck?"

"You're still alive, and that should be enough for you," she answered.

I realized the truth of her statement. I had, indeed, been lucky. With millions of Jews annihilated during the war, I was still alive. I should always remember that and rejoice.

In twelve days, I had a reply from Nathan. It was a cold, formal letter informing us why he had withdrawn his offer. It seemed that my next-door neighbor in Israel, Mr. Levine, had written to Nathan and offered him interesting information about me—"for a price."

Nathan, with his usual brotherly love, had paid the price. In exchange for his money, he had falsely learned that I had married a Polish Christian woman. Therefore my daughters were Christians, and Nathan in his religious zeal didn't want any part of the whole pack of us.

When I showed this malicious letter to Sabina, she burst into tears. What upset her was not the incorrect information that it contained, but the fact that my brother would have so little faith in me that he would pay someone for some "dirt" on me. And this was a religious man?

Sabina herself wrote a letter to my brother, informing him that she was the daughter of Professor Szimon Davidson, a Jewish surgeon who was executed by the Germans because he refused to work in a clinic where human beings were used in experiments as guinea pigs. Sabina pointed out that her father's whole family had been exterminated in concentration camps by the Nazis. She and her mother had been saved because they were secretly hidden by their Christian friends.

My brother replied to her letter two weeks later. His letter was not cordial; it had a military ring to it. He demanded a copy of a marriage certificate indicating that our marriage was performed according to Jewish law.

We were able to send Nathan the required documents. They were properly signed by a rabbi and we hoped that my brother would be convinced that Jewish law had been followed.

In three weeks we received a notice from the American Embassy that a visa was available—just for me. I was so enraged that my family's visa arrangements had not been made that I called the United States Embassy to see if there was some kind of a mistake. I received a devastating reply.

"Your brother has approved a visa for you, Mr. Shainberg," the official voice said, "but not for the rest of your family."

"This is an outrage," I heard myself saying. "I won't go without them." I slammed down the phone.

Sabina gathered what was wrong without my telling her. "He obviously doesn't want me or the children," she said bitterly. "How could a rabbi have such little compassion for members of his own family?"

"I wouldn't go without you and the girls," I said. "Let him answer to God for his prejudice and injustice."

"There is no use trying to work this out by correspondence," Sabina reasoned. "He will never give in. I think you should go to him alone, and then he wouldn't have the heart to keep us separated. Maybe you could appeal to his wife?"

"You don't know my brother. Once he gets something into his thick skull, it's impossible to change his mind. I absolutely refuse to leave without you and the children."

Our arguments continued for a few days more. Eventually, I came to agree with my wife. There was nothing to be gained by my refusing his offer. Perhaps if I pleaded in person, he would soften a bit.

I disliked leaving Sabina and the girls alone, but we were now living in a modern, well-protected complex, and I felt they would be safe.

"May this be our last separation," I fervently wished when Sabina and my daughters came to see me off at the airport. I promised to return as soon as possible. Hopefully I would have the necessary visas to bring them over to America.

That was March 20, 1959, another day in my memory that remains indelible. Naturally, I was excited about flying to New York. I had always dreamed of seeing America, but never thought I would have the chance to live there. If we had only moved to the United States before the war—my father certainly had the resources to do so—we would all be together and alive today.

I tried to sleep on the plane, but I couldn't. How would my brother greet me, I wondered, and how would his wife react to my pleas to back my family? Without their approval and financial assistance nothing could be done.

At the airport in New York I was delayed for two hours. First, I couldn't find my luggage, and then, the customs man went through every item in my bags. Another gentleman took me to a small room and asked me endless questions about my past and demanded to know precisely why I was coming to the United States. I was convinced that he had me pegged as a Soviet spy.

At last, I saw my brother. Although we hadn't seen each other for more than twenty years, I recognized him immediately. He hadn't changed much and was waiting for me alone without his wife. I rushed over to him to embrace him, but he pulled away. He had such a scowl on his face that I didn't attempt to kiss him. A handshake was all he could muster, and a limp one at that.

Instead of telling me that he was glad to see me after all these years, which was what I expected, his first comment was, "I thought you would be taller. You must be only five-eight or five-nine."

I was surprised by this irrelevant comment, but my brother really didn't know how to speak to me; he just issued commands. "You must send your family a telegram immediately to let them know you arrived safely!"

"Well," I said, "it's nice to know you care somewhat about my family since you wouldn't let them accompany me."

"This is not the proper place to discuss these matters. We will send them a telegram and then take a taxi to my apartment."

He escorted me to the cablegram counter and helped me compose a message. He paid for the wire. Then we proceeded to the cab stand and entered a taxi. Nathan gave the driver his address and took what looked like a large roll of bills out of his pocket.

"Here," he said, handing me the cash, "I don't want you walking around New York penniless."

As I later discovered, the large wad turned out to be seven one-dollar bills.

I had heard that New York was big, but I hadn't quite expected what I saw, especially after two years of living in a country whose entire population could be housed in any one of New York's five boroughs.

We rolled up to Nathan's apartment in the city's Lower East Side, a largely Jewish district that reminded me of old Warsaw's Jewish quarter. The buildings were aging and not well kept.

Once upstairs, he introduced me to his wife, but not by name. She was "the daughter of Rabbi Schwartzman, Chief Rabbi of Canada."

"Pleased to meet you," I said, summoning my most proper greeting. She acknowledged it with a nod and then showed me my room for the stay, a small alcove without the privacy of even a curtain. Whoever had paved American streets with gold must have missed my brother Nathan and his neighborhood.

We began discussing the subject of why Nathan had refused to allow my family to emigrate to the United States with me. He invoked the same explanation he had used in his letter—that American law would not permit them to permanently relocate until I was "established" and settled in the United States. He believed that it would be more difficult for me to become established and a success if I had to deal with the day-to-day pressures of my family's adjustments to American life, as well as my own. It was more important for me to get a job, learn English, and make the necessary sacrifices inherent in beginning a new life, before exposing my family to such complicated cultural changes. My brother's most persuasive argument was that I would be acting irresponsibly to burden him with the requirements of supporting my entire family before I even had the capability of supporting myself. In my entire adult life I had never been a burden to anyone and I didn't plan to become one now. I understood some of Nathan's points and I decided to concentrate my energies on finding a job. I wanted to become self-supporting as quickly as possible.

I started searching for work the next day, focusing on my specialty—carton-manufacturing plants. Since I couldn't speak English, Nathan agreed to accompany me on interviews.

Our treks around the city were exasperating. There was little work. My English wasn't good enough. I wasn't a member of a union. I wasn't a citizen. There seemed to be a hundred reasons why I couldn't be employed.

Then, on Nathan's suggestion, I started showing up at District 65, the union headquarters on Astor Place in Manhattan. I arrived every working day for a month until Peter Ivanovitch, the personnel manager, took pity on me. He told me to report to a Mr. Sinclair at Metro Corrugated in Brooklyn. If I worked out all right there for a month, I would be permitted to join the union.

I made my way to Brooklyn as quickly as I could and, after a brief interview, was hired. I was put to work immediately, as a grounds-keeper sweeping rubbish from the yard.

I explained to Mr. Sinclair, in my broken English, that I had been a chief in my father's plant and knew the industry well.

Three days later, I was still chasing a broom. I went to him again and said I wanted to work with the machines. I again reminded him that I had been a production chief and knew the profession well.

He said the plant had no kitchen, and he didn't need a "chef."

We both immediately realized the confusion from my poor communication. The next day he assigned me to set up the machines early in the morning for the day's production run.

The job worked out well until I received my first paycheck. I was getting paid a dollar an hour, and I knew the union scale was $2.10. I argued with Sinclair and we agreed on $1.70 until I was admitted into the union.

Working at this regular job, I started saving money to bring my family to the United States. I wrote Sabina frequent letters to keep her posted on my progress. In the evenings, I kept away from Nathan's apartment as much as possible and frequented the Polish-American Club on Manhattan's East 8th Street. I made several acquaintances there, and soon discovered how friendly Poles can be when they are not in Poland.

Indeed, I found that many Americans, particularly those who were first or second generation immigrants, were friendly and helpful to other new immigrants. They had left the old country for whatever their reasons, and they brought with them bits of their culture to the United States. In America, everyone seemed to understand that this was a country for sharing. New immigrants, like myself, even learned to share prejudice. There was anti-Semitism in America, that's for sure, but there was also anti-Polish sentiment, anti-German, anti-Italian, anti-Black, and anti-you-name-it.

Although my job at the carton plant was progressing satisfactorily, it wasn't returning enough money for me to bring Sabina and the children. After six months, I was beginning to miss them sorely. I had been rebuffed by American Jewish organizations when I went for help, so I turned to American Polish groups and met a Mr. Zachariasiewicz, who was very helpful. After a certain amount of questioning, a woman who worked for Zachariasiewicz took down Sabina's name and her Israeli address and promised that she and the children would be in New York within three weeks.

Exactly two weeks after this meeting, I received a telegram from Sabina. She had received her visa and airline tickets, free of charge, and would be with me in a few days.

I was overjoyed to see my wife and daughters again. I swore that this had been our final separation. We were in America now, and we would stay here as a family.

America treated us well, perhaps too well. We started with a modest apartment and soon were able to afford a better residence. Then we purchased an automobile and slowly acquired the accoutrements of contemporary American life. In Poland, Sabina had been happy with one new dress a year, but after a short time in America, she could afford four a year. Only then did she start complaining that she had nothing to wear.

As we settled into American life, we put the children into a Jewish school, but soon found substantial difficulty there. I had to work overtime at every available opportunity to pay the tuition, but still that wasn't enough. The school wanted us to sell raffle tickets to help them raise money. This disturbed me, but not as much as finding out that the teachers made no particular effort to help the girls overcome their language handicap. They spoke Hebrew and Polish fluently, but had trouble with English.

The problem was settled by placing the children in America's public school system, where they were better assisted in learning English and becoming Americans. Slowly we adjusted to our new conditions and finally entered what was to us the mainstream of American life.

I did well in my field and, within a decade, became the senior manager of one of the largest carton manufacturing plants in the United States. Our plant has had a record of productivity, high morale, and safety that few factories in the U.S.S.R. could ever match.

I've had the opportunity to participate in and study both the American and Soviet systems. Because I was personally involved in both, I feel especially qualified to evaluate them. From what I can tell, the Soviet system is theoretically more efficient, but it actually doesn't work as well. Communists are used to planned economies that assign their captive labor force to specific projects, according to priority. The totalitarian system gives them the political authority to do whatever it takes to achieve their ends. The capitalists, however, are subject to the unpredictable vagaries of the free enterprise system. In the end, the communists can't provide the one key element—incentive.

While the American system is subject to many other problems that are unheard of in Soviet-controlled countries, there is still the omnipresent incentive, the reason and the avenue for doing a better job. Capitalist competition may seem to be a more difficult way of getting things done than communist cooperation, but it isn't. Philosophers can argue for hours on end, but the true answer lies in the production statistics and the quality of the material produced.

I should not tout American industry too much, for it does have its faults. Nor should I be too critical, for its benefits clearly outweigh anything else in the world.

Today, I manage a plant not far from the Statue of Liberty, and it is a constant reminder that I am an immigrant who has struggled, like so many others, to become an American. And a few hundred yards from that famous statue is Ellis Island, the place where so many millions first stepped on American soil. It, too, serves as a constant reminder.

I feel so lucky to have the opportunity to work in, and to be a part of, the United States of America. For me and for the more than half-million survivors of the Holocaust who live here, America is the true Messiah. Here, we see no more hatred, no more discrimination, no more fear to walk freely on the streets. The American principle of equal rights for all citizens and all humanity is one of man's greatest achievements. Let us hope that forever on, America will continue to be the symbol of freedom for all nations and all nationalities.

I still have an attachment to Poland and to Israel, despite my problems with both places. But today, these attachments are overshadowed by my love of America. I want to be, and have worked to be, part of that immigrant stock that has helped to build this country.

I have been well rewarded for my work. I have grown professionally and have reaped the benefits of my labors. But beyond that, I have reaped a greater harvest. I have reaped the harvest of life. I have lived in peace with my family and helped it grow and prosper. I have clung to my Judaism in the American style—freely, without being coerced by community or family. And I can stand on the busiest street corner in Manhattan and shout, ''I am Maurice Shainberg, and I am a Jew.'' And it won't make any difference to anybody. I can be Maurice Shainberg in America. I can be Jewish in America. I can tell my story—yes, even the story of the Katyn massacre. Having told it, I'm still alive. And more important, I have a great reason for living.

Sometimes, one has to wait a lifetime for something. I have been fortunate. Two things I desperately wanted—freedom and family love—have finally come to me in this country.

In July of 1975, my brother Nathan invited my family and me to attend the wedding of one of his three sons, all of whom are rabbis.

It was an impressive ceremony conducted by a group of rabbis in a beautiful synagogue. But most unforgettable was something that happened after the ceremony was over.

My brother Nathan, after a half-century of almost coldhearted indifference toward me and all I stood for, approached me and gave me a kiss. It was something I had longed for all my life, and, together with my precious new freedom, it convinced me that being born ''with a hat on'' has truly made me a very lucky human being.

APPENDIX

Translated Verbatim Copy of Colonel Zaitzev's Diary

The following entries are from the section of Colonel Zaitzev's diary which I originally copied in Yiddish on brown Russian graph paper.

10-19-39 I received a telegram from HQ, summoning me to Moscow.

I could not finish dinner—I feel apprehensive as to what awaits me. At HQ, I saw Beria approaching me with a smile—I felt better. He said, "I have an important mission for you. You know those 17,000 Polish officers we took as P.O.W.s? We have to bring them over to our side as future cadres of the Polish Army." He took me to the personnel department to get me some help. I was given fifteen officers as my staff.

1. Mjr. Borchook—assistant to Col. Zaitzev
2. Col. Frolov
3. Capt. Piskunov
4. Capt. Ivanov
5. Capt. Kochetov
6. Capt. Alekseyenko
7. Capt. Lebiedev
8. Mjr. Prestupa
9. Mjr. Vakchetov
10. Dr. Capt. Kenski
11. Lt. Segalyevich
12. Capt. Koshalin
13. Capt. Kolisayev
14. Lt. Gryshenko

15. Capt. Dvoraninov

With Beria's instructions, I was to work out a plan to accommodate the 17,000 Polish officers. I was to guide their re-education, to make them pro-Soviet. I went to Smolensk, where I had difficulties obtaining a proper building for my purposes. I received little cooperation, but I finally convinced them to give me what I needed. I established three camps for Polish officers in the Smolensk forest: Kozielsk, Ostaszkow, and Starobielsk. The P.O.W.s had to build their own camps.

The camps were completed before May 1, 1940. I received a personal thank-you from Beria for a job well done.

The three camps are composed of 85 blocks with 200 men to a block. A block is a wooden building in which sleeping facilities are not beds but boards mounted on three levels called floors.

Mattresses and pillows are filled with straw, and each man is given one blanket.

Indoctrination of the P.O.W.s by my officers is not going well. Capt. Piskunov tells me that Chaplain Jozwiak is one of the leaders who resist any cooperation with us. He must be disposed of.

3-7-40   Chaplain Jozwiak has been given poison in his food.

3-15-40   It had been noticed that one of my soldiers, young Kostenko, was helping the prisoners. Col. Frolov reports that Kostenko has been liquidated. Well, one snake less.

4-13-40   Chaplain Jozwiak is dead.

6-22-41   The Germans have attacked Russia.

7-3-41   The plan to liquidate the camps has been approved by Beria.

7-23-41   I received a telegram from Beria explaining the procedures to be followed in liquidating the camps.

1. Transfer the hospital to army's jurisdiction.

2. Change security battalion. Replace it with 30-man groups of the secret, prisoner-liquidation detachment.

3. Empty adjacent 5-kilometer radius of civilian population. Explain evacuation as a military necessity.

4. Gather small firearms and ammunition taken from recently captured German prisoners.

5. Walk the Poles to the liquidation site in groups of 100.
6. The liquidation platoon should trail the Poles by 20 meters.
7. The prisoners should be contaminated with lice.
8. 5 kilometers from camp have prisoners dig fox-holes—use them for graves.
9. Make certain that the Polish officers are dressed in their own clothing.

Execute this plan a few days before the Germans enter Smolensk.

7-24 to	Liquidation of the Polish P.O.W.s completed.
7-26-41	Telephoned Beria that his procedures were followed to the letter.

ABOUT THE AUTHOR

Maurice Shainberg was born in Poland to a family of prominent rabbis. He graduated from the University of Gdansk and spent five years in the Moscow Military Academy. Under a false identity as a Polish Catholic named Mieczyslaw Pruzanski, he rose to the rank of colonel in the Soviet dominated Polish KGB. After the war, he revealed his deception to KGB authorities and was imprisoned. He eventually escaped with his family to the United States after a brief stay in Israel. He now lives with his wife and two daughters in New Jersey.

RUSSIA REVEALED!